Bernstein to Brandt

A Short History of German Social Democracy

Bernstein to Brandt

A Short History of German Social Democracy

Edited by
Roger Fletcher

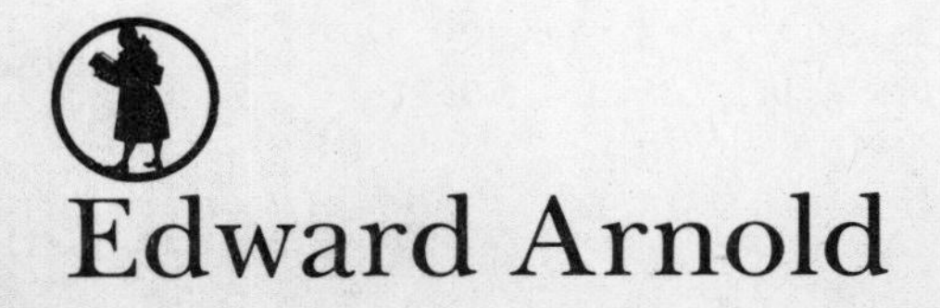

Edward Arnold

First published in Great Britain 1987 by Edward Arnold (Publishers) Ltd, 41 Bedford Square, London WC1B 3DQ

Edward Arnold (Australia) Pty Ltd, 80 Waverley Road, Caulfield East, Victoria 3145, Australia

Edward Arnold, 3 East Read Street, Baltimore, Maryland 21202, USA

British Library Cataloguing in Publication Data

Bernstein to Brandt: a short history of
German Social Democracy.
1. Sozialdemokratische Partei Deutschlands
—History
I. Fletcher, Roger
324.243'072 JN3946.S83

ISBN 0 7131 6480 8

Photoset in 10/11 pt. Linotron Baskerville
by Northern Phototypesetting Company, Bolton.

Printed and bound in Great Britain by
Biddles Ltd, Guildford and King's Lynn

Contents

Part IV: Renewal and Rebirth

Part V: Epilogue

Acknowledgements

This book is a collective effort in more than the customary sense, for a great many individuals and institutions have had a hand in its production, although, of course, final responsibility for any remaining errors or deficiencies rests with the editor alone. To each of the following, a special debt of gratitude is owed: to the Australian Academy of the Humanities, for a travel grant which helped significantly to accelerate the production process; to Klaus Loewald, for research assistance, advice and translation services 'above and beyond'; to Lisa Moloney and Margaret Ralph, who did most of the typing; to the Verlag Neue Gesellschaft, for permission to use, in English translation, Susanne Miller's 'Eduard Bernsteins Haltung im Ersten Weltkrieg und in der Revolution 1918–19', which first appeared in *Bernstein und der Demokratische Sozialismus* (1978), eds: Horst Heimann and Thomas Meyer; to the Fondazione Giangiacomo Feltrinelli, for permission to use part of H. A. Winkler's 'Eduard Bernstein als Kritiker der Weimarer Sozialdemokratie', which appeared in the 1983–84 issue of their *Annali*, pp. 1003–27.

Finally, but by no means least, sincere thanks are due to the publishers, whose keen interest, informed advice, patience and solicitude have been exceptional and invaluable at all stages of the production process of this book.

Abbreviations

ADAV	The All-German Workers' Association (*Allgemeiner Deutscher Arbeiterverein*), founded in Leipzig by Ferdinand Lassalle in 1863.
ADGB	National German Trade-Union Congress (*Allgemeiner Deutscher Gewerkschafts-Bund*): the socialist trade-union umbrella organization (previously known as the General Commission) founded at Nuremberg in 1919.
AWO	Workers' Welfare Organization (*Arbeiterwohlfahrt*), also the title of an SPD welfare and social-policy magazine in the Weimar Republic.
BDF	Federation of (bourgeois or non-socialist) German Women's Associations (*Bund Deutscher Frauenvereine*), founded in 1894.
CDU/CSU	Christian Democratic Union, consisting principally of former conservatives and members of the Catholic Centre Party: the main conservative party in postwar West Germany. Its Bavarian sister-party styles itself the Christian Social Union.
DDP	German Democratic Party: a Weimar middle-class party of former left liberals and some left-wing National Liberals.
DNVP	German Nationalist People's Party: extreme but 'respectable' nationalists of the Weimar Republic.
DVP	German People's Party: a Weimar middle-class party comprising, in the main, former National Liberals.
FDP	Free Democratic Party: a minority party representing liberal and business interests in post-1945 West Germany.
GDR	German Democratic Republic, as the East German regime calls itself.
GFR	German Federal Republic or Federal Republic of Germany (West Germany).
IISG	International Institute for Social History, Amsterdam.
ILP	Independent Labour Party: organization of British ethical socialists founded in 1893.
ISD	International Socialists of Germany (*Internationale Sozialisten Deutschlands*): German 'Zimmerwaldian' group led by Julian Borchardt.
IWMA	International Working-men's Association (First International).
KP	Karl Kautsky Papers, IISG Amsterdam.

KPD	German Communist Party, founded in January 1919.
NPD	National Democratic Party of Germany: widely regarded as neo-Nazi and seriously feared in the late 1960s but never a serious force electorally.
NSBO	Nazi Factory-cell Organization (*NS Betriebszellen-organisation*): the basic unit of Nazi labour organization in the Weimar Republic.
NSDAP	National Socialist German Workers' (Nazi) Party.
RGO	Revolutionary Trade-Union Opposition (*revolutionäre Gewerkschafts-Opposition*): Communist anti-SPD trade-union organization in the 1920s.
SA	*Sturmabteilung* or Stormtroopers: Hitler's private army of brown-shirted street-fighters; liquidated in the 'night of the long knives' in 1934.
SAG	Social Democratic Working Group (*Sozialdemokratische Arbeitsgemeinschaft*): First World War socialist dissident group.
SAP	Swedish Social Democratic Workers' Party.
SAPD	German Socialist Workers' Party (*Sozialistische Arbeiterpartei Deutschlands*): left-wing splinter group which left the SPD during the Great Depression.
SDAP	Social Democratic Workers' Party (*Sozialdemokratische Arbeiterpartei*): 'Marxist' labour party founded in Eisenach in 1869. After its union with the ADAV in 1875 it adopted the title of German Socialist Workers' Party (*Sozialistische Arbeiterpartei Deutschlands*).
SDF	Social Democratic Federation: organisation of British Marxists dating from 1881 and led by H. M. Hyndman.
SED	Socialist Unity Party, as the East German ruling Communist party calls itself.
SPD	Social Democratic Party of Germany (*Sozialdemokratische Partei Deutschlands*): the title adopted by the principal German labour party since the dropping of the anti-socialist law in 1890.
USPD	Independent Social Democrats or Independents: the SPD left wing which broke with the moderate majority over the war issue in 1917.
VDAV	League of German Workers' Associations (*Verband der deutschen Arbeitervereine*), founded in June 1863.
ZAG	Central working community or joint industrial alliance (*Zentralarbeitsgemeinschaft*) of trade unions and employer organizations formed in November 1918.

Notes on Contributors

Hans-Joachim Bieber is head of the planning staff of the University of Kassel and lecturer in modern history. His principal publication to date is his two-volume trade-union study, *Gewerkschaften in Krieg und Revolution* (1981).

Willy Brandt is a former mayor of West Berlin and a former chancellor of the Federal Republic of Germany. He was awarded the Nobel Peace Prize in 1971 for his efforts to promote international understanding and East–West détente. Until March 1987 he was SPD Party Chairman, and he is still a member of the West German parliament. Also prominent in the Socialist International, which he has served as president since 1976, he has recently attracted international recognition as chairman of the North–South Commission. He is undoubtedly one of the most able and widely respected democratic socialists of the postwar world.

John Breuilly is senior lecturer in history at the University of Manchester. He is the author of *Nationalism and the State* (1982) and (with W. Sachse) *Joachim Friedrich Martens und die deutsche Arbeiterbewegung* (1984).

William Carr was professor of modern history and head of the history department at the University of Sheffield until his retirement in 1986. He is the author of several books on German history, including a *History of Germany* (now in its third edition), *Hitler: A study in personality and politics* (1978) and *Arms, Autarky and Aggression* (1972).

Ute Daniel teaches history at the University of Siegen. She is completing her doctoral dissertation on women during the First World War.

Neil C. M. Elder is assistant director of the Institute of European Studies and reader in politics at the University of Hull. He is the author of *Government in Sweden* (1970) and co-author of *The Consensual Democracies? The Government and Politics of the Scandinavian States* (1982).

Geoff Eley was born and educated in Britain but is now professor of history at the University of Michigan, Ann Arbor. His major publications include his *Reshaping the German Right* (1980), (with D. Blackbourn) *The Peculiarities of German History* (1984) and *From Unification to Nazism* (1986).

Roger Fletcher is the author of *Revisionism and Empire: Socialist Imperialism in Germany 1897–1914* (1984) and (with Fritz Fischer) *From Kaiserreich to Third Reich: Elements of Continuity in German History 1871–1945* (1986).

Ute Frevert teaches history at the University of Bielefeld. She has published widely on women and medicine. Among her latest books is *Frauengeschichte zwischen bürgerlicher Verbesserung and neuer Weiblichkeit* (1986).

Dick Geary is head of the department of German studies at the University of Lancaster. He is the author of *European Labour Protest 1848–1939* (1981) and (with Richard Evans) of *The German Unemployed 1918–1936*.

Anthony Glees is a lecturer in contemporary history at Brunel University in West London. He is the author of *Exile Politics during the Second World War* (1982).

Karen Hagemann has published widely on various aspects of women's history in Germany, especially women's history in Hamburg during the Weimar Republic. The latter is the subject of her doctoral dissertation.

Harold James is professor of history at Princeton University. He has been a research fellow at the Institute for European History in Mainz, as well as fellow at Peterhouse, Cambridge. He is the author of *The Reichsbank and Public Finance in Germany 1924–1933* (1985) and *The German Slump 1924–1936* (1986).

Eugene Kamenka is professor of the history of ideas and head of the History of Ideas Unit in the Research School of Social Sciences of the Australian National University, Canberra. His major books include *The Ethical Foundations of Marxism* (1962 and 1972), *Marxism and Ethics* (1969), *The Philosophy of Ludwig Feuerbach* (1970) and – with his wife, Alice Tay – *Marxism and the Theory of Law* (1987).

Dieter Langewiesche is professor of modern history at the University of Tübingen. He is the author of numerous books on various aspects of modern German social and labour history.

Detlef Lehnert teaches politics at the Free University of Berlin. He is the author of several books (both monographs and surveys) on the history of German Social Democracy.

Alfred G. Meyer is professor of political science at the University of Michigan, Ann Arbor. Among his more recent publications is *The Feminism and Socialism of Lily Braun* (1985).

Susanne Miller has published several books on the history of the German labour movement and on German socialism. She is co-author (with H. Potthoff) of *A History of German Social Democracy from 1848 to the Present* (1986). Though retired since 1978, she continues to be an active Social Democrat. As such, she spent the war-years in exile in Britain.

John Moses is the author of a history of the socialist trade unions in Germany. He is associate professor of history and head of the history department at the University of Queensland, Australia.

Klaus Schönhoven is professor of politics and contemporary history at the University of Mannheim. He is the author of several books on the history of the German trade unions, the German labour movement and modern German social history.

Peter D. Stachura is reader in history at the University of Stirling, Scotland. He has published widely on the history of the youth movement in Germany, on the Weimar Republic and on National Socialism. His most recent book is his *Unemployment and the Great Depression in Weimar Germany* (1986).

Susan Tegel studied at Vassar College (USA) and the London School of Economics, where she received her MSc and PhD. She was also an Alexander von Humboldt Fellow at the Free University of Berlin. Her doctoral thesis was on the reformist Social Democrat, Ludwig Frank, and she is presently working on a study of reformist Social Democrats and the political mass strike. She teaches history at the Hatfield Polytechnic.

Volker Ullrich lives in Hamburg as a teacher, critic and independent author. He has published extensively on the history of the German labour movement, on the history of everyday life and on the First World War. Among his recent books is his *Kriegsalltag: Hamburg im ersten Weltkrieg* (1982).

Heinrich August Winkler is professor of modern and contemporary history in Freiburg. His books and essays have dealt with the history of liberalism, nationalism, Marxism, fascism and National Socialism, as well as the *Mittelstand* during the Weimar Republic. He is currently completing a trilogy on workers and the labour movement during the Weimar Republic.

Foreword

Willy Brandt

The history of democratic socialism in Germany did not begin with Eduard Bernstein and it will not end with Willy Brandt. In fact, however, a century will soon have passed since the traditional party of the German left emerged from the illegality of the anti-socialist law and adopted the name it now bears – the Social Democratic Party of Germany (SPD).

What connects the SPD of 1987 with the party of the same name which originated almost 100 years ago?

In my view, more than outward appearance would seem to indicate.

Just as capitalism and bourgeois society no longer bear the same aspect which they wore a century previously, Social Democracy has also been transformed. In essence, it remains nevertheless what it was at its point of origin in the nineteenth century: it is a party of the broad working masses whose programmatic perspective of democratic socialism aims at securing a new social order that is superior to the present one – superior in terms of the demands for liberty, equality and fraternity which marked the birth of modern society.

In an age in which dependent employees comprise over 80 percent of the workforce, when peace is threatened by an arms race which spans the globe, in which the destruction of our vital natural resources has assumed catastrophic proportions, it is self-evident that Social Democracy is, programmatically and in terms of membership, a people's party, a party of the entire populace. And, indeed, the maintenance of peace is no more a class question in the old sense than is the preservation of natural resources. Even the liberation of work, which most closely binds modern Social Democracy to its historical antecedent, can scarcely be misapprehended in the limiting context of class interest. Here the decisive factor is rather whether humanity – so to speak, in conscious realization of evolutionary necessities – can succeed in shaping and unleashing on an optimal scale its intelligence, imagination and vigour. Unless it does succeed, a solution to the manifold problems besetting the human species seems inconceivable.

Of this I am certain: whether this world becomes a peaceful one, whether our grand-children will still be able to breathe its air and drink its water, whether there is a place on it for humankind or for meaningful work that is productive of individuality and history, this will depend not least on the degree of progress which international Social Democracy can and does make along its road to mutual security and disarmament, to safeguarding natural life-support systems and to the creation of a humane work environment.

German Social Democracy is about to give itself a new party programme, working from a first draft, the so-called Irsee Draft, which has been in existence since summer 1986. I believe one is entitled to be optimistic regarding the outcome of these intellectual endeavours. At the conclusion of the discussion process there will be a programme which will bring the party fully up to date and enable it to assert itself in pursuit of these ends. It is within the bounds of possibility that international Social Democracy might also draw advantage from it.

Bonn, 1987

Introduction

Roger Fletcher

One of the principal objectives of this collection of essays is to offer to the 'Germanless' reader, to the undergraduate reader and to the lay or general reader an interesting, intelligible and at once original survey of the history of German Social Democracy from its inception in the revolutionary 1840s until the present day. In particular, the intention has been to make available to the non-specialist reader the best and latest fruits of recent research, including German-language work which might not otherwise readily come to the attention of interested students. In so doing, the contributors have consistently striven to take due cognizance of the German labour movement in all its phases and in its rich heterogeneity. Yet this book was conceived as something over and above the standard undergraduate textbook. Great care has been taken to ensure that all contributions, while intelligible to the lay-person, also meet the highest standards of international scholarship in presenting fresh and stimulating interpretations that will not only interest students of the German labour movement but also serve the needs of experts working in such fields as comparative labour history, political science, social history, intellectual history, political sociology, war and peace studies, trade-union history and women's studies. We have endeavoured to achieve these aims within a context of brevity, lucidity and compactness.

Organizationally, the present volume is a blend of the thematic and the narrative or chronological approaches. The principal institutions of the labour movement (the Social Democratic Party and the socialist trade unions) are studied in depth, but at the same time the German working class is given equal billing. Hence the rather strong focus on proletarian and labour-movement culture, as well as on women and the Social Democratic women's movement. All the major events which have shaped or reflected the development of democratic socialism in Germany find a place in this narrative. Beginning with the revolutionary 1840s and the birth of the proletariat as a social force, our story progresses through the stormy Imperial adolescence of the movement, through the watershed of world war and the test of revolution, on to the first German experience of democracy and its apparent collapse, taking us into the long dark night of National Socialism, and terminating with Social Democracy's revival and accession to power in the post-1945 half-century.

For a variety of reasons, Eduard Bernstein has been selected as the ideological centrepiece and personal fixative of this narrative. It is now widely accepted that Bernstein has an undeniable claim to be regarded as the father of democratic socialism in the sense that he was the first socialist theorist of note who attempted to adapt socialist theory to the social and political realities of advanced capitalism (Schuon, 1986, 18). Yet there are other, and more compelling reasons why Bernstein, rather than Bebel or Kautsky or another Social Democratic luminary, seems pre-eminently suited to the role of representative ideologue and focal point in a history of the German democratic socialist labour movement. For one, his life and work spanned almost a century of the movement's history in a way that was almost unique. He was born in 1850 in the shadow of the 1848 revolution (the son of a Berlin locomotive driver and the nephew of a liberal revolutionary); he came to manhood and to Marxian socialism under the anti-socialist law; he served, with August Bebel and Karl Kautsky, as one of the troika which made Marxism the official ideology of the German and international labour movements, at the same time editing the central organ of the party in exile, the newspaper *Der Sozialdemokrat*; he returned from exile in 1901 to fight for democracy and pragmatic reformism, never wavering in his fight for truth, even when his struggle cost him personal friendships, political influence, financial security and the public respect normally accorded old age; and he finally died just six weeks prior to the Nazi accession to power. As a theorist, Bernstein lacked the profundity of Marx, Engels, Lassalle, Kautsky and Rosa Luxemburg, to name but a few, but in the end it was he and his theory, rather than they and theirs, which, in the words of Professor Carlo Schmid more than a generation after Bernstein's death, 'triumphed all along the line'. The circumstances under which the German labour movement achieved power and wielded influence, no less than the policies it sought to implement once in a position to do so, have accorded more nearly with the vision of Eduard Bernstein than with the theories of Marx, Kautsky or any other socialist thinker. It is arguable that they continue to do so to the present day. As a practical politician, Bernstein was personally less effective than August Bebel, Friedrich Ebert, Hermann Müller, Otto Braun, Erich Ollenhauer, Kurt Schumacher, Willy Brandt or Helmut Schmidt. Yet men like Helmut Schmidt, no less than party intellectuals like Susanne Miller and Thomas Meyer, continue to do him homage. More to the point, their actions and policies, as much as their thoughts, reflect the spirit of Bernstein far more keenly than they do the ghosts of Kautsky, Bebel or Marx. For such reasons it seems perfectly legitimate to accord Eduard Bernstein a central place in the history of the German working class and its movement.

But is there a need for a book of this sort? In the English-speaking world there is certainly no shortage of interest in the history of German Social Democracy. Paradoxically, Lenin's slogan, 'Learn from the Germans', is seemingly as applicable today, or believed to be so by democratic socialists throughout the world, as it was in the era of the Second International, when the Germans gave the world-wide movement its principal ideologies, its best and bravest leaders, and its most impressive example of a cohesive alternative culture, not to mention its most seasoned, best organized, most numerous and apparently most successful political, trade-union, women's and working-class cultural movements.

While the subject is thus of enduring intrinsic interest, it may be argued with equal validity that it is also of substantial contemporary relevance. In the advanced capitalist world, and in parts of the Third World as disparate as India and Tanzania, democratic socialism has supplanted liberalism as the principal practical alternative to political conservatism and the surest bulwark against both fascism and Bolshevism – in whatever guise. For those democratic socialists seeking external models, the German experience has a very strong claim to be regarded as offering inspiration and valid social alternatives that are at least as pertinent to the problems confronting humanity in the last decade of the twentieth century as are the British, Swedish, French or Italian models. Whether concerned with resisting Communist bullying (as did Willy Brandt as mayor of West Berlin), whether seeking to cope with the problems of a divided nationhood within the context of non-violence and democracy, whether the task is that of developing, with limited resources, a viable mixed economy that is in fact neither a Russian nor an American colony, or whether it is a question of building or rebuilding from scratch a welfare state that is based on a flourishing, internationally competitive capitalist economy and successfully defending it against the deconstructive mania of cranky market-forces reductionists and other utopians of the 'new right', or whether one is fighting for hope while caught in the crossfire of the Cold War and trapped in the frontline of the environmentalist struggle for survival, the peoples of the world still have much that they might learn from the Germans.[1]

It is arguable, moreover, that the present volume does fill a gap. To be sure, there are plenty of good monographs now available to anglophone readers, and there are even a few good and up-to-date surveys, the best being those of S. Miller and H. Potthoff (1986), Willi Guttsman (1981), Helga Grebing (1985), Dick Geary (1981) and Albert S. Lindemann (1983). Yet the present volume may claim to be unique in that it seeks to offer the anglophone public a comprehensive survey of German Social Democracy from the 1840s to the present in the form of a collective effort comprising over 20 separate essays from the pens of two dozen specialists of international renown and vastly differing expertise.

The authors are all distinguished scholars and widely respected in their several fields, though not all are academics. Diversity is perhaps the other main characteristic of this international team. In keeping with the aim of familiarizing the anglophone reader with the best and most recent fruits of German scholarship, half the contributors recruited for this volume are Germans. Other German specialists have been recruited from the United Kingdom, the United States and Australia. The result is therefore a genuinely international piece of teamwork. One quarter of the contributors are women. In general, the contributors divide evenly between established scholars of the older generation and those who are still under 40 years of age. Ideologically, they range across the political spectrum – from those who might be considered radical or left-wing in orientation, through moderates, reformists and liberals, to one or two liberal-conservatives. In approach, most are either political or social historians, but intellectual historians, political scientists, political economists, feminists and 'barefoot' social historians (as distinct from academic practitioners of 'history from below') are also strongly represented.

None of the essays in this book has been published previously in English. Only two have appeared before – those of Susanne Miller and H. A. Winkler. Both of these appeared in German, and in a very different form. The remainder have been especially commissioned for this book.

Foot- or endnoting and much of the conventional apparatus of scholarship have deliberately been held to an absolute minimum. Those direct quotations which are acknowledged in this work are presented according to the author–date system. The production of a book such as this symposium has, of course, posed more serious problems than those raised by the scale and manner of footnoting. The constraints imposed by the need to keep the length of the project within manageable bounds have inevitably entailed some hard choices and reluctantly-made sacrifices. For instance, numerous eminent and fascinating personalities have been given less than their due, while certain important aspects of the topic (such as the technical and economic changes which have unquestionably helped to shape working-class experience) have had to be dealt with only *en passant* or not at all. Again, focusing on essentials has meant some skimping at both ends of the time continuum, and useful extras, such as documents, illustrations, statistical data and a chronology, have had to be dispensed with. Hopefully the right choices have been made.

Another problem obviously raised by an attempt to realize a collective effort involving a multiplicity of authors and topics and incorporating a plethora of interests, outlooks and approaches is the very great difficulty of bringing it all into unison, of achieving even a modest degree of cohesion. Instead of trying to square the circle or produce a narrow, sectarian work (of which there are already more than enough on the market), coherence has thus been sacrificed, to some extent, on the altar not of expediency but of theoretical pluralism and methodological variety. One may perhaps be pardoned for expressing the hope that the latter are still regarded, in some circles at least, as inherently desirable principles of intellectual discourse. Accordingly, the use of the editorial prerogative has been confined very largely to standardizing spelling, punctuation, style, etc. and to the minimization of avoidable and superfluous overlap.

Note

[1]As a British writer has speculated, 'Classical Marxism, in retrospect, seems to have been in many ways a strangely simplistic doctrine. Whether the experience of the twentieth century will lead to a revival of socialist ideas in a more relevant and sophisticated form remains to be seen. If this is to be so, Germany may well be the place' (Kendall, 1975, 139). Cf. G. Haupt, 1986, 48ff.

Part I
The Birth of a Movement

1 The Beginnings of German Social Democracy, 1835–1875

John Breuilly

The Emergence of the German Labour Movement, 1835–50

The term social democracy, already in use before 1848, did not have the specific political meaning that it was to acquire by the late nineteenth century. It is important not to project that later meaning upon this earlier period.

Mid-nineteenth century social democrats considered that purely political democracy would not be able notably to increase freedom and happiness unless social and economic problems were also directly tackled. But they continued to support democratic political demands. Although unclear and divided amongst themselves about aims and methods, it was this combination of social reform and political democracy which identified the supporters of social democracy.

This broad group lacked a clear social constituency or effective organization. Germany in 1848 consisted of some 39 separate states. The most important were Austria and Prussia. Neither of these states had a constitution, a parliamentary system of politics, or provision for free speech, assembly, publication and organization. In these circumstances it was impossible for open organizations to develop expressing political values and seeking support from within society. Agriculture still dominated the economy. What manufacturing activity there was concentrated itself upon small workshop production and rural industry. The 'factory' (a term which included many small units of production) covered only a tiny fraction of the labour force. Such establishments often simply centralized traditional methods of work. Thinkers such as Marx were struck by new technology and factory production but as yet this was of minor importance within the German economy. More important was the way in which competition and commercial production were increasing and a growing number of working people sold their labour for a money wage. This was linked to the rapid population growth of the time.

The first kinds of workers to be attracted to social democratic ideas were artisans, men who had trained for a particular trade which was fairly skilled, generally practised in small workshops, and not dependent upon advanced technology. These workers, especially journeymen and small masters, found that increased competition in the labour market and the penetration of commercial capital placed new pressures upon them. They had expectations of a respectable and secure living. They possessed organizations which enabled them to discuss and act together. This made them far more capable of responding to new ideas in some organized way than the mass of unskilled labour, the tiny élites of better placed factory workers, or the decentralized rural workers. Artisans sensed that they faced novel and fundamental changes. They found that the new ideas developed by social democrats could clarify their predicament and suggest courses of action. Thus the anti-capitalism of early socialist thinkers could be used against the excessive competition to which these workers were exposed. The ideas concerning the 'organization of work' (a popular phrase of the period) tended to be used to project a vision of many small workshops supplying fixed levels of demand in a non-competitive economy: the artisan idyll.

These new ideas first influenced German artisans who had left Germany. Tramping ('wandering') journeymen had formed associations abroad in London, Paris and parts of Switzerland in the late 1830s and early 1840s. From about 1844 it had been possible to form educational associations in some German cities. These associations concentrated upon educational work but they also engaged (often secretly) in political discussions. A few skilled occupations had some kind of trade-union organization but these also had to remain secretive. Many of these associations included small masters as well as journeymen and were often led by various middle-class figures. They were not class organizations in the modern sense of that term. Some of them stressed education as the way of changing their situation; some, a variety of associational activities (co-operative production was a popular idea); some, political methods, including sudden and violent revolution. None looked to the formation of specialized political parties or trade unions within the context of a modern state and industrial economy.

In the brief period of freedom during the spring and summer of 1848 it was possible for such workers to establish new and larger associations. But the very speed with which the old governments had collapsed meant that these associations did not feel the need to come together in any powerful political movement. Some working-men concentrated upon trade-union activity. Others combined with middle-class groups to press for political change in their particular state. Some loose umbrella organizations – notably the Brotherhood of German Workers – were formed. But the Brotherhood probably never had more than 23,000 members throughout Germany. More purely political organizations such as those of the liberals, democrats and Catholics, led and supported by various middle-class groups, dominated the oppositional politics of the period. Although the numbers of workers who organized expanded considerably, the bulk of them were artisans and they still represented only a small minority of the labour force. The tightest and most politically aware organization, the League of the Communists to which Marx belonged, was never more than a small sect.

The Response to the Failure of Revolution, 1850–62

The revolution disappeared almost as quickly as it had arisen. Organizations deemed suspicious by the restored governments were suppressed; censorship was reimposed; and a more effective political police was organized. The only kinds of organizations with worker involvement which could survive were educational associations, co-operatives and certain support funds. Even these were looked upon with suspicion and contacts between local associations were forbidden. What is more, the co-operatives increasingly took on a middle-class, business character, and some of the educational associations began to take in new middle-class groups, such as clerks, and to play down even the limited political role they had continued to perform.

However, the 1848 revolution had brought about important changes. In many states, such as Prussia, some kind of constitutional and parliamentary system remained in being, even if limited in its powers and electoral base. Rulers were aware of the need to respond to pressure from below before it became dangerous.

The 1850s witnessed the first rapid economic expansion of the manufacturing sector. Governments made concessions to economic liberalism. Expansion and economic liberalism in turn affected the labour movement. The boom of the 1860s increased the bargaining power of some skilled workers and led to an increase in strike activity. Increased labour migration made it difficult to prevent contacts between workers in different areas. The liberalization of the economy made it increasingly difficult to suppress organizations amongst workers, especially if it could be argued that these had a purely economic or educational purpose and did not seek to engage in political activity.

The first main political effect was the rejuvenation of liberalism. The growing and increasingly confident middle class took advantage of the new parliaments to increase their political strength. Some of their leaders helped workers' co-operatives and educational associations, partly in order to create some popular support for their politics, partly genuinely to help workers, and partly to prevent workers falling prey to anti-liberal ideas, whether from the left or the right. From the late 1850s a growing number of organized working-men, still mainly artisans, supported this growing liberal movement. Social democratic or socialist ideas were played down. Indeed, the liberal most popular amongst these workers, Hermann Schulze-Delitzsch, stressed his economic liberalism and insisted that the state should not intervene in economic matters. He stressed the development of privately funded co-operatives, thus linking liberalism and distinctive artisan values.

The Development of an Independent Political Labour Party, 1862–75

This expanding liberal movement faced its first major challenge in Prussia in the early 1860s. The attempt by the king to increase the size of the army and the length of service was opposed by liberals who feared that it would reduce the influence of parliament, which they dominated. However, most of these liberals, with the memory of 1848 still fairly fresh in their minds, had no desire to whip up popular opposition to the crown. They wanted organized workers to support them, but not to take political action directly. It was the impatience with the liberal hesitation which led in May 1863 to the formation of the first workers' political party, the All-German Workers' Association (*Allgemeiner Deutscher Arbeiter-Verein* or ADAV) under the leadership of Ferdinand Lassalle. Lassalle opposed the liberals and sought to mobilize a mass working-class movement in support of both political democracy and state-funded co-operatives. Lassalle took up the specific concerns of an artisan-dominated labour movement, but he sought to turn these against the liberals, to channel them into an independent political party, and to try to appeal to the interests of the whole working class.

It was a bold move, exploiting yet at the same time breaking with many of the traditions of the artisan labour movement. In Lassalle's own short time as flamboyant leader (he was killed in a duel in the summer of 1864) it largely failed. Most organized workers did not join Lassalle. For some time they preferred to work with liberals in a broader, safer and more promising political movement. Even here, however, they pressed for a greater emphasis upon their own distinctive social interests, and tried to push the liberals towards a more democratic commitment. In June 1863, partly as a reply to the ADAV and partly as an expression of this tendency, the League of German Workers' Associations (*Verband der deutschen Arbeitervereine* or VDAV) was established. The VDAV was concentrated in southern and central Germany, especially Saxony, whilst the ADAV was concentrated in northern Germany, especially in the Prussian Rhineland and in Hamburg. It was a less centralized or purely political movement than the ADAV, tending rather to emphasize labour interests within a broad liberal movement.

The events of 1866–7 had a major impact on these two small organizations. The defeat of Austria by Prussia signalled the victory of the Prussian 'solution' to the national question. The VDAV was concentrated in non-Prussian regions and largely opposed this solution, whilst the ADAV supported it. The divisions between the two organizations increased. The social democracy of the ADAV expressed illiberal ideas of mass democracy and state subsidies for co-operatives. The VDAV wanted cautiously to extend liberal democracy downwards and place some restrictions upon unrestrained economic freedom.

The formation of the North-German Confederation in 1867 brought together most of the German states north of the river Main (many of them directly annexed to Prussia). A lower house of parliament was established, based on universal adult male suffrage. Although the political organizations claiming to be working class received only a small amount of electoral support in early elections, this step did encourage the development of party organization and an appeal to a class constituency. It was difficult for established elite parties like those of the liberals to respond as effectively to these new opportunities as could the ADAV or political Catholicism.

The economic boom of the late 1860s did not collapse until 1873–4. In these circumstances some trade unions flourished and there was a veritable strike wave. This was helped by the fact that economically liberal legislation carried through in the North-German Confederation included extending the freedom to form trade unions and to strike.

In the face of these dramatic changes the liberal movement fell apart. Some liberals crossed over to support Bismarck because he was seen as solving the national question and laying the basis for national and liberal progress. Other liberals continued to oppose him, though they were divided amongst themselves. New kinds of political sentiment, such as ethnic nationalism and political Catholicism, as well as the appeal to class, began to displace the popular liberalism of the early 1860s. Liberals became more suspicious of labour organization as they fared badly in elections and observed with alarm the rising tide of strikes.

In these circumstances most of the VDAV, along with the breakaway group from the ADAV, formed its own independent political party, the Social Democratic Workers' Party (SDAP) in 1869. The ADAV element, and the need to make a class appeal, meant that the new party stressed social and political demands in ways which made it difficult to continue in alliance with liberal or even radical democratic groups. The SDAP affiliated to the International Working-men's Association (IWMA) in which Marx was closely involved. Marx opposed the ADAV because it failed to see that socialism could triumph only on the basis of capitalist development, which meant that workers should form an alliance with liberals to hasten economic and political progress. Marx remained critical of many of the preoccupations of the SDAP, such as its belief in democracy for its own sake, its anti-Prussianism and its restricted social vision. In certain ways the ADAV was closer to Marx – with its explicit appeal to the wage-earners as a distinct and progressive class interest and its recognition that ultimately liberal and proletarian democracy were incompatible. But Marx was closer to the SDAP leaders, August Bebel and Wilhelm Liebknecht, though one should not exaggerate his influence upon them.

The two small and conflicting parties tried to take advantage of the growing trade-union and strike movement. The ADAV, although theoretically of the view that strikes could be of little help to workers, supported them on political grounds. However, the ADAV, with its strongly centralized and authoritarian character, alienated trade unions when it tried to subordinate them to itself. There were also many splits within the ADAV. The SDAP developed as a looser organization, more tolerant of the autonomy of affiliated trade unions or local political groups. Liberal attempts to influence trade unions foundered on middle-class hostility to strikes.

But various forces were pushing the two organizations closer to one another. It seemed pointless to continue opposing Prussian domination once it was immovably established. The hopes of the ADAV that a conservative Prussian regime might make concessions to working-men had proved illusory. With the introduction of mass suffrage, both organizations had accepted the need for specialized political parties appealing to the working class. Their differences on state intervention or the role of trade unions seemed to be purely doctrinal. There was some pressure from rank-and-file members of both parties to bury their differences in the face of hostility from governments as well as much of the middle-class liberal movement.

The Franco-Prussian war and its aftermath increased this pressure. Prussian dominance was now sealed. The split between pro- and anti-Prussian liberals hardened, with the pro-Prussian element dominant. Members of both parties were subjected to repression because of their opposition to the prosecution of the war after the victory of Sedan. The collapse of the boom in 1873–4 increased the effectiveness of measures against strikes and trade unions and led workers to shift their attention to politics. Above all, the dominance of the partnership between Bismarck and the liberals at the expense of workers meant that labour unity against both the Prussian state and liberalism was urgently needed.

Faced with all these pressures, the leaders of the two organizations met in 1875 at Gotha to form a single party. The practical need for unity was more important than the precise programme on which they unified. Some of the ideas of the SDAP, especially on further extensions of political democracy and trade-union rights, were combined with ideas about state support for producers' co-operatives. It remained unclear what could be obtained by reform and what by revolution. The new party made demands upon the present state and outlined the need for laws on matters such as regulation of hours. Yet at the same time it condemned the whole structure of power above it as 'one reactionary mass', which hardly suggested that such demands would be heeded. In London, Marx fumed at the incoherence of the programme and its inability to see that the old regime and the growing middle class, the remnants of feudalism and burgeoning capitalism, represented different kinds of enemies and should not be indiscriminately lumped together. He also exaggerated the degree to which Lassallean ideas had been accepted by the SDAP in the negotiations. Such ideas had never been wholly alien to those within the SDAP.

Conclusion

By 1875, then, there was a single labour party in Germany. Its successor, the Social Democratic Party was, by 1914, the largest political party in the world, drawing its electoral support largely from the urban working class and with a Marxist programme. It is difficult to prevent knowledge of this influencing our understanding of early social democracy. East German writers stress the revolutionary Marxist current within the movement. West German historians focus upon more democratic and reformist ideas. Both views distort our understanding of this period. By 1875 the new socialist party was not a party of the industrial working class (this had yet to develop) committed to revolution. But neither was it a party of moderate workers seeking progressive reforms and forced into political isolation by the alliance between Prussia and liberalism. It was a small political grouping of largely artisanal workers committed to democracy and to numerous restrictions upon the free market. How it changed to become the mass party of the industrial working class is a story that other contributors to this book take up.

2 Working-Class Culture in Imperial Germany

Dick Geary

The Culture of Organized German Labour

The overwhelming majority of historians of German labour, at least until recently, have concerned themselves less with the culture of everyday life (*Alltagskultur*) than with the formal cultural organizations of the labour *movement*. This is no accident, nor is it simply a reflection of an historiographical tradition. It does correspond to a situation in which German workers joined cultural and leisure associations on a nation-wide level and in massive numbers. In 1914 several Social Democratic cultural or leisure organizations had over 100,000 members: the Choral Societies' Federation (*Deutsche Arbeitersängerbund*) mobilized almost 200,000; the cyclists' organization (*Solidarität*), over 130,000; and the gymnasts' association (*Arbeiter-Turn- und Sportverein*), 186,958. The Social Democratic Party also ran chess, ramblers' and educational societies throughout the Second Reich. This scale of nation-wide mobilization had no counterpart in Edwardian Britain or in *fin-de-siècle* France. These various German organizations were also politicized, at least to the extent that they were ancillary organizations of the SPD. Our first concern, therefore, must be to explain the success of the SPD and its cultural organizations in mobilizing so many workers in Imperial Germany.

Part of the explanation of Social Democratic success may lie in residential factors. Unlike the British case, where a significant percentage of skilled workers lived in single-family terraced housing from the turn of the century, and where they could thus enjoy a 'modest domesticity', the rapidity and scale of urbanization in Germany after 1870 led to cramped and overcrowded living conditions, often in large tenement buildings (*Mietskasernen*). In the Ruhr, where the situation was not as grim as in the older industrial cities and where company housing was often of superior quality to that found in the private housing market, it was none the less the case that few working-class families could survive without taking in lodgers, especially as there were few opportunities for female employment outside the home in this overwhelmingly heavy-industrial region. In 1900 in Essen 11 per cent of all households took in six or more lodgers, 15 per cent took in three lodgers, and 26 per cent took in two. In the Ruhr as a whole at this time 54 per cent of all families took at least one lodger; and of these families 70 per cent had at least one child of their own. Under these circumstances the development of a privatized life-style was scarcely possible, and such a fact, as Franz Brüggemeier has argued, may have served to generate working-class solidarity. It also meant that the enjoyment of leisure-time was more likely to take place outside the home and especially in the pubs, which, as Karl Kautsky commented, formed the backbone of Social Democratic survival and mobilization.

This context helps to explain the attraction of the choral societies, cycling clubs, educational associations and the like. That attraction was further enhanced by the *relative* absence of commercialized alternatives. It appears to be the case, with possible exceptions in the metropolitan centres of Germany, that mass spectator sports and commercialization were essentially postwar phenomena. Thus Ross McKibbin claims that the cultural organizations of German Social Democracy were able to be so successful precisely because they came to occupy a vacuum (McKibbin, 1984, 297–311).

Politics and Working-Class Culture

If the absence of alternatives and residential factors helps to explain the scale of cultural and leisure organizations in Imperial Germany, we need to look elsewhere to explain why those organizations had an explicitly *political* dimension, in so far as the majority of them were associated with the Social Democratic Party. Admittedly, the 'political' nature of sports clubs is open to question. Many workers joined for the exercise and for reasons of sociability rather than for expressly political motives. Attendance at educational associations was often generated by vocational needs rather than radical ideology. It is also the case that the SPD and the socialist or Free Trade Unions initially distrusted the leisure organizations, seeing in them a source of competition and diversion from more important industrial and political goals. In this sense these organizations were created from 'below'. Furthermore, it has been argued, often and at length, that the 'politicization' of working-class culture in the ancillary organizations of the SPD was merely superficial. Far from constructing a real *counter-culture*, Social Democratic cultural associations often simply reproduced the classic works of 'bourgeois' culture: at festivals and other meetings one heard the music not only of Beethoven but also Mendelssohn, Verdi, Léhar, Strauss and Wagner. Choral societies sang traditional folk-song as often as anything else, whilst theatre groups performed the masterpieces of Schiller and Goethe. From the trade-union and party libraries the works that were most commonly borrowed were rarely those of Marx or Engels but either popularizations of evolutionary biology or – more commonly – works of fiction. Co-operative stores ceased to be the seeds of a new form of social organization and became increasingly 'neutral' commercial organizations. In concerts, performance and professionalism became at least as important as any political message. The political content of Social Democratic celebrations generally decreased after 1906. Following this line of argument, therefore, it may be somewhat perverse to construct an explanation of the 'politicization' of working-class culture in Wilhelmine Germany, especially when a much-quoted authority (Guenther Roth, 1963) has even claimed that the very existence of this Social Democratic subculture served to 'integrate' workers into the social and political fabric of the Second Reich.

This is not the last word on the matter, however. First of all, the membership of these organizations overlapped to a very considerable extent with that of the SPD and the Free Trade Unions. Secondly, the very fact that these were *Social Democratic* clubs and associations meant that to join them was to cock a snook at the Imperial establishment – at the Kaiser, the army, the police and the employer – which might bring persecution and harassment in its wake. Indeed, the harassment of Social Democratic sports clubs actually increased in the years immediately before the First World War. It is also not without significance that most of the working-class cultural organizations included the word 'workers' in their title, thus demarcating themselves from the world of bourgeois leisure. The choral societies sang radical and revolutionary songs as well as more popular tunes. It should also be noted that the music played at many of the workers' gatherings was determined in large measure by the repertoire of a band or orchestra that had in fact been booked by the proprietor of the establishment rather than by the workers themselves. Few Social Democratic festivals were devoted entirely to apolitical activities. In fact, the activities of local organizations were given over to repeated discussions of revolution and rigorous propaganda against capitalism and the *Kaiserreich*, as Vernon Lidtke (1985) has shown in general and Mary Nolan (1981) in the specific case of Düsseldorf. The simple fact that workers, too, celebrated Goethe and Schiller should not mislead us into the facile assumption that such celebration merely reflected an 'hegemonic' bourgeois culture: for what workers took from Schiller was different, and markedly so, from his middle-class reception in the Empire. Superficial similarities in matters of dress may also tell us little about the political identity of the wearers: otherwise we would have to conclude that Rosa Luxemburg was thoroughly bourgeois and no socialist revolutionary. Above all, participation in the various Social Democratic ancillary organizations served to sharpen the political and social awareness of the participants and was often an actual liberation for the individual worker, who learnt independence and self-confidence through his activities in the clubs, which also served to foster a sense of solidarity. In any case, some of those clubs had been set up specifically to counter existing 'bourgeois' institutions, such as the virulently nationalist gymnasts' organization. There was even a workers' puppet-theatre, delivering a message considerably at odds with the traditional Punch-and-Judy show. In fact, this Social Democratic subculture did offer an alternative view of the world to its members, an alternative view of politics, work, education, religion, recreation and the family. To argue that it 'integrated' workers into the prevailing political and social fabric (however 'negatively') is somewhat problematical in view of the fact that some of the party branches with the most highly developed organizational subculture went over almost to a man to the left opposition in the revolutionary upheavals at the end of the First World War, as in Remscheid and in several Saxon towns.

The politicization of working-class leisure in Imperial Germany is thus to be taken seriously and requires explanation. It was, above all, a consequence of the role of authoritarian and interventionist government. Of especial importance were not only the discriminatory franchises of the most important states or *Länder*, particularly Prussia, not only the manifest discrimination in taxation and tariff policy, not only the repression and harassment of organized labour, especially but not exclusively in the years of the anti-socialist law (1878–90); equally significant was the state's intervention in areas which in Britain or elsewhere were often regarded as 'apolitical'. The often brutal intervention of the Imperial authorities in industrial disputes was contrasted unfavourably with the situation in Britain by Ernst Dückershoff, a miner who had lived and worked in both countries. He wrote:

> Politics are not in question [in industrial disputes in England] . . . Such hatred and mutual rage as in Germany is not to be met with. The capitalist exploits the same means as there, but he is not backed up in the same way by the authorities (McKibbin, 1984, 320).

State intervention into proletarian everyday life was not restricted to industrial disputes. Far from it, for German workers needed police permission to marry in some states, where cohabiting unmarried couples could be compelled to separate and could be prosecuted by the authorities. Almost all forms of working-class leisure were subject to the supervision of a suspicious police force, including the sports clubs and *Schnapskasinos* (drinking clubs). Raymond Fosdick, an American visitor, could not suppress his surprise at the extent of police regulation in Berlin in 1914, where even the colour of automobiles and the length of hatpins were decreed by official instruction (Fosdick, 1915, 27).

The politicization of Social Democratic subculture was thus to a large extent a response to governmental harassment and persecution. But the political identity of German working-class leisure was also expressed in the existence of specifically Catholic working-men's clubs, trade unions, choral societies and the like, which organizationally mirrored the SPD's ancillary organizations but which were committed to support for the Centre Party and preached a message markedly at variance with the Social Democratic image of state and society. The Polish working class in Imperial Germany built its own clubs, unions and political party, sang Polish folk-songs, honoured the heroes of Polish history, and frequently encountered police repression, but remained committed to the values of Polish nationalism. In short, despite certain superficial similarities, even the *organized* working class of Germany's Second Reich possessed several different cultures. But that is far from the end of the matter, for it is not at all clear that the organizational culture of the labour *movement* can be equated with 'working-class culture' more generally.

Labour-Movement Culture versus Working-Class Culture

The emergence of a relatively homogeneous working-class culture in Britain has been attributed to the growth of a social structure that was overwhelmingly urban and industrial by the late nineteenth century, when 85 per cent of the labour force were wage labourers and 75 per cent of these were manual workers of some kind or other. The situation in Germany was very different: in 1914 almost 30 per cent of the labour force still worked in the agricultural sector (compared with 11 per cent in Britain). Over half of those registered in the census as 'workers' lived in small towns and villages of under 10,000 inhabitants; and approximately one third of those employed in 'industry and crafts' were either self-employed or worked in firms employing five or fewer persons. Even more significantly, almost a half of the industrial labour force in Germany on the eve of the First World War were first-generation factory workers. Such factors made the emergence of a monolithic working-class culture most unlikely. Moreover, 'working-class culture' in Wilhelmine Germany, whether of a formal or informal kind, was an overwhelmingly male affair (at least in the way it has been portrayed by historians). The values of sport were often aggression and masculinity, whilst that pre-eminently male preserve, the public house, lay at the centre of working-class leisure outside the home. For the overwhelming majority of German working-class women before the outbreak of the First World War, the home and the family occupied what might misleadingly be described as 'leisure'-time. Finally, and most importantly, the organizational subculture of Social Democratic and Catholic workers in Imperial Germany was above all a culture of skilled workers enjoying permanent employment, and the content of that culture was 'improvement'.

Social Democratic cultural organizations saw themselves as the 'third pillar' of the labour movement, alongside the party and the trade unions. Their aim was not only to politicize workers but to 'educate' them, to raise them 'onto a new plane', to 'ennoble' them. Thus their concept of culture overlapped with a traditional view of 'culture' to some extent. The disadvantages of working-class life were to be compensated and 'new human beings' created. As a result, many Social Democratic militants had little understanding of or for behaviour that was not 'respectable', for petty criminality and violence. Such actions were regarded as the work of '*Lumpen*' and ascribed to 'immaturity' on the part of the 'unschooled' and 'unorganized'. Yet we must remember that no more than a quarter of the German working class belonged to the economic or political organizations of the labour movement. Even amongst the organized, participation in some aspects of Social Democratic culture was limited. In Hamburg only 3 per cent of organized workers made use of trade-union libraries. Amongst unionized dockers, transport workers and factory labourers the figure dropped as low as 1 per cent. For broad sections of the German working class, especially those which suffered regular unemployment or where there were high rates of fluctuation and mobility, it made little sense to develop a life-style geared to the future. Thus dockworkers in Hamburg and the highly mobile young miners of the Ruhr were more inclined to forms of direct action rather than to the cautious and long-term strategies of the official trade-union leaders.

As Michael Grüttner has argued, following the American anthropologist Oscar Lewis, there existed among some groups of German workers a 'culture of poverty', characterized by an absence of 'deferred gratification' or long-term perspectives. Here there existed a tacit acceptance of and sometimes active support for various kinds of 'self-help', including pilfering. Petty criminality was endemic in daily life. After the miners' strike of 1912, for example, 1750 miners were found guilty of offences by the court. No fewer than 35 per cent of these people had previous convictions, thus revealing both how difficult it was to steer clear of the law and that Geman workers were far from the timid creatures populating the pages of some history books. The life-style of these sections of the working-class was also often characterized by violence – against the authorities, against supervisors at work, but also against one another and in the home. For the SPD and the unions, however, such 'rude' manners were unacceptable; and the inability of Social Democracy to mobilize the *Lumpen* had not a little to do with the tragic division of the German labour movement in the Weimar Republic.

3 The SPD in Imperial Germany, 1871–1914

Susan Tegel

The Party to 1890

Four years after the unification of Germany the German labour movement, divided since 1869 between two distinct organizations, united to form the new *Sozialistische Arbeiterpartei Deutschlands* (German Socialist Workers' Party). In 1890 it changed its name to the *Sozialdemokratische*

Partei Deutschlands (German Social Democratic Party or SPD); by 1914 it had become not only the largest political party in Germany, but the largest socialist party in the world.

Government policy had encouraged unification. Germany's first independent labour party, the All-German Workers' Association, the Lassalleans (after their first leader, Ferdinand Lassalle), united with the Social Democratic Workers' Party founded in 1869 by Wilhelm Liebknecht and August Bebel at Eisenach, otherwise known as the Eisenachers. When the parties united in 1875 at Gotha, Marx criticized their new programme, later published in 1891 at Engels' behest as *The Critique of the Gotha Programme*. He assumed incorrectly that the 'Marxist' Eisenachers had capitulated to the more numerous Lassalleans. Though Liebknecht was for a time a fellow exile of Marx and Engels in London and Bebel had become acquainted with some of Marx's writings, neither personal nor literary acquaintance had turned them into Marxists. To the end of the 1870s Marxism was at best only dimly understood by a few and never propagated to the exclusion of other theories.

At the outbreak of the Franco–Prussian War in 1870 Bebel and Liebknecht, elected on universal suffrage to the North-German parliament or Reichstag, had abstained on the vote for war credits. After Napoleon III's overthrow all five Lassallean and Eisenacher deputies opposed further war credits and openly supported the Paris Commune. Thus began the Social Democrats' reputation as dangerous revolutionaries and traitors. Bebel and Liebknecht were later tried for high treason, convicted and imprisoned for two years.

After unification Bismarck turned on those hostile to the newly created empire – on the Catholics, against whom he directed his *Kulturkampf*, or anti-Catholic campaign, and the Social Democrats, whose vote increased in the 1874 elections from 3 per cent to 7 per cent. Persecution was stepped up. In the 1877 election the unified party's vote rose to 9 per cent. Two successive attempts on the life of the Kaiser the following year served Bismarck as a pretext for outlawing the party. Neither of the would-be assassins was a Social Democrat but the anti-socialist law was introduced initially for three years, renewed thereafter on four occasions, only lapsing in 1890. All Social Democratic organizations and almost all newspapers and literature were banned. The law was administered by the provincial police, harshly enforced in Prussia, less so in the south. Many Social Democrats were imprisoned, expelled or emigrated. At the same time Bismarck introduced social insurance, the first such legislation anywhere, but refused to extend protective legislation to regulate conditions of work. This failed to woo the workers away from an interest in political emancipation and reconcile them to an occasionally paternalist but mainly repressive state.

The anti-socialist law did not exclude the Social Democrats from contesting elections to the Reichstag or *Landtag* (provincial parliament), though Bismarck had on more than one occasion tried to extend the law. The Social Democratic vote initially declined to 7.5 per cent in 1878 just before the introduction of the law, to 6.1 per cent in 1881, 9.7 per cent in 1884, down to 7.1 per cent in 1887, rising to 19.7 per cent in 1890 when the law lapsed. The party only partly went underground, overtly attempting to work within the bounds of legality though contemptuous of this legality. It operated an underground distribution network of the party paper, *Der Sozialdemokrat,* which was first published in Switzerland and then, after pressure from the German government, in London.

The experience of the anti-socialist law radicalized the party. Marxism could now make inroads. The Lassallean confidence in the state was shown to be misplaced. The Gotha Programme had emphasized the need to employ 'all legal means', such as universal suffrage, to ensure a 'free state and socialist society: the abolition of the wage system' and all 'exploitation'. It also demanded the creation of producers' co-operatives with state aid, as a means of solving the 'social question', a Lassallean idea about which Marx was dismissive: 'It is worthy of Lassalle's imagination that with state loans one can build a new society just as well as a new railway!'. The appeal of Marxism lay not only in the aggressive language but also in its message: the irreconcilability of the working class to the bourgeois state and the certainty of the collapse of capitalism through class struggle. 'Legal' was erased from the Gotha Programme in 1880 to cope with the new circumstances. Isolation encouraged the view that emancipation was solely the task of the working class. Though Marxism began to gain ascendancy, the extent of its ascendancy must not be overestimated. Those who came to profess Marxism often understood it only very crudely.

Another legacy of the anti-socialist law was the emphasis on parliamentarism. The active leadership of the party was by necessity in the hands of the parliamentary group, who came to gauge their success by success at the polls. Thus the party was radicalized while conditions were created for a reformist practice.

The Transformation to a Mass Party, 1890–1914

The lapse of the anti-socialist law in 1890 did not eliminate the pariah status of the Social Democrats. They were still the 'enemy within'. Party members, especially the older generation who had survived the 'heroic years', never lost their fear of the reintroduction of repressive legislation. In 1894 they were threatened by a Subversion Bill which would have deprived socialists of the franchise; in 1898–9 a so-called Convicts Bill would have imposed heavy penalties on anyone trying to interfere with strikebreakers. Unable to secure the necessary Reichstag legislation, the government resorted to a more effective use of the existing law. Police harassment continued; Social Democratic meetings would be dissolved by the ever-present political police. Social Democrats were also often prosecuted in the courts for perjury and *lèse majesté,* the latter an occupational hazard for a Social Democratic journalist.

The unification of Germany facilitated industrialization, underway since 1850. Between 1870 and 1890 Germany became highly industrialized. In 1870, 65 per cent of the German population lived on the land. In the next 20 years there was internal immigration from east to west, from rural areas to the cities. Drawn to towns and industrial regions, the migrants worked in mines, heavy industry, on railway and canal construction and building generally. Urbanization and population increase – the latter almost doubled between 1870 and 1914 – contributed to a worsening housing shortage, high rents and rising food prices. Industrialization transformed the social as well as economic structure. The industrial working class expanded: between 1887 and 1914 their numbers doubled. Unemployment remained at about 2 per cent and wages rose higher than in other industrial countries. Wilhelm II, who ascended the throne in 1888, initially promoted the extension of social legislation to protect conditions of work and provide legal safeguards such as factory inspection, regulation of child and female labour and guaranteed Sunday rest. Additional provisions were introduced after the turn of the century. Economic reality remained grim. German industrialists, with few exceptions, were advocates of laissez-faire and hostile to state regulation of conditions of work, though a few were paternalist. In either case, they ruled their workers autocratically: any political or union activity was deemed dangerous and severely penalized as such.

The industrial working class increasingly turned to the party they believed represented their interests and offered them a sense of solidarity and hope. After 1890 the SPD developed into a mass political party. The trade unions, which suffered more than the party during the previous outlaw years, and were dependent on the political wing of the labour movement, gradually revived. Initially uninfluential, as their membership and funds increased, overtaking the party's, their influence grew. By 1906 they were in a position to circumscribe party policy on the mass strike issue; after Bebel's death in 1913 they exerted a decisive influence on the party leadership.

A new organization statute was agreed at the first conference after the lapse of the anti-socialist law, later modified in 1905. Two groups elected by the party conference constituted the party leadership: the executive or *Vorstand,* consisting mainly of party officers, dealt with business matters and conference decisions, prepared the agenda for the annual congress and vetted membership, and a control commission which reviewed the work of the executive, including finance and expulsions, and monitored the extensive party press. Policies and tactics were decided at the annual party.congress, attended by mandated delegates from individual Reichstag constituencies. Reichstag constituencies were never redrawn in the period 1870–1914, and this had political consequences not only for representation in the Reichstag but also at the party congress. Overpopulated industrial areas were under-represented, distorting the extent of party support on a given issue.

In theory the party congress was dominant. The parliamentary party was responsible to it but in practice retained the strong position derived from the period of repression. The congress could hardly predict and lay down decisions in advance to cover every eventuality. Resolutions were submitted to the annual congress and vigorously debated; votes were taken and the majority became congress decisions and hence party policy. This was normally not the end of the matter. Certain resolutions repeatedly popped up at subsequent congresses. Thus the lid could never be put down finally on the mass political strike or on the votes for state budgets, to cite but two examples.

The SPD was the first democratic mass party and the best organized, as contemporary sociologists like Max Weber and Robert Michels observed. Michels, then a young SPD member, became so disillusioned he formulated his 'iron law of oligarchy' that an organization, no matter how democratic in theory, was not so in practice, because of domination by those in positions of authority. Certainly Bebel, who was party co-chairman until his death in 1913, was most adept at sensing the party mood and then helping to direct it. Rarely did the party go against a resolution Bebel identified with. In the disputes between left and right Bebel occupied the centre, and as a centrist attacked and reconciled opponents from either direction.

The bureaucratization of the party took place after 1905. Before then there had been a strong tradition of local autonomy, a legacy of the Eisenachers, reinforced by the experience of repression, which taught that the fewer officials a party had, the harder it was for a repressive state to prosecute. Each local organization elected from one to three persons to liaise with the leadership. As early as 1893, especially in the south where association laws were freer – a uniform Imperial association law was not introduced until 1908 – regional organizations developed to deal with common problems. As the south seemed intent upon a 'deviant' course, party radicals tended to support centralization and uniformity to keep the party on its 'revolutionary' course, in contrast to developments in the trade-union movement where centralization was implemented to curb radicals. Intermediate levels of organization were created, manned by paid officials. A complex bureaucratic structure developed, approved by the party left, unaware of the extent to which the bureaucrat could have a vested interest in the status quo. Party organization became an end in itself, a development welcomed by a liberal like Max Weber precisely because it deflected the party from revolution. Friedrich Ebert, later President of the Weimar Republic, elected to the executive in 1905 and co-chairman of the party executive after Bebel's death in 1913, was a stereotypical party functionary, in party-paid employ since the age of 29, dour, efficient and unimaginative.

The party has often been criticized for not making use of this vast potential, preferring verbal radicalism to action. It has been argued that the excluded Social Democrats were 'negatively' integrated into Wilhelmine society through a network of cultural organizations linked to the party which created a subculture. Other factors must not be ignored: a genuine fear of a repressive state and the further possibility of a coup were among them. The influence of Karl Kautsky encouraged 'political immobility'. Editor of the party's theoretical journal, the *Neue Zeit* (founded 1883), author of numerous volumes explaining Marxism (hence his epithet, 'the Pope of Socialism'), Kautsky, like Bebel, was a centrist, but he was also very doctrinaire. His Marxism was 'orthodox' rather than revolutionary. Revolution would arrive one day, he believed: one need only wait ('revolutionary attentism'). Finally, the party was itself a product of German political culture and its lack of a successful revolutionary tradition.

Reformist possibilities

In 1891 the party at Erfurt adopted a new programme, the Erfurt Programme. Divided into two parts, principles and demands, its first part (drafted by Kautsky) contained a Marxist description of the inevitable decline of bourgeois capitalist society (through a class struggle) into socialist ownership of the means of production. The second half (drafted by Eduard Bernstein) contained demands for reforms, the roots of which lay in the Enlightenment or the abortive revolution of 1848. None of these was implemented before 1918. They included universal direct suffrage for all men and women over the age of 20 (the Reichstag suffrage applied to all men over the age of 25); proportional representation, redistribution, direct democracy such as initiative and referendum, freedom of speech and assembly; abolition of legal discrimination against women; abolition of a standing army; secularization of state and education; free medical care; graduated income tax; and measures specific to labour, such as the eight-hour day.

Were the two parts compatible – one specifically Marxist, the other reformist and not even specifically socialist? Marx, in any case, was not averse to the introduction of democratic demands which, if implemented, would create the fully developed bourgeois society from which socialism was to emerge. There was a tension between the two parts, but much depended on which part received emphasis and whether to the exclusion of the other.

Shortly before the Erfurt congress such an attempt was made by the Bavarian Georg von Vollmar, one-time editor of *Der Sozialdemokrat,* imprisoned twice during the outlaw years, and recently elected to the Reichstag. In his El Dorado speeches he called on the party to address itself to the immediate tasks of social and economic improvement on the basis of the present political and social order. Tactics or practice were more important than principles. Vollmar was a practical politician, best described by the term reformist, and his El Dorado speeches were a reformist manifesto. Like most other reformists, he came from south Germany (those states south of the Main River), where milder social and political conditions encouraged optimism about the possibility of reforms.

Reformists were often described by their contemporaries as 'revisionist' but there is an important distinction, aside from the fact that reformism preceded revisionism. Revisionism is closely associated with Bernstein's attempt to revise Marxist theory. In exile in England and Engels's executor, Bernstein, a year after Engels's death, suggested in a series of articles in the *Neue Zeit* between 1896 and 1898, and in a later publication entitled *Presuppositions of Socialism* (1899), the need to update Marxist theory. But his views were overwhelmingly rejected at Party congresses in 1899 and 1903, and he could not rely on reformist support, despite his attempt to reconcile theory with practice or revise theory to accomodate reformist practice. Reformists were not interested in theory. If they occasionally invoked theory, this was no more than engaging in conventional party discourse. They did not want their practice to be limited by theoretical considerations, Kautskyan or Bernsteinian. Revisionism was often used as a blanket term for non-Marxists but there were important differences between reformists and revisionists, and even amongst revisionists themselves. Revisionist intellectuals, south German politicians, most party and trade-union functionaries, though differing from time to time on individual issues, belonged to the party right, and generally supported the reformist tactic.

South Germany was less industrialized than the north, and south German Social Democrats were keen to increase their electoral base by attracting the votes of rural workers and small farmers. In the 1890 Reichstag election 27 per cent of the SPD vote had come from rural areas. Alarmed by the formation of the Agrarian League in 1893, which agitated against the SPD in rural areas, they felt disadvantaged by the Marxist view contained in the Erfurt Programme that the peasant and artisan were anachronisms, due to disappear. Led by Vollmar, they were instrumental in getting the party at least to consider the 'agrarian question' in the years 1894–5, with the possibility of an addition to the Erfurt Programme. But the attempt foundered on the beliefs of the majority that the SPD was the party of the industrial working class. For Kautsky, any concessions were incompatible with Marxism; for a radical like Clara Zetkin, it would dilute the party's 'revolutionary character'. But Bebel, realizing the implications for the party's electoral strategy, in the end supported concessions.

Electoral success was thus to be confined to urban, industrial areas, and though the party had over a million members by 1914, this was still a minority of the working class. Its electoral support far exceeded its membership numbers (members were ostensibly committed socialists) and included a political protest vote from some rural areas, as well as from the lower middle class. After 1903 it became more difficult to capture the floating vote. The party also attracted intellectuals and Jews but had difficulty in making inroads on the Catholic industrial working class. In the 1912 Reichstag election the party received four and a quarter million votes, but saturation point seemed to have been reached. There were limits to its electoral appeal.

The influence of the south Germans exceeded their actual numbers. Approximately half the membership came from Prussia with 13 per cent from Greater Berlin, the latter roughly equal to Baden, and Bavaria and Württemberg, together at 15 per cent. But by 1912 the party had a total of 231 deputies in the *Landtage* and nearly 11,000 Social Democrats on municipal and district councils, proportionately more from the south. Imperial Germany was a federal state consisting of 22 single states, three Free Cities and Alsace-Lorraine, each with separate electoral laws. In Prussia, the largest and politically most influential state, no Social Democrat was elected to the *Landtag* until 1908 because of the notorious three-class franchise, based on the amount of tax paid. Three per cent were in the first class, 85 per cent in the third. The Conservative parties won almost half the seats while polling less than the Social Democrats who won only six. The chancellor appointed and removed by the Kaiser appeared before the Reichstag and before the Prussian *Landtag* as a Prussian minister. He needed the support of both. Legislation could be temporarily blocked by the Reichstag but not initiated. The reform of the Prussian suffrage became of paramount importance and led a reformist from Baden, the Reichstag deputy Ludwig Frank, Vollmar's successor as 'leader' of the south German reformists, to advocate extra-parliamentary action, the political mass strike. Some states like Saxony, alarmed at the growth of the SPD, introduced restrictions on their suffrage as early as 1896. In contrast, in the south electoral reform broadened the suffrage, so that by 1906 Baden, Württemberg and Bavaria had direct universal manhood suffrage.

Germany had a multi-party system and a two-round system of voting which in practice encouraged electoral alliances, for if no candidate received a majority on the first ballot, there was a run-off election. In Baden, National Liberals and left liberals feared the Catholic Centre Party more than the SPD and joined the latter in an official alliance for the run-off elections in 1905, 1909 and 1913, the first such alliance ever. This was condemned by the party because it involved the Baden Social Democrats in instructing their voters to vote for a bourgeois party. (There had been unofficial alliances hitherto and in practice no Social Democrats would vote for a conservative.) This alliance, known as the Baden Grand Bloc, led to co-operation in the *Landtag* on certain pieces of legislation. The Baden Social Democrats also voted for the state budget, a practice associated with the south Germans, off and on since 1891, and condemned by the national party as a vote of confidence in a bourgeois government. Since reformists were willing to work within the bourgeois state and co-operate with bourgeois allies, as a means of breaking out of political isolation – and they were less isolated in the south – they opposed what they deemed self-defeating empty gestures. In occasionally voting for the budget, they incurred the wrath of their northern colleagues. A fierce debate at the 1910 party congress led to a threat of expulsion, though this was further than Bebel wanted to go.

Attempts to transfer the Baden Grand Bloc to a national level met with little success. In the 1912 Reichstag election, an electoral alliance which included the left liberals and, indirectly, the National Liberals, foundered on the reluctance of left-liberal voters in the north to vote for the SPD. Within the Reichstag itself there was no chance of a Bloc from Bassermann (the National Liberal leader) to Bebel, as desired by some left liberals and reformists. The decision of the SPD Reichstag delegation in 1913 to vote for military credits because it established the principle of direct taxation for defence expenditure was an abandonment of the party principle of 'Not one man, not one penny for this system!' as Wilhelm Liebknecht had once declared. To a limited extent, south German practice was beginning to influence the Reichstag delegation where the right was over-represented, compared to the party congress.

Opposition to reformism which deflected the party from its revolutionary course came from the party left, beginning with the anarchist-inspired *Jungen* or 'Young Ones' in the early 1890s, who were hostile to parliamentarism. Others like Rosa Luxemburg and Parvus (Alexander

Helphand), exiles from the Russian empire, were quick off the mark to attack Bernstein in the 1890s, and Rosa Luxemburg was already then attacking reformist practices such as budget votes. The outbreak of the Russian revolution in 1905 led to a radical upswing and calls for a mass strike. Again in 1909–10 a revival of interest in the mass strike, linked to the Prussian suffrage protest movement, drove a wedge between the diverse opponents of revisionism and reformism. For Kautsky the SPD was a 'revolutionary' but not a 'revolution-making' party, and he defended the parliamentary tactic and strategy of attrition. The left was strong in urban centres like Bremen and Berlin, but not all were in the north (Stuttgart in Württemberg was also important). Radicalism is not synonymous with Rosa Luxemburg, despite her prominence, nor is it synonymous necessarily with Marxism. Until 1914 the party left was divided between a revolutionary left (including Rosa Luxemburg), which was hostile to parliamentarism, concerned to escalate mass action and to teach the German masses to 'speak Russian', and a left-of-centre group which included Karl Liebknecht. The revolutionary left were rather isolated, while the left-of-centre, which constituted the 'radicals' within the Reichstag delegation, were alert to the fact that even if the party rejected revisionism and some reformist practices, reformism was stealthily taking over the party.

Except for the 1907 Reichstag election, the so-called Hottentot election, when the SPD, vulnerable to accusations of lack of patriotism, opposed German policy in south-west Africa, and lost some seats, there was a steady rise in votes, proportion of votes and seats from 1890 to 1912: 35 seats in 1890, to 44 in 1893, 57 in 1898, to 81 in 1903, down to 43 in 1907, to 110 seats (out of 397) in 1912, with 35 per cent of the votes. What did these numbers signify? Was the party any nearer its goal? Or, given the semi-absolutist nature of the German constitution and the absence of parliamentary government, were they merely providing actors for the Reichstag stage?

4 Socialist Trade Unionism in Imperial Germany, 1871–1914

John A. Moses

The dominant political culture of Imperial Germany was even more hostile to the existence of trade unionism than that of the classic industrial nation of Great Britain. This was because the German power elite feared organized labour as the breeding ground of revolution and therefore resisted the introduction of legislation which would have accorded the trade unions the status in industrial society that they had won for themselves piecemeal in the parliamentary island kingdom. The fact that there the power elite was more liberal enabled the gradual, albeit grudging, but ultimately positive integration of the labour movement into the state. In Germany, while the trade-union movement managed to grow virtually to equal that of Britain's by 1914, it succeeded only in being 'negatively integrated' into the state.

It is this phenomenon of so-called negative integration – a concept first employed by Guenther Roth and applied with great effect by Dieter Groh – that concerns us here. The concept is a most useful explanatory device since it indicates how the trade-union movement could grow and function and still be regarded with great suspicion by both the power elite and the educated middle class of Germany, a factor which had disastrous long-term effects for German society.

Apart from that, the history of trade unionism in the *Kaiserreich* and its frustrated efforts to modernize industrial relations at a time when Germany was at the height of her imperial and economic power is of crucial importance in trying to account for some of the peculiarities of both German foreign and domestic policy. Because the *Kaiserreich* tried to impede the growth of organized labour, it prepared to a great extent its own internal and external collapse. This chapter will sketch the growth of socialist trade unionism in Germany in three stages in the period 1871 to 1914, a subject concerning which there is only limited literature available in English.

Trade-Union Beginnings in a Reactionary State

The period 1871–90, coinciding with Bismarck's chancellorship, constitutes the first stage. Bismarck was a decided enemy of organized labour. His attitude was determined by generally anti-liberal, authoritarian, patriarchal, monarchical values which were commonly held by the Prussian Junker landowning elite. Bismarck simply reflected the social and political views of his class, and these were also shared by the industrial power elite, as well as the *Bildungsbürgertum* (educated middle classes).

These power relationships were fixed by the Reich constitution which Bismarck devised in order to perpetuate the monarchical order in Germany. Apart from blatantly reactionary features in the Reich constitution, such as the principle of monarchical sovereignty expressed by denying the popularly elected legislature (Reichstag) the right to control the executive, the German government was not responsible to the legislature but to the emperor, and there existed a reactionary industrial code (*Gewerbeordnung*) which was applied to disadvantage organized labour. On top of all this, the judiciary, when handling litigation on industrial relations, was notoriously biased against the trade-union movement. For example, the industrial code expressly guaranteed, in paragraph 152, the right of all individuals in a particular business or trade to form associations for the collective benefit of that business or trade, but paragraph 153 of the same code foresaw penalties for the 'misuse' of this right if pressures were exerted on persons to join or to prevent persons from withdrawing from trade unions. The provision was, as it was interpreted at least, a serious limitation on the right of association. This meant that trade unions had to be particularly cautious, especially in organizing strikes. In fact, the application of the industrial code by the Reich judiciary practically denied the full right of association to trade unions, whereas businessmen's associations made virtually untrammelled use of it. The bias against organized labour in Imperial Germany was particularly crass.

There were two main reasons for official hostility towards trade unions. First, ever since the 1848 revolutions, at the lastest, the German middle and upper classes had feared the revolutionary potential of the masses. This was intensified in 1870–1, when the Reich was founded, by the publicity given in Germany to the Paris Commune of that time. As a consequence of France's defeat in the war against Prussia and her German allies, the working class of Paris had risen up with great violence against the established order and for a short time won control over the city of Paris. This episode was described in the Reichstag by August Bebel, a leader of the then minuscule Social Democratic movement, as a small outpost skirmish compared to the inevitable uprising of the working classes in Germany against their exploiters. It thus became part of the myth of German political culture that the working class was bent upon the violent overthrow of the monarchical-capitalist order. Secondly, and no less central, was the widespread notion expressed by the Reich Minister for the Interior von Puttkammer in 1886 that behind every strike lurked the hydra of revolution. In other words, organized labour in Imperial Germany had to fight against the assumption that it was preparing the violent overthrow of the state.

Indeed, Bismarck's strategy in the mid to late 1870s had been to exploit the general bourgeois fear of socialism so as to weaken the liberal movement as well. He did this by cynically attacking the Social Democratic labour movement which was so small at that time that it in no way posed a threat to the existing order. Part of Bismarck's reasoning was that he could discredit and demoralize liberalism by inducing the liberals in the Reichstag to vote for an illiberal law, i.e. to deprive a section of the community of its basic rights on the pretext that its political ideology threatened national security. In this, Bismarck proved successful. His anti-socialist legislation was finally passed through the Reichstag, with liberal support, in 1878. It remained in force till 1890, during which period the German Empire took on the characteristics of a police state, at least as far as trade unions and Social Democrats were concerned. For 12 years these groups struggled under a remarkably repressive piece of legislation which accorded the police the power to exile persons suspected of socialist agitation. Hundreds of trade unionists were victimized under its provisions, and virtually all trade-union organizations were declared illegal under the act. This put an abrupt end to the efforts of far-sighted trade-union leaders to centralize the entire movement on a nation-wide basis. It is important to note these plans that were being discussed and partially implemented prior to the passing of the anti-socialist law because they provided the model for the organizational plan that was implemented after that law had lapsed in 1890.

In the period 1871–8, leading German trade unionists were concerned with interrelated organizational and ideological issues as they affected the efficacy of the class struggle. Ideologically they were torn between Ferdinand Lassalle's application of the 'iron law of wages', which taught that strikes for higher wages were useless as they only drove up the price of commodities, and the Marxist doctrine of class struggle, which encouraged militant trade-union organization, since Marx and Engels regarded unions as 'the first military school of the proletariat'. So, while Lassalle's doctrines (initially more widespread in Germany than those of Marx and Engels) accepted trade-union organization primarily as a means of recruiting workers for the Lassallean socialist party, Marxist doctrine urged the formation of trade unions precisely because they were the natural strike organs of the working class. For Marx, strikes served to raise the class-consciousness of the proletariat. Trade unions were therefore both natural and necessary instruments of class struggle. In them, workers became socialists without realizing it.

Two socialist parties had emerged in the period 1863–75. It was in this situation that Marx (in the famous Hamann interview) recommended that the socialist or Free Trade Unions should not affiliate with any particular political party but simply organize separately and proceed with the class struggle. Moreover, the German industrial code prohibited the affiliation of any kind of business or trade-union organization with a political party. So there were two compelling reasons why trade unions had to be organized separately from any socialist parties – one ideological and one legal. To complicate matters further, there were individual labour leaders who did not believe in trade unions affiliating to form a separate national organization. These thought it sufficient that there be local craft unions scattered independently from one another throughout the country, in which case there was no legal barrier to their being affiliated to a political party.

Trade-union discussion prior to 1878 thus centred on the issues of independence from political parties, i.e. 'neutrality', and whether there should be a unifying national trade-union federation. By 1875 a 'union' plan had been devised, chiefly due to the efforts of Theodor York (1830–75), a joiner from Harburg near Hamburg. He envisaged the affiliation of all craftsmen engaged in working in one product or commodity for which there existed a range of separate craft unions. As, for example, there were all manner of trades associated with wood, York's plan foresaw a federation of these in an all-encompassing wood-workers' union. Similarly, there would be a metal-workers' union, and so on. Some unions with a long organization and craft tradition, such as the printers or tobacco workers, would also be affiliated alongside the quasi-industrial unions into a federation known as 'the union' (*die Union*).

The virtues of this arrangement would have been to enable the more efficient planning of strikes, the prevention of the use of strike-breakers, the nation-wide organization of lodging for members travelling in their journeyman's years, the better administration of unemployment relief and job listing, and so on. In short, York argued for the adaptation of the existing guild-conscious craftsmen of Germany to the changing requirements of a rapidly industrializing country that had only recently become a political unit.

York's proposals, however, encountered much official bureaucratic obstruction, and his organizational plan could be only partially implemented before the passing of the anti-socialist law in 1878. He himself had died in 1875, but his colleagues pressed on with his plan until Bismarck's policies eventually frustrated it. What must be noted about York's initiative is his perception that the new political and industrial situation in Germany demanded the institutionalization of protection for the industrial worker by means of a national, politically independent trade-union body. It was a far-sighted vision that was kept alive all through the 12 years of state oppression by those who shared York's perception.

The 'Legien Era', 1890–1914: Trade-Union 'Neutrality' and Autonomy

The period of the anti-socialist law, far from destroying the drive of workers to organize into craft unions, or to vote for the SPD, rather served to intensify it. Initially, after 1878, virtually all craft unions were dissolved by police action. However, by the mid-1880s, craft unions were being re-formed, provided they could demonstrate their political neutrality, i.e. evince a solely craft-orientated purpose, which formation was allowed under the industrial code. By 1890 there were some 50 craft unions in existence with a membership of just under 240,000. The state had no objection to non-militant craft organizations. The printers' union, for example, survived the anti-socialist law period entirely unscathed as it maintained a thoroughly non-militant, politically neutral stance. Indeed, it was emphatically pro-monarchical. This was Bismarck's ideal – subservient, non-political labour organizations. But such a situation could not be maintained; the industrial conditions were so oppressive that strikes were inevitable, as the example of the great mine workers' strike in 1889 demonstrated. The massive, spontaneous strike of that year, originating in the mines of the Ruhr, spread to other mining regions in the nation and encompassed 150,000 workers. And although this, the largest strike ever to take place in Imperial Germany, was defeated by the mine-owners, it spawned in the short term the new mine workers' union and in the long term accelerated the formation of a coalition of existing unions after the anti-socialist law had lapsed.

Bismarck's labour policy had proved in all respects a gigantic failure. He had tried to eliminate both political and industrial labour organizations, first by banning them and then by instituting his famous social-service legislation. The purpose of the sickness, accident and old-age insurance legislation of the mid 1880s was to persuade the working class that the paternalistic state would take care of their welfare, and consequently there would be no need to bring about a revolution in order to get justice for the working class. In short, Bismarck's much vaunted social-service legislation was merely a tactical move to preserve the monarchical-capitalist system from the looming threat of socialist trade-union militancy. Indeed, he had said quite openly in the Reichstag that social-service legislation would not have been introduced had it not been for the existence of a Social Democratic movement. This observation caused the socialist party leader, August Bebel, to observe that, if the existing grossly inadequate social services were the consequence of labour militancy, then even more militancy should result in better social services! Indeed, the character and philosophy of the Bismarckian system was both an affront to, and a provocation of, the labour movement in general. And by the beginning of the final year of the anti-socialist law, i.e. 1890, it was abundantly clear to all parties that Bismarckian tactics on the domestic front had failed to contain, let alone eliminate, the 'internal enemy' of socialism and its industrial manifestation, trade unionism. It was in the context of solving the all-important 'social question' that Bismarck clashed with the young emperor, Wilhelm II, and found himself forced to resign as chancellor. Wilhelm II had cultivated the illusion that he could win over the working classes to the state by more generous inducements rather than harsh repression à la Bismarck.

The technical reasons for the rejection of a more Draconian form of the anti-socialist law by the Reichstag on 25 January 1890 formed the background to Bismarck's dismissal by the emperor on 19 March that year. The existing law had to run until September 1890, after which it was possible for the Social Democrats to hold their first national congress on German soil since 1877 – at Halle. During 1891 and 1892 the advocates of a unified trade-union movement had been at work, especially in Hamburg, to revive the organizational plan of Theodor York so that their efforts to improve working conditions and to avoid such debacles as the 1889 miners' strike might be given some chance of success. The concept that 'organization was everything' was advocated by the young Carl Legien, the most eloquent champion of the union plan of Theodor York in 1892. Legien was the *spiritus director* from then on, until his death in 1920, of a centralized German trade-union umbrella organization. His aim was to concentrate the weak and fragmented socialist or free trade unions as the 'second hammer' of the labour movement, i.e. to complement the now free political party. It was a rational enough objective, but at the time Legien's concept, as had been the case in York's time, encountered unexpected opposition from within the ranks of labour. This came from those who cultivated quasi-anarchistic notions of the class struggle as well as those Social Democratic officials who did not see the need for an autonomous trade-union organization which pursued economic goals within the existing capitalist system instead of concentrating efforts on the political struggle to change that system.

Legien's concept of an independent trade-union federation in Germany took a good 10 years to gain acceptance even from his own party. The basic reason for this was the perception by the Social Democratic leadership in the 1890s of the nature of capitalism and the advent of socialism. Friedrich Engels had taught the SPD to expect the great imperialist struggle of the Powers by the turn of the century, after which the proletarian revolution would eventuate, allowing the SPD to assume power in Germany. It was therefore inopportune to expend significant effort on building up the trade-union movement when really all that was required was the increased recruitment of Social Democratic voters among the working class. The SPD, because of Engels's 1890 analysis of the world situation, became virtually a party of 'revolutionary attentism', i.e. simply waiting around for the inevitable to happen and then being in a position to exploit it and assume power. This ideology was applied in the SPD by Karl Kautsky and August Bebel, and it presumed that the industrial wing of labour would always be ready to behave as the 'artillery' of the party, i.e to be employed at their behest in tactics deemed by them to be opportune. This concept of trade unionism neither accorded with political-economic realities nor with the aspirations of the Free Trade Union leaders themselves, who, under Legien in 1892, had implemented a diluted version of York's union organization plan. What was to be the first viable forerunner of the modern trade-union federation in Germany was called in the 1890s the Gerneral Commission of the Free Trade Unions of Germany.

Not even the most enthusiastic supporters of the General Commission in the years 1892–6, with the possible exception of Legien himself, could envisage how significant a force it would become in the German, and indeed in the international labour movement. In those foundation years there was much scepticism concerning the purpose of a centrally administered and independent trade-union organization. As indicated, the Social Democratic leadership itself rejected the concept of two 'hammers' in the labour movement. They could not yet accept the notion of trade-union autonomy. Above all, the party fought to control the direction of the movement, for it was feared that independent trade unions would concern themselves chiefly with immediately realizable goals within capitalism rather than with its overthrow. This issue continued to bedevil relations between the political and industrial wings of labour until the party leadership came to realize that capitalism was not going to self-destruct according to the timetable prepared by Engels in 1890. But even then the SPD found it hard to abandon its belief in the 'primacy' of party authority.

Other factors, however, assisted in ensuring the position of the General Commission in the mid-90s. The Great Depression since the mid-70s was nearing its end, and the rising buoyancy of the economy led to an increase in both union membership and central funds. Further, after Engels's death in 1895, Eduard Bernstein's revisionist ideas could be ventilated, and these positively encouraged trade-union activity as a normal and essential part of the labour movement. Thirdly, by the turn of the century the Roman Catholic Church had succeeded in founding its own Christian trade unions in competition with those affiliated with the putatively socialist General Commission. This was a powerful argument for the insistence upon the latter's autonomy and independence from the SPD because it had to be seen that the General Commission really was politically neutral (as it was asserted) if it were to attract workers without regard to their political or religious allegiances. All this assisted the General Commission enormously in its struggle to assert its *raison d'être* during the 90s.

Legien's concept of organized labour triumphed over its detractors by virtue of its essential pragmatism. Workers still needed defending, and strikes had to be organized while one was waiting for the advent of socialism. No one could ever say precisely how long that wait would be. In the meantime, the overriding task was to organize. Legien's conviction was that to have any chance in the oppressive Wilhelmine society, the workers needed the systematic organization that the trade-union movement could provide. Indeed, Legien's analysis of the virtually militaristic German power structure and its legal system convinced him early that it could be changed not by confrontation, i.e. by quasi-anarchistic action, but rather by attrition. The existence of large and self-sufficient trade unions would have to be taken into account by governments whose predominant concern was to stabilize the system. In short, the General Commission pursued a policy of 'negative integration' to the extent that it advocated the patient adaptation to existing forces with the ultimate aim of winning piecemeal concessions from both government and management.

The General Commission, composed of men who had emerged from the major trade unions, had no utopian illusions about sudden and dramatic changes in the power relationships of either industry or the state. They realized full well the determination of the ruling classes (an alliance between conservative landed nobility, the army and industry) to protect 'the nation' from the evils of socialism – with which trade unions were identified. It was understood, too, that the ruling classes were waiting for the opportunity to stifle the growing power of organized labour, as this was manifest in the apparently inexorable expansion of the SPD as well as in trade-union membership and financial strength. Indeed, ever since the lapse of the anti-socialist law in 1890, governments had been at their wit's end to devise means to contain the growth of organized labour. This was the major political issue for the Reich. When inducement failed, repression was threatened, such as the projected ban on socialist newspapers in 1894 and the anti-strike legislation of 1899. None of these measures passed through the Reichstag, to the chagrin of the government. Indeed, Wilhelmine political practice was an undisguised provocation of organized labour. However, neither the political nor the industrial leadership would be drawn. No excuse was to be given the Reich government to reintroduce anti-socialist legislation.

The Preconditions for 'Positive Integration'

Nothing illustrates better the characteristic caution of the trade-union and socialist party leadership towards the Prusso-German military monarchy than the tactics they adopted with regard to the Second International. The German Social Democrats, and behind them the trade unions, were the most prestigious element in the Second International, both in terms of sheer parliamentary numbers and organized membership, on the one hand, and by virtue of ideological authority on the other. However, despite the obligation to play a leading role in the International, the Germans successfully withstood all pressures to implement policies at home that could possibly provoke their government to institute measures that would restrict the relative freedom now accorded to organized labour. For example, the Second International repeatedly urged the marking of a May Day demonstration with a one day strike for the eight-hour day. That, in the eyes of the General Commission, would have been a most counter-productive provocation. Eloquent non-German firebrands in the Second International believed that the Germans, by virtue of their apparent strength, ought to be taking the initiative in this campaign. What they failed to appreciate was the anxious nature of the German power elite. An aggressive action on the part of organized labour would have resulted in confrontation with the military. Even with the increased membership after the turn of the century, the General Commission judged that their influence over only a fraction of the work-force was far too inadequate to guarantee the success of any political strike action. Striking unionists would be faced with wholesale dismissals, and their organizations could not sustain the consequent financial blood-letting.

This situation became even more evident during the so-called mass strike debate (1905–6), when the Second International, as well as Marxist luminaries such as Rosa Luxemburg within the SPD, urged the use of the mass or general strike in Germany for political objectives. Governments in other West European countries had been responding to widespread strike action by making concessions to the demands of organized labour both in electoral law and social policy. Consequently, the political use of the mass-strike weapon recommended itself. As in the case of the Russian revolution of 1905, significant constitutional changes might be wrought by what began as a series of mass strikes. Rosa Luxemburg in particular polemicized vigorously against the German unions for their traditional reluctance to provoke the authorities. Basing her views on the Russian example, she advocated the open encouragement of strikes in the belief that they educated the proletariat for revolution and thus led the working class to seize their historic role and bring about their own emancipation from wage slavery. The main impediment to the working-out of this process, in Luxemburg's view, was the General Commission, which kept a restraining hand over undisciplined strike action. In reality, in

Luxemburg's assessment the organization and tactics of the German trade-union movement were veritable obstructions to the ultimate liberation of the toiling masses.

Rosa Luxemburg's vitriolic criticism of the General Commission represents, alongside her attack on the revisionist Bernstein, the ideological division between the self-proclaimed orthodox Marxist revoluntionary theorists in the German labour movement and the pragmatic trade-union functionaries, who assumed the day-to-day task of organization, as well as confrontation with management. There was no doubt in the mind of the trade unionists that they represented the real labour movement, whereas those who advocated the foolhardy provocation of the militaristic regime were unrealistic dreamers who had no conception of the hardships which a protracted strike could impose on workers' families. That the theorists in the movement ignored this real problem and placed all their faith in the far from predictable workings of history was incomprehensible to the trade-union leadership for whom 'general strike' was 'general nonsense'. The 'muscle' of organized labour was opposed to carrying out any directive from the self-appointed 'brains' who did not have to suffer the consequences of their untried political ideas.

The mass strike debate within the German labour movement was brought out into the open at the Mannheim congress of the SPD in 1906. As indicated, the party had been under pressure also from the Second International to discuss the strike question since it was now considered a practical means of preventing a war between the then aligned rival power blocks. If the working classes of Europe committed themselves to a general strike, in concert, then their national ruling classes would be unable to go to war against each other. It was a noble concept which the SPD felt obliged to place on the agenda. This it did with obvious reluctance because it was well known that the General Commission opposed the idea and that any test of wills between the party and the union movement would be embarrassing for the party, since by 1906 the union organization was by far the stronger, in both numbers and resources. Under these circumstances it would be difficult to uphold the fiction that the SPD was morally the leading organ of the German labour movement.

The outcome of the mass strike debate at Mannheim was a milestone in the history of party-union relations. It solved in principle the question whether the trade-union movement was really an autonomous section of it, i.e. the 'second hammer', or whether it was simply the artillery under the command of the party generals. The resolution that was worked out between Carl Legien for the unions and August Bebel for SPD made it plain that the party could not call a political strike without first getting the approval of the General Commission. Thereby the General Commission had not only established its undisputed leadership over the unions; it made the point that it, rather than the party, determined the essential priorities of the movement.

In reality, then, by the eve of the Great War, the German socialist movement had been effectively 'trade-unionized'. The pressures of the wartime economy and the attendant political stresses further advanced trade-union autonomy to the extent that trade unions became both indispensable economic and political factors influencing the 'governability' of the Reich.

5 Women Workers, Workers' Wives and Social Democracy in Imperial Germany

Ute Frevert

The 'woman question' and the 'labour question', these emotive terms of the 1860s and 1870s, constituted focal points of social movements which, despite different class bases, were at first closely intertwined. When middle-class women first assembled at Leipzig for a national women's conference in 1865, the choir of the local workers' education association welcomed them with a serenade. The women's education association of Leipzig conducted its Sunday class in the rooms of the workers' education association; the respective chairpersons, August Bebel and Louise Otto, knew each other well. Whereas the bourgeois women's movement concentrated increasingly on the educational and occupational interests of its own class, it remained sensitive to the problems of women of the lower strata, which it intended to tackle through social welfare programmes. The workers' movement in turn discovered a 'woman question' in its own ranks and faced it with great ambivalence: it wanted to enrol proletarian women as allies in the class struggle, but many male members nevertheless recoiled from this sort of politicization, which they thought unwomanly. Women's gainful employment, welcomed by some as economic liberation and as the prerequisite of women's capacity to organize, struck others as the capitalist work of the devil.

This ambivalence runs like a red thread through the history of changing relations between Social Democracy and women. It was grounded in the specific social structure of the workers' movement and its tense relations with the Enlightenment- and progress-oriented concept of social development and human history. In its political ideology, Social

Democracy was clearly a child of the modern and industrial age, even though many of its adherents continued for a long time to be formed and influenced by pre-industrial traditions, as regards concepts of life and values.

Industrial Women's Work: Bone of Contention for Early Workers' Associations and Trade Unions

At their first organized appearance in 1848, middle-class women had shown concern with living and working conditions of proletarian women and had considered measures designed to improve the socially and economically depressed position of women workers and workers' wives. Louise Otto, editor of a women's journal and eventual founder of the bourgeois women's movement, even then asked female servants, factory and home workers to form collective associations, and she simultaneously appealed to existing workers' associations adequately to consider the interests of women workers.

Her suggestion went largely unheeded. The Brotherhood of German Workers, the first national and trans-occupational workers' organization, founded in 1848 and dissolved by the police in 1850, did declare its readiness to accept female members, but this was hardly more than lip service. The Brotherhood, after all, like the local workers' associations, consisted of journeymen who retained their earlier organizations, especially the emergency funds, merely widening their aims by a unionist and occasionally political dimension. In most of the trade branches women were not formally employed at all and did not, therefore, require union representation. But where women also worked for wages, as in tailoring or cigar making, the most resolute opponents of women's work assembled. The Association of German Cigar Workers, founded in 1848, at its second congress in 1849 demanded the exclusion of women from factories; at the time, a factory was understood to mean both centralized and decentralized (that is, home) production. Cotton printers and tailors also opposed female colleagues and bombarded the government with many petitions demanding the abolition or at least considerable reduction of women's employment. As the reason, they listed the strong competition they faced from the women, who worked for lower wages and would ruin the entire trade in the end.

A relatively liberal trades policy, to which most old-fashioned guild adherents succumbed, and the fast growing demand for workers in an expanding industrial economy caused the protests of male colleagues against the wage-depressing female 'dirty competition' to fail. The number of women employed in the textile and tobacco industries rose meteorically. In the tailoring trade, women were on the march after the expansion of the store system in the 1840s. The mechanical spinning and weaving mills, the underwear and clothing enterprises, which could operate with workers trained on the job, employed women predominantly. Consequently, the unions of cigar workers and tailors, newly founded in the 1860s, continued their struggle against women workers in their own ranks. The agenda of the first General Cigar Workers' congress at Leipzig in 1865 registered as point ten 'the removal of women and children from the work-places in the interest of morals and morality', and the All German Tailors' Association, founded in 1867, explicitly excluded women from membership.

Both trade unions were linked politically to Ferdinand Lassalle's All-German Workers' Association, which resolutely opted against an increase in industrial work-places for women. The Lassalleans, placing hope in the future socialist state rather than trusting to improvements within the existing system, interpreted women's industrial work as a disgrace liable to undermine the workers' economic and social resistance to capitalism. The leaders of workers' education associations which, after the failed revolution, developed a busy political activity mainly in Saxony and southern Germany, argued more pragmatically. These groups, mostly founded and led by liberal-progressive bourgeois, usually took the view that, as a resolution of the third Workers' Association congress said in 1865, 'women are entitled to any occupation of which they are capable'. The manufacturer Moritz Müller of Pforzheim, especially committed to this view, went farther and encouraged the delegates to improve the earning capacity of women through concrete educational measures and thus to open to them (almost) all professions and activities. Müller's opinion did not find general acceptance. Several local groups were ready to accept it with restrictions and argued for the limitation of women's work to specifically female branches of occupation and to home work, lest male work positions and the wage level men had achieved be endangered. Others demanded, like the Lassalleans, the removal of women from the factories, their preparation for becoming good housewives through domestic service, the payment of higher (family) wages for men, and thus the liberation of wives and daughters from the yoke of 'mechanical labour'.

It would distort the historical perspective to classify such views collectively as 'proletarian anti-feminism', and it would mistake the motives leading workers to these evaluations. The workers' associations of the 1850s and 1860s primarily contained journeymen, many of whom worked in production units mostly shaped by specific trades, and who perceived the industrial system as a threat to their traditional form of work and of life. Even if already employed in factories, they maintained their scepticism and rejection of the new order which cancelled traditional rules and rhythms of work and life. It was one of the old-fashioned matters of course that women worked in the home, looked after meals, gardens, children and domestic fowl and, if necessary, aided husbands in their trade. Women's factory work then struck men as a blatant offence against morality and custom; if men were forced to get accustomed to work-places outside their homes, women at least ought to stick to tradition and safely transfer a piece of the 'sane world' into the new state of affairs. Wherever this was impossible for economic reasons, they were to adopt such activities as were clearly defined as female occupations by tradition. It was such backward-oriented wishful thinking, rather than the adoption of the modern bourgeois family concept, which to the workers lacked realism, that underpinned the protests and resistance against women's work outside the home in trade and industry. Of course, fear of competition and professional concepts of exclusivity played their part, but the particular severity of the women debate is not explained solely by these objections and motives, which were used also against unskilled male workers.

It was completely different socio-cultural values and views that distinguished the middle-class mentors of the workers' education associations, those liberal-progressive lawyers, professors, entrepreneurs and teachers who stood for the women's right to gainful and factory employment. To their minds, industrialization meant progress above all, liberation of human energy and work from artificial limits and stagnation. Their arguments in favour of industrial women's work were national economic benefit, social justice and personal freedom. Although their views could command majorities at central congresses, the excited debate about principles continued. In subsequent years, as before, people differed on whether the workers' movement should approve and welcome women's industrial work as an economic and social medium of emancipation or whether it was to oppose it as conducive to lower wages and the destruction of the family. The founding congress at Eisenach of the Social Democratic Workers' Party, emerging from the workers' association movement in 1869, faced motions to abolish women's employment but also a proposal demanding equal wages for men and women. The delegates eventually adopted a compromise promoting 'restriction of women's work'. The unification congress of the Lassalleans and the Eisenach Social Democrats at Gotha in 1875 employed both a more rigid and a more differentiated language when deciding to forbid all 'women's work deleterious to health and morality'.

In the new trade unions, created in the context of socialist party formation, the fight about women's wage-work and organization continued as well. The All-German Cigar Workers Association resolved in 1869, after acrimonious debate, to admit women so as to end wages competition. But many locals resisted and succeeded in being exempted from the new statute. The trade-structured professional organizations above all – lithographers, book binders, glove makers, hatters etc. – stuck to their exclusive principles of organization which admitted neither women nor unskilled workers to membership. There were clearly fewer reservations against the joint organization of the sexes in the weaving and spinning factories: thus the Trade Co-operative of the Manufacturing, Factory and Manual Workers, founded in 1869, recruited men and women simultaneously and in 1870 had more than 1,000 female members in addition to about 6,000 men. But among the socialist-oriented unions of the 1870s and 1880s this was a glaring exception. In 1892, the Free Trade Unions counted 4,355 organized women representing 1.8 per cent of the membership, while the number of female workers in the industrial sector amounted to over 20 per cent at that time. The first general trade union congress asked all member organizations in that year to admit women at once and to regard recruitment of female members as the 'demand of self-preservation'. Most professional associations adopted this recommendation, and four years later, 15,265 women (4.6 per cent) were trade-union members. This increase pertained mainly to the newly emerging industrial associations – textiles, metal, timber – which placed less emphasis on the distinction between skilled and unskilled workers and faced women with fewer reservations.

Socialist Concepts of Theory and Organization

The persistent opposition of male unions against recruiting women and representing their interests was one reason why middle-class women adopted the cause. In 1869 they founded an 'Association for the Education and Mental Stimulation of Working Women' in Berlin, with the aim of creating a trade continuing-education school as well as living quarters and a support fund for female workers. Associations of this kind appeared in other cities as well, defining themselves mainly as organizations for education and social aid but excluding trade-union aims and wage struggles in the narrow sense.

As, however, the bourgeois women's movement proceeded to regard women workers and workers' wives as mere objects of social policy and welfare rather than as subjects of autonomous interests, such as Louise Otto had envisaged in 1848, proletarian women looked for other allies. For their problems and their forms of protest they took increasing guidance from the trade-unionist and political organizations of male workers. This became evident in the 1880s when, first in Berlin and then in many other cities, women workers' associations came into being and either independently or with the help of middle-class 'deserters' like Gertrud Guillaume-Schack or Emma Ihrer gave first priority to the wage question and even considered strikes to obtain better pay. The anti-socialist law, providing penalties for Social Democracy's 'efforts constituting a public danger', spelled a quick demise of these women's groups: they were prohibited and their members fined and taken into custody. It was possible even to apply the Prussian law of 1850 pertaining to associations in order to dissolve women workers' organizations: if they were shown to be politically active, pursued political aims or maintained contact with political parties, paragraph 8 applied: it forbade women, as it did apprentices and minors, to attend political meetings and to join political organizations. This exclusion paragraph remained in force until 1908 and badly impeded the Social Democrats, especially in their party-political women's activities.

It is true that at first the Socialist Workers' Party (existing since 1875) did not evince much interest in female adherents. Rather, the initiative came from the proletarian women themselves as they strove for closer contact and support on the part of the Social Democrats. Beginning in 1889, they created informal women's agitation commissions which called meetings and sent delegates to Social Democratic congresses. They also founded occupational and general women workers' associations which devoted themselves mainly to women's continuing political and cultural education, thus forming a link with the tradition of workers' education associations of the 1850s and 1860s. In 1893 there were in Germany at least 33 local women workers' associations with more than 3,000 members. Almost all of them were dissolved by the police, despite their explicitly unpolitical character; they were then founded anew, so that in 1907 there were 94 of them with more than 10,000 members. As in the associations initiated by the middle-class women's movement in the 1860s, women convened regularly for lectures and meetings, discussed literature, child rearing, religion, prostitution and divorce, and maintained 'stimulating sociability'. Separate women's functions were maintained after 1908, when women could become party members with equal rights. Just as women SPD activists were, by statute, to devote themselves primarily to 'women's agitation', party congress resolutions authorized the women comrades to arrange local meetings for the purpose of theoretical and practical training.

Next to the journal *Die Gleichheit* (*Equality*), published since 1891 under the editorship of Clara Zetkin by the Social Democratic Dietz Company and starting with 2,000 copies, the most important training and agitation text was August Bebel's book, *Women and Socialism,* first published in 1879 and reprinted for the fiftieth time in 1909. It paved the way to the Social Democratic movement for many workers' wives and women workers as well as for women from bourgeois and petit-bourgeois strata. Women, Bebel told his readers, were doubly disadvantaged in capitalist society: they suffered both 'from social and societal dependence on the men's world' and from the 'economic dependence in which women in general and proletarian women in particular find themselves together with the proletarian men'. A successful struggle for occupational, juridical and political equality might moderate this double oppression but could never fully eliminate it. A solution of the 'woman question' was possible only within the framework of an overall 'removal of social antagonisms'. Once the 'social question' as a whole had been solved and the capitalist economic and social system had been dislodged, 'sexual slavery' would finally disappear. But Bebel's book offered more than succinct analyses and visions of a socialist future: it furnished concrete directions for action and pointed to methods by which proletarian women could free themselves from their lamentable position. First they were to prepare themselves, together with the bourgeois women's movement, to achieve complete equality of all women in existing society; secondly, the proletarian women's movement was to struggle 'hand in hand with the world of proletarian man' for provisions to 'protect the working woman against physical and moral degeneration and secure her capacity as mother and educator of the children'. Finally, the proletarian woman was to take her position in the common class struggle of the proletariat 'to create a state of affairs which makes possible, through relevant social institutions, full economic and spiritual independence for both sexes'. It followed that class-conscious workers' wives and women workers found their political home in Social Democracy, the sole party, as Bebel emphasized repeatedly, which drew the proper conclusions from the human rights discussions of the eighteenth century. Indeed, the Socialist Workers' Party had demanded the ballot for all citizens during its foundation congress at Gotha in 1875. The Erfurt Programme of 1891, formulating this demand with more precision, asked for the extension of the suffrage to all citizens 'irrespective of sex'; it also asked explicitly for 'the abolition of all statutes discriminating against women in matters of public and private law'. At the time this was a spectacular move; no other party of Imperial Germany condescended to such far-reaching demands for equality before 1918.

Even the SPD, however, did not always speak with one voice on this question. There were in the party decided opponents of demands for women's equality. It was above all in the interest of the proletarian family, they argued, that women manifestly had no business in factories. It must be the aim of the socialist movement to return women to their families, Edmund Fischer wrote in the *Socialist Monthly* in 1905; their 'natural occupation' lay in 'the care and upbringing of their children and the better structure and fortification of family life'. Whereas this 'natural doctrine' provoked severe contradiction, mainly among active party women, it cannot be denied that many Social Democratic families practised precisely what socialist theory was officially attacking. The more highly paid skilled workers, who formed the hard core of the organized workers' movement, did not wish their wives to follow occupations outside the home. Even August Bebel, who had asked 'women to step beyond the narrow circle of domesticity and fully to participate in public life and the cultural tasks of mankind', left no doubt that the future socialist society was to provide a clear separation of roles between the sexes, which left to men 'the defence of the country' and to women 'the care of home and hearth'. He was never able to commit himself to the emancipating function of female gainful employment as unambiguously as Clara Zetkin, the first leader of the proletarian women's movement.

Daughter of a village teacher and a trained teacher herself, Clara Zetkin had joined German Social Democracy early in the 1880s. At the International Workers' Congress in Paris in 1889, she made a speech 'For the Liberation of Women', which became famous and thenceforth the manifesto of the proletarian women's movement. It contained a categorical stand against any ban and any restriction of female gainful employment, for it was work 'outside the family' which made the woman worker economically independent, and this independence of women, she said, was the necessary precondition of their social and political equality. 'Full emancipation', however – and here Bebel and Zetkin agreed completely – could be attained only under socialism; therefore women were to join Social Democracy. Clara Zetkin did not ignore the difficulties of such collaboration in practice: 'Women followed the socialist banner without male aid, often, indeed, against men's wishes'. Just as within the party, for example, during nominations of convention delegates, women were always placed at the bottom of the lists, so male Social Democrats initially opposed the recruitment and mobilization of female members. They did not even wish to have their own wives and daughters in the party. But this negative attitude, still prevalent in the 1890s, weakened gradually. At the beginning of the twentieth century, the majority of women SPD members was recruited from among Social Democrats' wives. Their daughters usually organized themselves in the socialist workers' youth movement so as to enter the party at 18 years of age.

Women Social Democrats in Action: Welfare, Family Care, Women Workers' Protection

The Social Democratic environment now provided increased opportunities for women's organized activity, combining political education, social gatherings and social welfare commitment. These opportunities were exploited primarily by non-employed women: far more than half of all female SPD members had no work outside the home and, therefore, could more easily find time for conventions, demonstrations and women's meetings. Employed women, trying to harmonize their occupations with daily home and family duties, had more than enough to do. After the enervating factory labour their second working day began: food had to be prepared, the home cleaned, groceries bought and children cared for. The Sunday of 'leisure' was reserved for laundering and the necessary mending and sewing. This left no time for political or trade-unionist commitment. Nor could unmarried women workers dispose of their 'free time' as freely as their male colleagues. Their evenings were largely filled with housework as well, while the men spent time at the pub, at the football stadium or in political meetings.

The social composition of the female SPD membership – close to 10 per cent of all members in 1909 – shaped the policy of the Social Democratic women's movement. While it had initially constituted itself as a movement of women workers and defined women's gainful employment as the most important condition of women's emancipation, from the turn of the century it adapted itself increasingly to the needs of its client housewives. From 1904, *Die Gleichheit* published a housewife's and children's supplement, thus catering to the 'family egoism' of its women readers. Social Democratic local and trade papers developed 'women's corners' with sewing patterns, fashion tips and advice on home management and child rearing. Leading party and union women kept opposing the restriction of women's political work to specifically female concerns and the exclusion of general political topics, but this type of 'division of labour' gained quick acceptance in practice. Apart from the agitation for the female suffrage, the Social Democratic women's movement after 1900 concentrated on a field of activity for which, as the local government programme of the SPD in 1911 explained, women were 'quite particularly fitted': the commitment to welfare.

Table 5·1: Women in the SPD and in the Free Trade Unions

Year	SPD Women Members	%	Trade Unions Women Members	%
1892			4,355	1.8
1900			22,844	3.3
1906	6,460	1.7	118,908	7.1
1910	82,642	11.5	161,512	8.0
1913	141,115	14.4	223,676	8.8

After involving itself, especially in southern Germany, in local-government politics and obtaining a share of power in city halls, the SPD developed a stronger interest in the tackling and solution of concrete current problems. Socialist revolution, which was to remove all social ills at one stroke, had taken a back seat. It appeared to be more sensible to act in practical politics than to wait for D-day. The Social Democratic women supported these efforts, for in the realm of community affairs they perceived promising openings for constructive aid to proletarian women and families. Klara Weyl, an infant and welfare nurse in Berlin, suggested that women comrades work for the welfare of the sick, the unemployed, the orphaned and infants, agitate for the establishment of nursery schools and crèches, and shoulder tasks in school policy, health affairs, home inspection and food control. This would make it possible 'to alleviate, at least somewhat, the many-sided misery of the working class through social care and thus to contribute to its spiritual and physical rebirth'.

This opened up a field of women's endeavour in which, like their middle-class 'sisters', they could function with broad independence. They need not compete with men nor suffer defeat in the struggle for greater participation and influence. The high level of practical work in this area provided concrete experience of success and the feeling of real improvements and progress. Finally, it was undeniable that such person-to-person service activity was very congenial to the experience and interests of many Social Democratic (house) wives, more, at any rate, than agitation directed primarily at women factory workers. In the direct aid from woman to woman, in social service to the sick, needy, indigent women and families, they could beneficially apply their own experience both to themselves and to their 'clients'. It was their own cause they fought for, small but effective steps away from the misery which characterized the daily lives of all too many workers' families. Before the First World War the Social Democratic women's movement strongly committed itself to mother- and childcare. It organized excursions and holiday hikes for workers' children, created commissions for child protection and published numerous pamphlets on child rearing, thus emphasizing the political significance of motherhood properly understood: by conscious educational work, women could exert a powerful influence on their children's development, thus helping eventually to determine the long-term successes of the workers' movement. In this perspective, the Social Democratic family appeared as the germ-cell of the movement, and the mother as its main bastion.

In contrast, employed women, the erstwhile first and preferred objects of the proletarian women's movement, receded from the forefront of members' work even though, as before, Social Democratic women agitated for the concerns of women wage-earners, for shorter hours, equal pay and healthier work conditions, using leaflets, pamphlets and petitions. It was women workers' protection above all which formed part of the central and controversial demands of the proletarian women's movement after 1896. In 1889 Clara Zetkin had resolutely rejected special protective regulations for women and instead emphasized the principle of equality of men and women as the yardstick for socialist policy, but she, too, promoted them in the 1890s. The argument that this would reduce women's work opportunities to the advantage of 'unprotected' men counted for less than the insight that, given their triple burden as wage workers, house-workers and mothers, proletarian women stood in far greater need of protection than male proletarians. Pregnant women and those in childbed especially were to be exempted temporarily from their wage-work, both in their children's interest and to avoid excessive health strain. A law of 1891 demanded six weeks' interruption of work after a birth, but women frequently circumvented this ban because of insufficient financial security. These new protective measures, moreover, pertained to factory workers exclusively; domestic servants, country and home workers had no claim to a 10-hour working day, to Sunday or night leisure or to the pregnancy leave of eight weeks provided in 1908.

Given the oppressive work conditions to which women, usually being unskilled workers, were primarily exposed – work-places detrimental to health, low wages, long hours, monotonous labour requiring increased strain and concentration as the work-pace kept accelerating – the Social Democratic women's movement retreated step by step from its original theory of emancipation. In political Sunday speeches women's employment continued to be saluted in principle as conducive to an enlarged horizon or as 'preparation for the political life', but in their practical party activity women Social Democrats, like the bourgeois women's movement, accepted the thesis that the profession of motherhood was the most important task which women in society could and should undertake. No doubt the ideological transfiguration of the housewife's and mother's not exactly carefree existence agreed with the feelings of most proletarian women, who preferred family work, as a more need-related form of life, to an occupation determined by strangers. 'Occupation', after all, for girls and women of the working class almost always meant unskilled, dirty, badly paid, physically exhausting labour of demonstrably doubtful value to individual development. Activity in a spinning mill or a paper factory was hardly ever identical with satisfying 'self-realization'; its value was measured solely by the contents of the pay envelope. No wonder that most women gladly renounced this freedom to take gainful employment as soon as their husbands' earnings sufficed to support their families. To be a housewife and mother seemed infinitely more sensible than alienated factory work.

Bourgeois and Social Democratic women found theoretical and practical points of agreement in the high value they placed on motherliness and motherhood as the 'natural female profession' and also in their commitment to social care, but they confronted each other as 'hostile sisters' (Bebel). The bourgeois Federation of German Women's Associations (BDF) did not invite Social Democratic women to its founding congress in 1894, partly fearing to lose the good will of the police and the authorities, and partly in consideration of conservative member groups. A motion of the organization of progressive women's clubs at the general congress of 1900 to support collaboration with socialist women was decisively rejected. Social Democratic women also distanced themselves sharply from the bourgeois women's rights advocates, reproaching them with halfheartedness and reformism. They stuck to the principle that, as Clara Zetkin had said in 1891, 'the final cause of the low social position of the female sex throughout the millennia is not to be found in the respective "male" legislation but rather in property relations determined by economic conditions'. The final emancipation of women was possible only after change in these property relations under socialism. They therefore rejected official contacts or open collaboration, just like the BDF. The first Social Democratic women's congress in 1900 gave individual comrades permission 'to co-operate occasionally and temporarily with women's rights advocates and other bourgeois elements' and left it 'to their taste, to their tact' to evaluate each case.

Hence there occurred occasional concerted action by bourgeois and Social Democratic women at the local level while the leadership committees insisted on the differences in principle between their operations and aims. Thus the SPD women participated only marginally in the debate over the Civil Code (enacted in 1896 and operative as of 1900), whereas the women of the BDF evinced greater (if belated) commitment to the juridical equality of women. *Die Gleichheit* supported most of the legal-political demands of the bourgeois women's movement but simulataneously emphasized the far-reaching class differences most clearly apparent in the example of the law regarding masters and servants. While the women Social Democrats argued energetically for the abolition of these statutes, such a demand was not to be found in the protest resolutions of the BDF. Middle-class women also strongly opposed unionization of domestic servants, just as they stood solidly against the introduction of the eight-hour day for their personnel.

Despite many a point of contact in the struggle for political and juridical equality, the 'class view' remained finally decisive for the philosophical and political orientation of the two women's movements. Women Social Democrats above all kept fending off the embrace of middle-class women in the name of 'general sisterhood' (Zetkin). Their programme did not envisage the dethronement of male domination and the appropriate participation of the 'female element' in society, politics and culture, but first and foremost the liberation of proletarian women from their economic oppression under capitalism. Behind this revolutionary rhetoric of leading party women, however, tendencies were developing since 1900 towards a pragmatic, socio-political reformist commitment which, during the First World War, created the link to bourgeois-female social work.

6 The Life and Work of Eduard Bernstein

Roger Fletcher

It is an indisputable fact that no socialist revolution has yet taken place in a single advanced capitalist country. In the 100 years since the death of Marx the only socialist revolutions to have occurred – and it is a moot point whether they can all be lumped together meaningfully under this label – have usually come about in backward agrarian societies, and then, typically, with the aid of some powerful extraneous force, such as a national liberation struggle against some form of colonial or neo-imperialist domination. In the First World of capitalist Western Europe, Japan, North America and Australia, the only form of socialism that has yet come to power, or seems likely to come to power, is democratic socialism or social democracy. It has normally done so by non-violent means and, once in office, it has consistently and successfully practised the politics of gradual, piecemeal reform. It might therefore be assumed that here, at least, the life and work of Eduard Bernstein, the father of democratic socialism, would be more widely known and appreciated than they are. The purpose of this chapter is to go some distance towards remedying this anomaly.

Life of Bernstein

Eduard Bernstein was born in Berlin on 6 January 1850, the son of a Jewish locomotive driver. His family tree was none the less replete with rabbis, physicians, mathematicians and other distinguished personages, including his uncle Aaron Bernstein, a religious reformer and liberal newspaper publicist. As an adolescent Bernstein became a bank clerk and joined the Social Democratic movement. He abandoned the faith of his fathers on the day after his mother's death and never relented in his atheism (Bernstein to Karl Kautsky, 16.12.1927, KP, DV 545). All his life he steadfastly insisted that he was and remained a true disciple of Marx and Engels, 'a supporter of the theory itself', as he wrote to Kautsky on 16 December 1927. In 1875 he participated actively in the Gotha unity congress, helping to bring together the supporters of Ferdinand Lassalle and the followers of Marx and Engels.

In 1878 he accepted an appointment as private secretary to the ethical socialist or neo-Kantian philanthropist Karl Höchberg, accompanying him to Switzerland. With Höchberg's financial assistance he helped to found, in 1879, an illegal *émigré* newspaper, *Der Sozialdemokrat* – henceforth the official organ of the SPD. After a trip to London to allay the reservations of Marx and Engels, Bernstein became its editor in chief in

1881. Enjoying the confidence of Marx and Engels (Engels designated him, jointly with Bebel, as executor of his literary estate), Bernstein *qua* chief party scribe served, together with Bebel and Kautsky, as one of the three individuals who were principally responsible for the acceptance of Marxism as the official party ideology during the heroic years of socialist struggle and repression. When Bismarck's anti-socialist law was lapsed in 1890, Bernstein and Kautsky jointly drafted the famous Erfurt Programme, the first self-consciously Marxist programme of the SPD and one which was to remain in force for three decades. While the SPD was now free to operate openly in Germany on an equal footing with the non-socialist parties, Bernstein was not: the warrants for his arrest were renewed annually until 1900, and Prussian pressure on the Swiss authorities forced Bernstein to leave Switzerland in 1887.

In 1888 he arrived in London, where he remained until his return to Germany in 1901. Here a new world opened to him. Supporting himself with the aid of a regular SPD party stipend (in return for contributions to the Berlin Social Democratic central organ, *Der Vorwärts,* and to Kautsky's theoretical journal, *Die Neue Zeit*) and as a freelance journalist, Bernstein was not only in almost daily contact with Engels, but he was soon deeply immersed in and expert on British left-wing politics. He quickly became well-acquainted with SDF Marxists like H. M. Hyndman and Ernest Belfort-Bax, with eminent Fabians like Shaw, Wallas and the Webbs, with ethical socialists like Keir Hardie and Ramsay MacDonald, with trade-union and ILP leaders, with social liberals like J. A. Hobson, with Radicals like H. W. Massingham, E. D. Morel and H. N. Brailsford, and with scholars of the Great English Revolution. (In fact, he claimed to be the discoverer of Gerard Winstanley and was a great admirer of 'Freeborn' John Lilburne.) In Britain he learnt that there were many possible roads to socialism and that the ethical impulse might well provide, in the long term, even for Continental socialists, a more fruitful tactic than the violent dogmatism that he had begun to recognize in the Hegelian dialectic well before the death of Engels in August 1895.[1] Between 1896 and 1898 he ventilated, in a series of articles entitled 'Problems of socialism' and published in *Die Neue Zeit* (later issued in book form as *Zur Theorie und Geschichte des Sozialismus* [*On the Theory and History of Socialism*], 3 vols, Berlin, 1901), his growing doubts regarding the validity of key elements in the Marxist theoretical legacy. In 1899 he followed this up by publishing *Die Voraussetzungen des Sozialismus und die Aufgaben der Sozialdemokratie* (*The Presuppositions of Socialism and the Tasks of Social Democracy*).[2] Thus began the 'revisionism' debate.

When Chancellor Bülow made it possible for Bernstein to return to Germany – he did so, of course, in the hope that Bernstein's return would split the socialist movement – the revisionist heretic threw himself into the practical work of the German labour movement, principally as an SPD Reichstag deputy. Between 1902 and 1908, and again from 1912 until 1918, he represented Breslau. From 1920 until 1928 he succeeded Georg von Vollmar as the representative of one the Berlin electorates. During this time he kept up his journalistic activity but added nothing of substance to the body of theoretical work which he had commenced in the late 1890s.

In 1897 he had married Regina Schattner née Zadek. The union produced no children, but the available evidence suggests that Bernstein was an excellent father to his step-children, who evidently elected to remain in Britain after their parents' return to Germany. In 1892 he suffered a nervous breakdown and had to be sent to Zurich for a cure. Thereafter he was afflicted by indifferent health, especially in the last decade of his life. In 1925 he suffered a minor stroke which kept him bedridden for some time. Personal circumstances, including the death of his beloved 'Gine' and the suicide of his step-daughter Käthe, combined with his disappointment over the direction taken by the SPD after 1914, did much to keep him chronically gloomy and pessimistic throughout the 1920s. In his letters to Kautsky, whose youthful friendship was renewed by their common opposition to German policy during the Great War, Bernstein often complained of being 'without a literary homeland' and of his 'political death' (Bernstein to Kautsky, 10.12.1925 and 9.11.1927, KP, DV 535 and 543). He resigned his Reichstag seat in 1928 and died on 18 December 1932, six weeks before the Nazi *Machtergreifung*. The urn containing his mortal remains was placed in the Berlin trade-union headquarters, where it was soon desecrated by Nazi hooligans.

Bernstein and Revisionism

Bernstein's theoretical work has always been misunderstood. It continues to be so, partly because of the long shadow cast by the deliberate and tactically motivated misrepresentation of his position by such contemporary enemies as Rosa Luxemburg, and partly because his admirers persist in inflating his profundity, coherence and consistency well beyond that which the circumstances allow.[3] Bernstein himself accurately summed up his own contribution to socialist theory in a letter to Kausky dated 26 July 1924, where he underlined the main and long-standing difference between himself and 'the baron': 'from a theoretical starting-point you press forward and penetrate ever more deeply into the realm of theory, while I burst forth from praxis and land suddenly in the midst of theory, where I give a guest performance' (KP, DV 525).

As Susan Tegel has remarked, there were many reformist heretics before and after Bernstein. Old 'Ede' was simply the first person who attempted to draw together publicly, in a more or less coherent analysis, doubts that many party comrades had long nurtured privately regarding key aspects of the Marxist prognosis of capitalism, and to draw tactical inferences from these observations. Three decades after he first gave expression to these doubts, Bernstein was still referring to 'premature conclusions of Marx and Engels in consequence of their seduction by the Hegelian dialectic' (Bernstein to Kautsky, 16.12.1927, KP, DV 545), and he never ceased to condemn the SPD's chronic failure to bridge the gulf between theory and praxis as a source of great mischief for the party and for the class which it represented.

Central to Bernstein's revisionism was this rejection of the Hegelian dialectic, which, in his view, exaggerated the importance of conflict and force while underrating the crucial role of the co-operative principle in past and present social orders. Bernstein proposed to replace the dialectic in socialist theory with the principle of ethical right (*Gerechtigkeit*). While he accepted much of Marx's economic analysis, he could not endorse the labour theory of value and he maintained that capitalism had evinced important progressive tendencies that had been inadequately foreseen by Marx and Engels. In Bernstein's estimation these tendencies were unlikely to produce a breakdown in the capitalist system, which, on the contrary, showed unexpected vitality in its capacity for curing its own ills. Far from having anything to gain from insurrection and class conflict, the toiling masses could and should achieve emancipation only through a steadily widening application of the democratic principle at all levels of social activity. Bernstein prized democracy, in the broadest sense, both as a means and as an end, forming an integral part of the socialist ideal. In his estimate, socialism and democracy went hand in hand, socialism being a more advanced sibling of liberalism. These ethically desirable objectives could be realised only gradually and by non-violent methods. He believed they were already well on the way towards realization in advanced societies like that of Britain.

Such was Bernstein's revisionist theory. Conceived almost entirely in the course of his London sojourn, it was pretty unexceptional stuff and, at the time, caused hardly a stir outside the more dogmatic Marxist left wing of the German Social Democratic movement, going largely unnoticed elsewhere in the Second International and among ordinary workers everywhere. Bernstein himself never attached great importance to it, and it certainly never gave him a position of leadership within the reformist wing of German or international Social Democracy. Bertrand Russell once summed it up in the remark, 'Bernstein's work, as is common in Broad Church writers, consists largely in showing that the Founders did not hold their doctrines so rigidly as their followers have done' (Russell, 1919, p. 27).

Bernstein as Practical Politician

After his return to Germany in 1901 Bernstein, at the age of 51, became a practising politician for the first time in his long life. It was a role which he cherished, even if he performed it rather awkwardly and ineffectually. He became involved in a great variety of practical work – in the party school, in trade-union affairs, in Berlin local government, as a party journalist and as an SPD Reichstag deputy. Here he specialized in fiscal policy and in international relations. By virtue of his long residence in Britain and his close familiarity with British affairs, he became increasingly worried about the Anglo-German antagonism that had developed by the turn of the century. As an anglophile and a 'pacificist', he made it his task to reverse this dangerous process of estrangement. This, rather than his correction of Marx, formed the principal subject of his speeches and writings between 1901 and the outbreak of the First World War.[4]

His long crusade against the international mischief-makers of Imperial Germany – for this is largely how he approached the task of educating

German Social Democracy for a more responsible and active role in public affairs – had its alpha and omega in his passionate attachment to free trade, 'pacifism' and cosmopolitan patriotism. Condemning protectionism as a vain attempt to preserve the antediluvian Junkers from extinction, he defended free trade along lines very similar to those of Cobden and Bright a generation before him. Whereas protectionism divided nations and classes, free trade was alleged to be conducive to the material and moral improvement of all humanity, as well as productive of peace among nations. In the tradition of 1848, he deplored certain types of nationalism – and internationalism – as atavistic, parasitic and reactionary, but at the same time he insisted that the worker did have a fatherland and could be, even ought to be, in a progressive sense both patriotic and internationalist. Although he rejected militarism as another ephemeral manifestation of anomalous, antiquated Junker hegemony, he was not an unconditional pacifist. Under certain conditions, he believed, the worker could and should take up arms – for instance, in defence of the fatherland against Russian imperialism, or in order to bring the blessings of 'civilization' to 'backward' peoples – but he was unable to envisage any circumstances in which a war among 'civilized' European powers might be justified. On the other hand, he could not bring himself to underwrite drastic measures, such as use of the general strike, to prevent or halt such a war, putting his trust instead in the 'grand panacea' of commerce and in the extension of democratic controls over foreign policy and military establishments.

His perception of imperialism strikingly paralleled the theory which Joseph Schumpeter was to expound in his 1919 essay on the sociology of imperialisms. Considering imperialism to be essentially a throwback to more primitive stages of historical development, he regarded it as being only marginally and incidentally related to capitalist interests. It could be progressive or reactionary, depending on the kind of society practising it. The imperialism of Periclean Athens, for example, or of Republican Rome and, in the modern era, of liberal Britain were obviously of a different and higher species from those of Chinggis Khan, tsarist Russia – or Wilhelmine Germany. The *Weltpolitik* of Kaiser Wilhelm II he condemned as thoroughly reprehensible and in no way deserving of working-class support, for he deemed it to be scarcely more than a costly expedient to uphold Junker influence in German government and society. It fanned the flames of suspicion and hatred among peoples and classes, needlessly burdened consumers in general and the working class in particular, and it simultaneously impeded long-overdue social reform at home and abroad. Colonialism, on the other hand, was something which Bernstein divorced from imperialism and endorsed almost without reservation. He seems to have contemplated it in terms of 'the white man's burden', believing it to be generally beneficial – to the colonial peoples and to humanity at large, no less than to the ruling and working classes of the colonizing power. Indeed, he frequently defended colonialism in the brutal terminology of Social Darwinism. Somewhat uncharacteristically, he strongly urged German Social Democrats to support the colonizing activities of even the Kaiser's government.

Such was the critical perspective from which Bernstein judged and found wanting the foreign policy of Wilhelmine Germany. Since Wilhelmine *Weltpolitik* was protectionist, militaristic, nationalistic, imperialistic (in the worst sense) and had been a poor achiever in the realm of colonization, he saw little to commend and much to condemn in the policies of Chancellors Bülow and Bethmann Hollweg. In his view the net result of their follies was that Germany, through ineptitude rather than design, was drifting towards a disastrous and unnecessary conflict with Britain and her allies.

What he advocated in place of this suicidal lunacy was a kind of Continental and pro-Western liberal imperialism. Again in the tradition of 1848, he was obsessed by the 'Russian peril', believing that Germany should counteract it by means of an anti-Russian Near Eastern free-trade imperialism aiming ultimately at the dismemberment of the tsarist empire and the liberation of its capitve nations. In the West, he wanted to see Germany working earnestly towards an understanding with republican France and liberal Britain, preferring the word entente to the terminology of alliance. As a step towards the conciliation of France he counselled the granting of home rule to Alsace-Lorraine, that is, home rule within the German Empire, and his proposed stepping-stone to Anglo-German amity was some form of naval détente.

In Bernstein's mind, this policy was closely bound up with domestic political considerations. He was firmly convinced that the achievement of greater democracy in Prussia and the Reich would act as a powerful stimulus to a Western alliance and that this, in turn, would accelerate the pace of domestic reform. Once Germany and Britain had buried the hatchet, he believed, a massive colonial redistribution would become possible, France would be pacified, Russia contained, and Germany's supine middle-class parties would recover their nerve and align themselves with their natural Social Democratic allies in a bloc 'from Bebel to Bassermann'. The days of the Junker–big business symbiosis would be numbered and a social-liberal alliance for peace and progress would become unstoppable. Socialism on the instalment plan, or social revolution without blood, sweat or tears, would at last be a real option rather than a utopian dream. Like Joseph Bloch (editor of the chief revisionist organ, the *Sozialistische Monatshefte* or *Socialist Monthly*), Friedrich Naumann and others, Bernstein also hoped to achieve a solution to the 'social question' by means of a 'revolution in world politics' (the title of Bloch's posthumously published book). In many ways, he was the working man's Bethmann Hollweg. For all his vague allusion to the need for world government and a league of nations (before 1914, his pronouncements on this subject were decidedly vague), Bernstein's proposals for a socialist alternative foreign policy amounted to little more than a programme for 'German world policy without war' (the title of a pamphlet published by the liberal imperialist Hans Plehn in May 1913). In other words, he wanted to have his cake and eat it too.

With the outbreak of the First World War in August 1914, Bernstein, like almost every other German Social Democrat, allowed himself to be swept up by his patriotic russophobia. Although he voted in favour of war credits on 4 August, within a matter of weeks he was at loggerheads with Joseph Bloch and other revisionist and reformist comrades of long standing. German annexationist demands and the brutality with which the German High Command waged the war soon convinced him that the conflict was, or had become, yet another East Elbian war of conquest. After March 1915 he no longer voted in favour of war credits, and his journalism and speeches now clearly marked him as an anti-war activist. In June 1915, for example, he published, together with Hugo Haase and Karl Kautsky, a ringing denunciation of the war, and Germany's part in it, entitled *Das Gebot der Stunde* (*The Demand of the Hour*). As his pacifism and his internationalism took on a more consistent and determined appearance, his relations with erstwhile enemies of the party centre and the left improved dramatically.[5] (By the end of the war Bernstein and Kautsky were back to addressing each other by their youthful nicknames – Ede and Baron.) From this point onwards, he was again to be found attacking the party majority for its inability to marry theory with practice and for its betrayal of socialist principles. These considerations led him to join the USPD in 1917, beside most of his bitterest foes of the prewar era.

Viewing class war as being no less objectionable than violence among nations, Bernstein played no active part in the German revolution of 1918–19. He merely sought to mediate between the SPD and the Independents, which had the effect of deepening his own isolation. The left still had no love for 'the old flour-sack', while the right was now fully confident of being able to fend for itself. Bernstein's most active role in the revolution was probably his service as a Treasury *Beirat* (two such supernumerary officials were appointed to assist each minister). In March 1919 he left the USPD and returned to the Majority SPD. He did so because he wished to underscore the need for working-class solidarity and in disapproval of the increasingly radical positions being adopted by the USPD. He mistrusted the council system, for instance, would not have a bar of proletarian dictatorship and was thoroughly convinced not only that Bolshevism must be combated within Germany but that it would also prove to be an unmitigated catastrophe for the Russian people. (His position here went back to his quarrel with Parvus-Helphand at the turn of the century). So intense was his hostility towards Bolshevism that it could even induce him to defend the conduct of Noske (see Tucholsky, 1975, vol. 4, 407).

During the Weimar Republic Bernstein took it upon himself to campaign for a frank acceptance of the German government's primary responsibility for the outbreak of the world war. In view of the severe burdens imposed by the Versailles Treaty, this seemingly Quixotic stand exasperated his friends without winning him any new allies within or beyond the ranks of the SPD. He continued to champion the cause of coalition with bourgeois parties, even with Stresemann's DVP. This, too, must have struck a raw nerve with many contemporary socialists, for the DVP played host to many of the bourgeois imperialists who had done most to ensure that a global war could scarcely be avoided in August 1914. He also resumed his prewar campaign against sectarian dogmatism and on behalf of the realities of power. In the new Görlitz Programme of 1921, replacing the Erfurt Programme of 30 years before, he seemed to have triumphed, but it was a Pyrrhic victory in that it was soon superseded by the 1925 Heidelberg Programme, which bore the stamp of Kautsky rather than Bernstein. The latter went on complaining about the many 'contradictions between our language and our practical behaviour' (Bernstein to Kautsky, 29.4.1926, KP, DV 538) and about the harmful consequences of the SPD's neglect of political education. To Kautsky he lamented that 'truly socialist thought has become completely alien to many [party comrades]' (ibid., 10.12.1925, DV 535). Both publicly and privately, he repeatedly affirmed that 'praxis, i.e. the practical struggle, has taken hold of me again and so dominates my every thought and feeling that I have no real taste for anything else' (ibid., 26.7.1924, DV 525).

Conclusion

True to himself to the very end, Bernstein remained in several respects his own worst enemy – a man of impeccable intellectual honesty and moral probity, yet often led astray by his pragmatic eclecticism, his confused empiricism and his moral idealism. Within the party and movement in whose service he had laboured selflessly for half a century, his death passed almost unnoticed in December 1932. He departed unsung, virtually unknown, apparently a complete failure. In the next generation great changes and deeds of almost unprecedented and certainly inconceivable infamy seemed to erase his memory from the historical record. Yet in Germany today, or in that part of it which enjoys free access to its past, it is no exaggeration to say that of the Social Democratic founding fathers Bernstein has emerged as a more respected figure than Marx himself and that his views are widely believed to have stood the test of time far more effectively than those of more erudite, prolific and charismatic pioneers like Marx, Engels and Lassalle. Outside Germany, Bernstein is still relatively little appreciated, despite the fact that the early rediscoverers of Bernstein were all foreigners – Peter Gay, Pierre Angel and Bo Gustafsson, for example. This deficit represents a loss which the cause of humanity and decency might profitably begin to make good.

Notes

[1]Some writers persist – quite needlessly, it appears to me – in attempting to pinpoint Bernstein's journey to Damascus. See, for example Kendall Rogers, 1983, 320–25.

[2]Translated into English by Edith C. Harvey in 1909 as *Evolutionary Socialism,* but without annotation and minus the key chapter on the 'snare of the Hegelian dialectic'.

[3]Determined to 'beat that flour-bag Bernstein so fiercely that the thick powder dust rises into the air and the periwigs of the Bernstein school are blown from their heads', Luxemburg, in her letters to her 'comrade and lover' Leo Jogiches in

the late 1890s, repeatedly appealed for ideas, arguments and suggestions that would facilitate this task. In this context she announced that 'the world does not stop with Bernstein' and that it was her intention 'to strive . . . for the most influential place in the [German Social Democratic] movement'. See Bronner, 1978, 64–5, 70–8. An instance of exaggerated and misplaced respect for Bernstein's sagacity is Thomas Meyer, 1977.

[4]See Roger Fletcher, 1984, 128–82; S. Miller, 1978, 213–21; H. A. Winkler, 1983–4, 1003–27.

[5]See Lukàcs, 1924, 591–7, for some perceptive commentary on 'Bernstein's victory'.

Part II
The Crucible of War

7 Everyday Life and the German Working Class, 1914–1918

Volker Ullrich

For a long time the history of the German labour movement in the First World War was considered almost exclusively from the point of view of the schisms within Social Democracy and the ideological clashes which accompanied them. The Bielefeld social historian Jürgen Kocka broadened this perspective with his study *Klassengesellschaft im Krieg* (1973), to which socio-historical research on the First World War is indebted for vital impulses.[1] Kocka's idea of explaining the genesis of the November Revolution through socio-economic processes of change and wartime distribution conflicts in a class society has been taken up in a number of local and regional studies. In these studies special interest has been devoted to the various manifestations of social protest and social conflict during the world war and revolution, such manifestations being subsumed under the common heading of 'mass movements'. From here it was only a small step to ask how the changing living conditions between 1914 and 1918 were experienced and interpreted by those concerned: the everyday life of wartime came under the scrutiny of scholarship.

The Working Class and the Outbreak of War

One of the most astonishing shortcomings of labour history is that to this day there has been no comprehensive investigation into the attitude of the German working class at the outbreak of war. On the basis of what we now know, however, we may safely assume that the picture of a general enthusiasm for war as commonly presented in the literature does not accord with reality. Rather, there is some evidence that the reactions of the working class to the outbreak of war were highly contradictory and complex, and thus cannot readily be reduced to neat formulas. Among the workers there was obviously no 'August experience', in the sense of an intoxicating feeling of community that transcended all social barriers, comparable to that in bourgeois circles. The mood among Social Democratic supporters in the early weeks of August was in fact characterized by currents of bewilderment and resignation. The about-turn of the party leadership on 4 August had occurred too suddenly to be universally implemented without problems. On a wave of emotionally based hostility to tsarism, which was systematically fanned by the Social Democratic press, sections of the working class were also dragged into the maelstrom of chauvinism. The subjectively sincere but factually erroneous conviction that Germany had to defend itself against an enemy attack awakened among SPD members dormant nationalistic feelings previously implanted by school and by the army. These had been only superficially overlaid by the party's declamatory anti-militarism prior to 1914.

One thing is certain: wherever patriotic fervour may have been in evidence among the workers, the everyday life of wartime rapidly exerted a sobering effect. Although a large proportion of able-bodied men had already been called up in August 1914, the country soon experienced mass unemployment on a scale which it had not seen for a long time. In some large cities it affected up to 40 per cent of men fit for work. In the absence of any state benefit, many of the unemployed had to turn to private charities, or – which was even more humiliating – to public poor relief. As early as 21 August 1914 the *Hamburger Echo,* the Social Democratic party newspaper in Hamburg, reported that in the poorer districts 'there is extremely severe hardship, indeed many people are actually starving'.

But even in many families whose breadwinners had been conscripted poverty made a rapid appearance. The statutory levels of benefit were totally inadequate, so that the local authorities were forced to make considerable supplementary provisions. This, however, lagged quite clearly behind the rise in the cost of living. For this reason, many women were soon obliged to look around for work in order to support themselves and their children. After the relative economic stability of the pre war years, which had brought the workers a modest but steady improvement in their standard of living, the hardship which suddenly descended on them was experienced by the families affected as a disaster – an experience which was in glaring contrast to the nationalistic exuberance of these months. The very first weeks of the war revealed how deceptive and fragile the 'internal truce' (*Burgfrieden*) really was. The effects of this experience were still felt even after October 1914 when, as a result of continued conscription and the developing war economy, unemployment declined and soon gave way to a labour shortage. The normality of everyday life before the war was never restored. On the contrary, as the war progressed, it increasingly deployed its destructive power on the 'home front' as well. The Moloch of matériel battle, which determined the development of the war following the transition to trench warfare in autumn 1914, not only consumed ever increasing quantities of manpower and equipment but also demanded the ruthless exploitation of all material and human resources. It was above all the workers who suffered from this, but other groups such as clerical staff and public employees were also obliged to endure the effects.

The Development of the Material Situation of the Working Class in Wartime

The factor which affected the situation of the working class in wartime in the most direct and lasting way was the scarcity and rising price of food supplies. In the early days of mobilization there had already been an onslaught on the food stores in all the major cities which had driven prices sky-high. True, the law passed by the Federal Council on 4 August 1914 permitted the governments of the individual states to fix maximum prices for foodstuffs. But in practice it proved to be largely ineffective. For it encouraged the tendency of the agricultural producers to withhold their produce until better prices were offered to them by government buyers, or, alternatively, to sell in secret to customers with the means to pay. Thus the city authorities were obliged to keep on adjusting the maximum price upwards, so as not to have their food supplies cut off. In January 1915 the rate of inflation was already 19 per cent, in July 1915 over 50 per cent and in July 1916 more than 100 per cent. By the summer of 1915 more nutritious foodstuffs such as meat, butter and eggs had already become unattainable luxury goods for the mass of the urban population. Alongside the rise in prices, irregularities in supply – caused by poor organization and confusion over areas of responsibility – were a constant source of discontent. One minute bread and potatoes, the single diet of the 'small people', were unobtainable; the next minute the market was flooded with them, with the result that much of the food was spoiled and went to waste. The shortcomings and inequalities in the system of distribution actually led to more anger and bitterness than a situation of continuous scarcity would have done.

Food supplies became not only scarcer and dearer, but they also deteriorated in quality. From January 1915 potatoes had to be used to make the bread 'go further', and from 1917 turnips were similarly used. More and more frequently the populace had to make use of substitute foodstuffs whose nutritional value was open to doubt and whose taste only faintly resembled that of the orginals. In many cities public war kitchens were set up, in which cheap, though not very nourishing, dinners were dispensed. At first, many workers showed a definite aversion to these 'beggars' soups', as such food was generally known. But sheer need forced them, and also impoverished members of the middle class, to abandon their resistance to these soup kitchens.

Wages were not able to keep pace with the rise in the cost of living, particularly food prices. The reduction in unemployment of the first few weeks of the war and the reflation of the war economy did bring about a rise in nominal earnings, but there were considerable differences between various branches of industry. Wages rose fastest in industries vital in the war effort – engineering, machine-making, the chemical and electronic industries – whereas they definitely lagged behind in the textile and foodstuffs industries and in the printing trade. But even among the highest earners in the armaments industry there were only a few, chiefly highly skilled specialists, who managed to maintain their standard of living, that is, to compensate for the loss of purchasing power caused by inflation. The general trend was very noticeably in the opposite direction, towards a marked loss in real earnings. According to calculations made by Kocka, the average real annual wage of a worker fell by 23 per cent between 1914 and 1918 in the war industries; in the peace industries the drop was no less than 44 per cent.

Anyone with no other wage-earners in the family often had to work overtime to the point of exhaustion. In the majority of armaments factories the hours of work rose to 12 hours per day and more. Night work and Sunday work also increased. Physical over-exertion and an inadequate diet led to a rapid deterioration in health. The number of sickness cases increased dramatically.

Despite the forced overtime, earnings were generally barely sufficient to cover essential expenditure on rationed foodstuffs, rent, heating and taxes. There was scarcely anything left for clothing and other everyday necessities. The consequence was that by the end of the war workers were forced to go around literally in rags.

If one takes all these factors into account – the decline in wages, chronic undernourishment, excessive hours of work, inadequate clothing – it is, indeed, possible to agree with Kocka that the war 'created for the working class a situation of shortage, deprivation and exploitation such as had not existed since the beginning of industrialization' (Kocka, 1984, 26).

In general, the manifestations of impoverishment first appeared among those wage-earners who were not employed in the war industries. Armaments workers were given priority over other workers not only with regard to wages but also with regard to food. Most major armaments firms set up their own works canteens to cater for their employees. In addition, from 1916 the War Nutrition Office (*Kriegsernährungsamt*) approved special supplements for armaments workers and heavy workers, which provoked a great deal of resentment and envy among those not employed in the armaments industry. Nevertheless, the theory of the dissolution of the German working class into two strata – the 'contented' (because well-fed) armaments workers, and the 'discontented' and hence easily radicalized non-armaments workers – is not tenable. In fact, all the indications are that the improvements in the position of the armaments workers promoted by the military authorities and the entrepreneurs did not have the effect of reducing conflict and uniting the classes. On the contrary, it strengthened the self-confidence of these groups of workers and facilitated the militant assertion of their interests. However, the structural changes in the working class must also be subjected to scrutiny.

Social Restructuring Processes within the Working Class

The deterioration of material conditions was accompanied by a thorough-going process of restructuring within the working class. Because of the initial lack of co-ordination in military conscription, industry was deprived of a large section of its old core of skilled workers, without regard to their qualifications and importance for maintaining production. Even though some of the conscripted workers were soon released again ('reclaimed') for work in specified armaments factories, the armaments industry suffered from a chronic lack of manpower, especially skilled workers, since the beginning of 1915. In order to plug the resultant gaps, entrepreneurs had recourse to those employed in the branches of industry less vital to the war effort, but also increasingly to the army of semi-skilled and unskilled workers. In this way groups of people who had hitherto stood aloof from the industrial work process entered the expanding armaments economy: small tradesmen and artisans who had been forced to close down their businesses or workshops; farm labourers attracted to the armaments industry by the higher wages: young people (school-leavers) who were obliged to contribute to the family income; but, above all, women who were unable to support themselves and their children on the paltry war benefit. The proportion of women working in industry rose from barely 22 per cent in 1913 to 34 per cent in 1918. Towards the end of the war many armaments companies employed more women than men. Female labour was particularly widespread in the munitions industry, where men and women worked in sometimes highly dangerous conditions.

The changes in the internal structure of the working class – the supplanting of older and more experienced workers by semi-skilled and unskilled women and young people, the constant succession of 'reclaimed' workers, the employment of prisoners-of-war – resulted in a degree of mobility and fluctuation in the workforce that was almost unprecedented. The effects of this restructuring process were ambivalent. For one thing, they promoted tendencies towards disintegration within the workforce. Many of the newcomers were unable to identify either with the strange new company or with a job for which they were not trained and which they often considered to be a transitional stage. This lack of attachment to the industrial and social environment heightened the element of sensitivity to the worsening working and living conditions. In his memoires Karl Retzlaw describes what everyday life was like for a workforce thrown together at a Berlin factory that had been switched to the production of shells:

> The working conditions were like they must have been under early capitalism. There was always 'something wrong'. Especially during the night shift. Never a night passed without one or more of the women collapsing at their machines from exhaustion, hunger, illness. . . . On many days in winter there was no heating, the workers stood around in groups, they could not and would not work. . . . In the canteen there were almost daily screaming fits by women, sometimes even depressing fights between them, because they claimed 'the ladle had not been filled'. (Retzlaw, 1971, 72)

On the other hand, there were also integrative processes among the workforces of the armaments companies. The concentration of thousands of workers, both male and female, led to the gradual erosion of traditional occupational differences and the elimination of many of the obstacles which had hitherto barred the way to common action. Where existing communication structures were not destroyed by massive attacks from without, and a skilled core of industrially experienced engineering workers belonging to the trade-union opposition was able to assert itself – as in the large concerns of Berlin or the Hamburg shipyards – the strong fluctuation of incoming workers obviously did not impair militancy but favoured it. Feldman, Kolb and Rürup are probably right in assuming that this encounter between a self-confident, militant tradition of local organization and an influx of unskilled and semi-skilled workers, cut off from their social environments and not yet accustomed to trade-union organizational discipline, was one of the most important constituent factors of the mass movements of the First World War (Feldman *et al.*, 1972, 87).

Social Protest during the War

When trying to describe the birthplaces and the various forms of social protest during the world war, one must first point to two general conditions of a restrictive nature. Firstly, it should be taken into account that with the declaration of a state of war, executive power in the interior had passed to the military commanders in the separate regions, the so-called acting general commands. They used the far-reaching powers of the state of siege in order to transform Germany 'into a collection of tyrannies'. The right of association and assembly was largely suspended, and the press was subjected to strict censorship. In practice, these measures were principally directed against the oppositional sections of the labour movement. Secondly, as the leaderships of the trade unions and the Social Democrats had voluntarily bowed to the yoke of the 'internal truce', discontent and resentment at the worsening living and working conditions could not be articulated in the usual way through the workers' organizations and the Social Democratic press. Two other fields of alternative publicity therefore became all the more important: the street, that is, the place where the struggle for the increasingly scarce food supplies was enacted, and the big industrial concern, particularly the expanding armaments factories. These became the venue of new forms of labour conflict.

Since late 1915 and early 1916 queues outside the grocers' shops had been a feature of everyday life in the big cities. They formed focal points of discontent and protest, which the authorities feared could easily trigger off disturbances and riots. In the discussion between the starving, work-weary women many things were said which found no echo in the press, committed as it was to the 'internal truce'. Nowhere else, except within a big company, were the opportunities for relatively natural communication, free of surveillance, so favourable in the conditions imposed by the state of siege; the women seized the chance of giving vent to their anger.

In the summer of 1916 most German cities experienced the first major food riots of the war, during the course of which numerous shops were looted. As a general rule, these were spontaneous outbreaks of militant self-help, not prepared or directed by any organization but springing from an acute bottle-neck in food supplies. After the 'turnip winter' of 1916–17, which sorely tried the patience of the populace, the hunger riots were repeated, but this time (unlike those of 1916) they extended to the smaller towns in the vicinity of the industrial centres, a sign of how widespread resentment at the appalling state of supplies had become in the meantime. Statements made by police officers at the time agree that those involved in the riots were above all working-class women and young people. This is scarcely surprising, since, apart from women, it was young people who were subjected by the world war to the most violent upheavals in their former way of life. As their fathers were at the front, and their mothers had the worry of obtaining food after a tiring day in a factory, the youngsters were left to their own devices. They were often forced to forgo an apprenticeship and take a better-paid but hazardous and mind-numbing job in the armaments industry in order to contribute to the upkeep of the family. Here we find the social roots of the innumerable complaints of the authorities about the lack of discipline and wild behaviour of the city youth, about the formation of gangs and juvenile criminality.

In his comparative study of Brunswick and Hanover, Friedhelm Boll has divided the mass movements of the war period into two phases: a first, from 1916–17, marked by food riots; and a second, linked with it, characterized by the political mass strikes, culminating in April 1917 and January 1918 (Boll, 1981, 204f.). This two-phased model is in need of correction because of its over-schematic nature. It can be established that as early as 1916 food riots could turn directly into strike movements and vice versa. It is, however, correct that the strike activities of 1916 remained limited, and, apart from the brief sympathy strike for Karl Liebknecht at the end of June in Berlin and a few other places, had as yet no clear political tendency. As a rule, they were initially fairly small actions which generally ended after a few hours and affected individual branches of industry or groups of workers, and no more. The demands made were chiefly economic ones: the workers demanded compensation for inflation or additional food rations, and soon resumed work if the employers (frequently under discreet pressure from the military authorities) signalled some willingness to meet their demands.

The reasons for this reticence with regard to strikes are obvious: any strike in wartime implied a major breach of the 'internal truce' in the eyes of the political and military leaders, and was therefore criminalized by every means. The strikers could count neither on the sympathies of the bourgeois media nor on the moral and financial support of the trade-union organizations, which had, of course, pledged to abstain from political strikes at the outbreak of war. Moreover, there were special risks involved in striking in wartime, since those taking part were bound to fear that they might be conscripted into the army. The 'threat of the trenches' (the employers' most effective instrument in securing industrial discipline) was particularly applied to the 'reclaimed' workers, who, if found engaging in political activity at work, were immediately conscripted once again.

All this explains why discontent and protest at factory level had to seek less spectacular manifestations which were close to the base and independent of organizations. Below the dangerous strike threshold many other forms of industrial action, both individual and collective, are known to have occurred during the First World War – for instance, deliberate go-slows, refusal to do overtime, absence from work without good reason, lack of co-operation with foremen and bosses, thefts and so on. These cases of everyday resistance have only recently engaged the attention of historians and still require more thorough research.

Social Protest and Social Criticism: The Politicization of the Mass Movements

The first expressions of dissatisfaction and protest in the working class were largely a result of economic hardship, though the longing for freedom may already have been visible as a driving force in the background. As the war dragged on, bitterness at the economic distress and war-weariness combined with resentment against the privileged and the rulers, with social criticism and social protest. Three factors, in particular, helped to give economic discontent a political dimension.

Firstly, since 1916–17, the spectacular failure of the state authorities in the sphere of food supply had led to illicit trading that was constantly expanding. Hordes of city-dwellers combed the country areas at weekends to buy additional food supplies or to obtain them by barter. It always aroused special indignation when police officers relieved the small hoarder of his laboriously acquired food supplies, while the big speculators and professional black-marketeers escaped unscathed. The lion's share of the goods that appeared on the black market ended up in the pockets of the rich. Because of this, the effect of illicit trading was to reveal the class divisions in society. Feelings of social resentment were activated by rumours which were now circulating everywhere. For example, in the Berlin armaments factories there was a story in the winter of 1916–17 that 'the crown princesses bathed in milk, while small children could not get any to drink'. Such rumours fell on fertile ground – despite official denials – because they were quite in keeping with the visible inequalities in food distribution and the markedly better situation of the wealthy strata of society.

Secondly, the news of the outbreak of the February Revolution in Russia made a great impression in the spring of 1917. In the conversations of the women in front of the grocers' shops, revoluntionary Russia became a symbol of hope for fundamental changes in their own situation too. Thus a police report from Hamburg in April 1917 remarked: 'Events in Russia, it seems, have not failed to have an effect on the masses, for in various places remarks were heard to the effect that "We only have to do as they have done in Russia, then things will be different".'

Thirdly, the public discussion of war aims which had been led by influential annexationist groups since 1916 increased working-class doubts as to whether the war was really a war of defence, as the government maintained, or whether it was, after all, a war of conquest in the interests of the ruling class. The report of a policeman from Saxony in May 1917 provides a good illustration of this mood: 'Understanding of the need to hold out is dwindling away. Among the people the comment is often heard: "Who are we really fighting this war for, if not really for big business?"' The fact that the strictly annexationist Fatherland Party

(*Vaterlandspartei*) was able to indulge in public agitation without hindrance, whereas opponents of the war of all shades were mercilessly persecuted, could only provide further grounds for such views.

The politicization of the mood of the masses in an anti-establishment direction was clearly shown in the April strike of 1917, but even more so in the January strike of 1918, the biggest strike movement of the war period. All the economic and political sources of irritation coincided in the January strike, and this very fact bestowed on it a great proto-revolutionary impetus. In Berlin alone, the centre of the strike, over 400,000 workers came out. At the top of the strike programme of the Berlin Workers' Council, which was adopted in many other places, was the demand for a peace without annexations and reparations, on the basis of the rights of nations to self-determination. Further demands were for improvements in food supplies, suspension of the state of siege, restoration of the rights of association and assembly, release of political prisoners, and a thorough democratization of all the state institutions in Germany.

The extent, intensity and duration of the January strike in the separate industrial centres were greatly dependent on the relative strength and political orientation of the labour movement in each area. A factor of major importance was the degree to which the USPD had succeeded in developing its own profile as a serious rival to the old SPD. Where it possessed a functioning system of elected officials in the factories it obviously found it easiest to mobilize the workers for the strike. The revolutionary left – the Spartacus Group and the left-wing radicals in the North German coastal towns – were, however, unable to exert any substantial influence on the preparation and execution of the January movement. On the contrary, this strike exposed the relative isolation of these groups from the industrial base and the revolutionary representatives of the trade-union opposition.

For the trade-union executives and the Social Democratic party leadership, the January strikes signified a grave setback. For the first time, plainly revealed to all, was the extent to which the decline in the government's authority spread to the leadership of the organizations of the labour movement. In order to fortify their position in the face of attack, they considered it necessary in many places to form a strike leadership together with USPD representatives and factory shop-stewards. To outward appearances the unity of the labour movement seemed to have been restored. This coincided with a deep-rooted need among the workers to entrust themselves to the established authorities of the old Social Democracy, so long as they were mindful, as seemed to be the case in January 1918, of their militant traditions. This constellation was to be repeated in the November Revolution of 1918, and would seem to go some way towards providing us with an explanation for its failure.

The Road to the November Revolution

Even the crushing of the January strike and the massive wave of repression that ensued could not re-stabilize the society of Wilhelmine

Germany, which had been shaken to its very foundations. There was no longer any let-up in the succession of strikes and demonstrations. After the failure of the Western offensive in the summer of 1918, the symptoms of collapse, which were visible everywhere, spread to the army and the navy. Rumours were rife of refusals to obey orders and of mass desertions. On 8 August 1918, the day of the British breakthrough on the Western front, which ushered in the last phase of the war, the view was widespread among the workers at the Vulcan shipyard in Hamburg 'that German militarism is going to its death': soldiers returning from the Western front detailed to do labour service at the shipyard are reported to have said that things looked bad on the Western front. It was even said that whole German units had gone over to the enemy. What a police spy overheard of a conversation between two patients in a military hospital in Bremerhaven in mid-August 1918 was probably a good indication of the mood of most soldiers: 'You see, comrade, we are finished, nobody thinks of victory any more, what it says in the papers is all lies and deceit. . . . If we put an end to it now, we can still save a lot – money and men. Should we allow ourselves to be shot to pieces just because the top brass still have an appetite for this insane butchery? . . . We'll get our comrades to do what they did in Russia, we've got nothing left to lose.' The moment military discipline broke down, the authoritarian state of Wilhelmine Germany was at an end; revolution could no longer be averted.

Notes

[1]This seminal work is now available in English translation as *Facing Total War: German Society 1914–1918* (Leamington Spa, 1984). For additional German-language literature, see Volker Ullrich, *Kriegsalltag: Hamburg im Ersten Weltkrieg* (Cologne, 1982), and Adelheid von Saldern, *Auf dem Wege zum Arbeiterreformismus: Parteialltag in sozialdemokratischer Provinz Göttingen (1870–1920)* (Frankfurt, 1984). Still useful is the classic Gerald D. Feldman, *Army, Industry, and Labor in Germany 1914–1918* (Princeton, 1966).

8 The SPD in War and Revolution, 1914–1919

Geoff Eley

The outbreak of the First World War confused the place of the labour movement in German society. From being the enemy within, self-evidently beyond the boundaries of legitimate consensus, it became part of a broad patriotic front, upholding German security against foreign aggression (as it was claimed), and maintaining the *Burgfrieden* or domestic truce while the war was on. Together with other aspects of the war – the tangible reality of imperialist aggrandizement, the changed relationship of state and economy, the power of the military, the divisions within the non-socialist camp, and the new corporative decision-making structures – this admission of the labour movement to the legitimate nation formed a new configuration of German politics. For liberals it opened possibilities of a lasting realignment, based on an expanding manufacturing economy, limited socio-political reform, and an incorporated labour movement, for which Germany's impending continental hegemony would deliver the material conditions. For the right, on the other hand, this was precisely their worst fear, the historic compromise the imperialist breakout was supposed to prevent. The resulting field of conflict, as it seemed, defined an unparalleled space for Social Democratic manoeuvre, but at the cost of repudiating an existing socialist political tradition and engendering potent sources of conflict with the socialist rank and file. How the SPD dealt with this situation had a decisive impact on the future course of the 1918–19 revolution.

Politics at War

Once the immediate drama of August 1914 had passed, the SPD's new position revealed some important ulterior agendas. A social-imperialist conception of working-class emancipation, which sublimated the earlier class analysis in an argument for the anticipated benefits of Germany's European and colonial hegemony, was one of these, and crystallized around the journal *Sozialistische Monatshefte*, which had already acquired a reputation for such perspectives before 1914 (see Fletcher, 1984). But for the main body of the SPD leadership the principal motivation was a kind of hard-headed but class-conscious pragmatism which was certainly infused with nationalism (the 'ideas of 1914', or 'social patriotism', as its left-wing opponents called it) but which counted on a reformist breakthrough now the labour movement had shown its patriotic reliability. As Eduard David, one of the party's leading reformists, said during the key talks with the government in the early days of the war, 'the hundreds of thousands of convinced Social Democrats who are giving their all for the war effort expected some acknowledgement of their own wishes in return'; consequently, 'a great gesture' by the government, 'not of words, but of political deeds', was 'essential' (Kuczynski, 1957, 207ff.).

Specifically, this meant the long-demanded introduction of universal suffrage in Prussia, together with a substantial package of social reform. In trade-union affairs it meant a legally sanctioned system of collective bargaining and full trade-union involvement in the running of the war economy. In both cases, it was thought, the concessions of the wartime emergency could become the lasting basis of the labour movement's acceptance into the nation. The 'purely' nationalist motivations were inseparably bound up in this reformist calculation. Reformists spoke of converting Social Democracy into 'national democracy', of drawing the labour movement into 'monarchist' waters, and of achieving a 'parliamentary democratic form of government headed by the monarchy' (see Fischer, 1967, 330–3; Boll, 1980, 119–20).

The most forthright and consistent exponents of this new course were the individuals who had opened contacts with the government in 1914: Eduard David, Albert Südekum and Max Cohen-Reuss. But they had powerful allies in the party Executive (Friedrich Ebert and Philipp Scheidemann), and together with the national trade-union leadership (especially Carl Legien), this grouping quickly set the tone in the Reichstag fraction and the SPD's public statements. Moreover, they were quite prepared to use wartime conditions and their new influence with the state authorities to settle accounts with the left in the party. By early 1915 Karl Kautsky complained to Victor Adler that the trade-union and party right were taking 'control of the whole party apparatus', were ready to 'use terrorism with no holds barred' against their opponents, and were seizing the chance to cleanse the SPD of Marxism (Kirby, 1986, 45; Carsten, 1982, 45f.).

At first the left were marginalized by the decision of 4 August into a hampered minority: the fourteen opponents of the war credits voted publicly with the majority, and it was not until the second Reichstag vote on the war credits on 2 December 1914 that Karl Liebknecht broke ranks as a solitary opponent. But the left-wing deputies also sat for some of the SPD's major regional strongholds (e.g. Berlin, Bremen, industrial Saxony) and broader disquiet was not slow to emerge. During the autumn of 1914 signs appeared in Stuttgart (where the SPD formally split), Düsseldorf, Bremen, Hamburg, Dresden, Leipzig and Berlin. On 4 August a small circle of radicals immediately took stock in Rosa Luxemburg's Berlin flat, and on 10 September 1914 Liebknecht, Luxemburg, Franz Mehring and Clara Zetkin issued a public statement to the Swiss, Swedish and Italian socialist press contesting the party's official line. While this drew negligible support inside Germany, an alternative politics had at least been defined. By the third vote on the war credits on 20 March 1915, Liebknecht was joined by Otto Rühle (representing Dresden), with another 30 SPD deputies abstaining.

The spring of 1915 proved an important watershed. Food shortages and the introduction of rationing produced the first popular demonstrations against the war in Berlin, mainly of women. Then on 5 March 1915 leading left-wingers formed the Group International, the first organizational nucleus of the opposition, with its own organ of opinion, *Die Internationale.* In early June the Group issued a leaflet calling for resumption of the class struggle on the basis of the SPD's prewar programme. This finally tempted the moderate opposition into distancing themselves publicly from the leadership, in a manifesto issued by Bernstein, Haase and Kautsky called *The Demand of the Hour,* and by galvanizing the troubled political conscience of the former party centre, the left successfully shifted the moral terms of the discussion. This also forced the leadership to speak out, and on 23 June 1915 it officially disavowed a war of annexations.

For the first time this placed the SPD's right-wing leadership at a relative disadvantage before the party. The original justification for supporting the war – national defence against tsarist aggression – now seemed very thin. In the fifth war credits vote in December 1915 the fraction divided more evenly at 58 to 38, and this time another 18 deputies joined Leibknecht and Rühle in the public opposition, with a further 24 absenting themselves from the vote. Concurrently, the left made the first moves for reconstruction on an international front with meetings of women's and youth representatives in neutral Switzerland, followed by fully fledged conferences at Zimmerwald (September 1915) and Kienthal (April 1916). Each of these meetings afforded the German left a limited platform, but unlike the Bolsheviks,neither the extreme radicals around Luxemburg nor the more equivocal opponents of the war were willing to break with the existing Social Democratic tradition.

In the event, a split was imposed by the right. On 12 January 1916 Liebknecht was expelled from the Reichstag fraction by 60 to 25 votes, whereupon Rühle resigned in solidarity. On 24 March 1916 another 18 deputies voted against the government's emergency budget and were promptly expelled by a vote of 58 to 33, reconstituting themselves as the Social Democratic Working Group (SAG) within the framework of the existing party. In the meantime, the Group International had strengthened their organization, acquiring the name Spartacus from the pseudonym attached to the first of their political newsletters. Then, after a special party conference on 21–3 September 1916, the executive moved rapidly against the left's strongholds, seizing control of *Vorwärts* unconstitutionally on 17 October and repeating similar actions elsewhere. The opposition convened a national conference on 7 January 1917, and when the executive expelled the participants there was no choice but to form a separate party. The Independent Social Democratic Party (USPD) was launched in a congress at Gotha on 6–8 April 1917.

The Divisions of the Left

There were now four groupings or currents within the German left. First was the SPD or SPD majority, with its base in the party apparatus and parliamentary fraction and increasing dependence on the trade unions. By 1917 the SPD leaders were firmly committed to a gradualist perspective of parliamentary evolution and social reform. The old materialist certainties remained – the confidence that history was moving securely on one's own side – but were now wedded to a sense of civic responsibility and patriotic *gravitas,* the belief that the SPD was now carrying the destiny of the 'whole nation' on its shoulders. This involved a recurring logic of compromise which measured SPD policies against an existing 'interest of state' and inevitably defused much of the party's radical thrust. In the wartime circumstances it also gave the leadership's priorities a strong nationalist, not to say imperialist, colouration. More disturbingly, it aligned the SPD not only against the anti-war dissidence of its own left wing, but also against the growing expressions of unofficial militancy among the working-class rank and file. The leadership fully intended to cash the reformist cheque in at the war's end. But to do so required not only continuous pressure on the government and existing forces of order. It also meant keeping general working-class aspirations in line. Imperceptibly, this was turning the SPD into the policeman of the working class.

By comparison, secondly, the USPD was an extremely incoherent phenomenon. For its national leaders, the split with the SPD had a moral rather than a clearly thought-out political basis. The new party was held together mainly by distaste for the SPD's collaboration in what was clearly a war of aggression, behind policies that were increasingly oppressive for the mass of the workers, and in ways that compromised the movement's proud traditions. But its leaders had little desire to break permanently from the existing movement, and their separatism was mainly imposed by the ruthlessness of the SPD's new internal regime. It was extremely unclear how the USPD would actually differ from the parent party, because talk of returning the movement to its revolutionary traditions usually implied the old prewar politics as opposed to the full-scale revolutionary strategy being advocated by Lenin. In that sense, they were reaffirming the old as opposed to proclaiming the new. The USPD was the SPD's troubled conscience, trespassing from an earlier era. Moreover, as yet there was little relationship to any organized popular support.

The third of the four groupings, the revolutionary circles of Spartacus and the extreme left, amounted to more of a coherent basis for alternative politics, but with scarcely any greater popular support. The Spartacists should not be disregarded: the Group's small paper membership is not the only measure of its influence, given the growing popular volatility and the interruption of normal public life by the war, and in such circumstances the determined vanguardism of a few agitators could go a long way. But the Spartacists had certainly not broken the hold of Social Democratic traditions on politically conscious workers, as opposed to reaffirming their continuing validity with a view to a future renewal of the whole movement. In this respect, the so-called Bremen left, with their greater readiness for a full split and neo-syndicalist orientation toward shop-floor militancy, represented more of a radical departure and formed the main basis for the shadowy International Socialists of Germany (ISD) set up in the wake of the Zimmerwald conference.

The fourth current within the left is much harder to specify, because it consisted of a slowly developing grass-roots opposition to a continuation of the war. The latter's basic hardships provided one explanation for this. But an equally important motor of discontent came from the massive changes in the working class wrought by the war economy. The increased regulation of labour (partly via the policing functions of the trade-union bureaucracy) was one form of these changes, dramatized by the Auxiliary Service Law of December 1916, which gave the trade unions a new degree of recognition at the expense of significantly militarizing the labour market. At the same time the trade-unionized minority of skilled male workers were swamped by the unprecedented influx of rapidly trained semi-skilled and unskilled labour into war-related industry. Thus, not only did the war place the labour movement in a very different relationship to the whole working class, which was itself in a process of drastic recomposition; but even its best tried supporters – skilled male workers in the metalworking trades – were becoming resentful of the war's effects.

This changing sociology of labour was the key to the grass-roots militancy of 1916–18. For both the previously unorganized 'new' labour and the politically conscious 'old' labour proved increasingly hard for the labour movement's existing institutions to contain. Where the one lacked the socialization into the movement's pre-1914 traditions, the other found those traditions damaged by the war economy and the accompanying consequences of the *Burgfrieden*. In this sense wartime conditions engendered contradictory effects for the working-class movement. The centrally regulated war economy's corporative structures brought real gains for the trade-union and SPD leaderships by opening unprecedented access to the state, to government politics and to managerial decisions in industry. For the SPD right, this created political capital that could be converted into postwar reforms by astute management of the newfound bargaining power. But for most rank-and-file workers, these institutional gains were mainly experienced as hardship. Quite apart from the long war's disastrous effects on living standards, the official labour movement's gradual incorporation was bought at the expense of the ordinary worker's shop-floor interests. If the growing regulation of the war economy was a form of 'socialism' for the right-wing SPD leader or trade-union bureaucrat, for the worker it meant speed-up, the suspension of factory regulations, lower safety standards, the suspension of basic trade-union rights and a general loss of control.

This contradiction became the source of popular radicalization. Whereas the labour movement leaderships around Legien and Ebert wished to strengthen existing gains via constitutional reform and a drive for parliamentary power, rank-and-file militants were reaching for more radical objectives. In the first instance this meant peace, but opposition to the war was now inextricably linked to attacks on its unequal burdens, and this was an obvious basis for reviving the movement's anti-capitalist critique. Between the protest actions of June 1916 (in solidarity with Karl Liebknecht) and the metalworkers' strike of January 1918 an accumulating movement of popular militancy increasingly sought new forms of expression. When the metalworkers' strike receded, it left a permanent organization in place, namely the Berlin Committee of the Revolutionary Shop Stewards.

The November Revolution

This completed the organizational configuration with which the left entered the German Revolution in November 1918. When the Imperial order collapsed amidst Germany's military defeat in October–November 1918, the divisions came quickly into play. The SPD right saw the constitutional transition as the consummation of its policies. The measures converting Germany into a constitutional monarchy, which passed into law on 28 October 1918, would already have satisfied the SPD leadership around Ebert and Scheidemann, on the grounds that parliamentary dominance would now guarantee the future of social reform. When the popular radicalization of early November outpaced the management of reform from above, with the naval mutinies of Kiel and Wilhelmshaven, the chain reaction of workers' and soldiers' insurgency in the rest of Germany, the forming of a revolutionary government in Munich on 7–8 November, and the Kaiser's abdication following the escalation of left-wing activity in Berlin on 9 November, the SPD perspective did not change. The leadership shifted its sights to the calling of a constituent assembly and concentrated on holding the fort for an orderly transition. Inevitably, this replicated the political logic of the wartime incorporation: an emphasis on patriotic discipline and public order; exaggerated fears of mass activity; angry contempt for the irresponsibility of the left and its agitation; practical compromise with representatives of the old order.

It is hard to detect many signs of doubt in the behaviour of the SPD leaders during the revolution, which still betrayed the familiar inevitabilism of the prewar tradition. They made a virtue of hard-headed realism, of taking the tough decisions the dreamers of the left were unwilling to take, beguiling the masses instead with unattainable utopias, playing to their worst instincts and flirting with chaos. 'The path from 4 August 1914 to 5 October 1918 was difficult', David recorded in his diary, 'but what would have been achieved by a revolutionary tactic?' Only 'the most frightful dangers and suffering', he answered, ending 'in the triumph of reaction' (Kirby, 1986, 227). Moreover, the SPD leaders enjoyed the complacencies of power. They had become the arbiters of a rapidly disintegrating situation, in which the agencies of the dominant classes had lost their popular legitimacy. By comparison, their left-wing rivals lacked the same kind of certainty, resources and support. The USPD acquired a stronger profile in the freer circumstances of October, with closer links to the Berlin shop stewards, but was still less than a convincing alternative to the SPD. The Spartacists and the far left were too fragmented and lacking in support. Liebknecht personally commanded enormous popular sympathies, but he was preoccupied with the purity of his revolutionary stance and was consequently refused a place in the new provisional government.

The SPD were clearly calling the shots. The Council of People's Commissioners formed during the night of 9–10 November in negotiations between SPD and USPD notionally gave parity to the left, with three nominees of the SPD (Ebert, Scheidemann and Otto Landsberg), two of the USPD (Haase and Wilhelm Ditmann) and one from the Berlin shop stewards (Emil Barth), the chair being held jointly by Ebert and Haase. On the afternoon of 10 November an assembly of workers' and soldiers' delegates met in the Circus Busch in Berlin to confirm the provisional government, and it, too, elected an Executive Committee on the basis of parity. But although the left successfully passed general socialist resolutions – for 'the speedy and thorough socialization of the capitalist means of production', as the Circus Busch meeting put it (Carsten, 1982, 227) – it was the SPD that defined the limits of the immediate situation.

This became clear in the first week of the provisional government's existence. Most notoriously, Ebert formed an 'alliance' with the army, which established a common front against 'Bolshevism' and pre-empted any democratization of the military through the soldiers' councils. Simultaneously, civil servants were urged to stay at their posts, and the government made no attempt to purge the bureaucracy or the courts. Significantly, the detailed programme of 12 November also made no mention of specifically socialist measures. Finally, the unions reached an agreement with the big employers on 15 November, which brought the eight-hour day and official recognition but eliminated the more radical option of nationalization.

In the abstract, the changes of October–November seemed an impressive achievement. But in the concrete, they were meant to pre-empt something else, and the actual circumstances of 1918–19 – of widespread working-class insurgency, whose democratic aspirations raced beyond the SPD's constitutionalism – tarnished the lustre of the success. At first, the opposition was confined to the political left – the USPD and the Spartacists and other groups of the radical fringe – who enjoyed limited popular support. Moreover, the overwhelming rank-and-file impulse was towards unity, towards healing the bitter wartime divisions. In practice, this current flowed strongly in the SPD's favour during November, and it was only with renewed SPD–USPD conflicts that the unity of popular opinion fractured. These occurred in a series of dramatic incidents between 6 and 28 December, which aligned the SPD increasingly with the reassembling forces of order and culminated in the USPD's secession from the government.

The Balance Sheet of Revolution

Superficially, the SPD's strategy had achieved striking success. They had consistently outmanoeuvred the USPD, from the formation of the Council of People's Commissioners on 9–10 November, through the Congress of Workers' and Soldiers' Councils on 16–20 December and the election of the latter's Central Council (which the USPD misguidedly boycotted), to the USPD's final resignation from the Council of People's Commissioners on 28 December. They had equally consistently controlled the central organs of the council movement in Berlin. In addition, the trade unions had secured a powerful corporative place for themselves via the ZAG. Most importantly of all, the parliamentary-democratic parameters of the revolutionary process had been secured by making the constituent assembly the fixed point of the general discussion. The advocates of a more 'Bolshevik' understanding of the revolution – the call for an exclusively socialist government in the form of the dictatorship of the proletariat based on the councils, to the exclusion of parliamentary forms of representation – had been consistently marginalized in the forums of the labour movement. The climax of this process came in January 1919, with the suppression of the Spartacist rising of 5–13 January and the elections to the National Assembly four days later. The outcome seemed a resounding popular vindication: the SPD polled 37.9 per cent of the vote, with 163 out of 421 seats, and together with the German Democratic Party (18.5 per cent, 75 seats) and Catholic Centre (19.7 per cent, 91 seats), had the basis of a clear republican majority. By comparison, the USPD managed only 7.6 per cent of the vote and 22 seats. The Communist Party (KPD), formed from the Spartacists and ISD (renamed IKD immediately before the fusion) on 30 December–1 January, boycotted the elections.

By other criteria the SPD's achievement was less secure. First, by adhering to a rigidly constitutionalist strategy and tying specifically socialist measures to the arrival of the future parliamentary majority, the leadership denied itself the opportunity for a reckoning with all the traditional objects of Social Democratic criticism since the party's foundation: the socio-political power of the army and civil service, the associated system of 'class justice', and of course the private economic basis of the societal power of the Junkers and the big capitalist bourgeoisie. By refusing a confrontation with militarism, by neglecting to reconstruct the bureaucracy and judiciary, by abstaining from an ambitious land reform, and by temporizing on the subject of socialization, the SPD leadership deprived the republican political order of solid social foundations beyond the ZAG and the associated corpus of welfare-state legislation, which (as the events of the late-1920s were to show) were by no means immune to reversal. Debilitated by a sense of constitutionalist responsibility and patriotic mission, constrained by traditional anxieties about the undisciplined instincts of the non-Social Democratic masses, the SPD's political imagination failed to escape from a remarkably moderate legalism.

Secondly, holding the revolutionary process to a narrowly demarcated constitutionalist path involved restraining the aspirations of the popular movement. The workers' councils became the main embodiment of the revolution's popular-democratic vitality, and while never institutionalized into a system of 'dual power' on the soviet model, they continued to resurface in various forms in each of the left's regional centres during the subsequent moments of radicalization, during the Kapp Putsch in March 1920 and the March Action of 1921. Much has been made of the councils' potential as the basis for a 'third way' between the SPD's constitutionalism and the insurrectionary politics inspired by the Bolshevik Revolution, and Ebert and his collegues certainly showed a lamentable lack of imagination in failing to harness this popular democratic upsurge. Here was the energy and institutional leverage precisely appropriate for the further-reaching democratization whose neglect proved so fateful for the Weimar

Republic's foundations. But not only did the SPD fail to grasp this positive opportunity; the party's own preferred strategy required the councils' active liquidation. A counter-revolutionary logic deepened the SPD leaders' practical dependence on the representatives of the existing order. In the name of one kind of democracy – parliamentary constitutionalism – another kind of democracy had to be suppressed.

From this contradiction – thirdly – came a popular radicalization that rendered much of the SPD's achievement nugatory. The signs were already there in January 1919 – in Berlin itself, and in large areas of industrial Germany – and as repression of the left continued and the government failed to act decisively on the socialization issue, the SPD's hold on working-class allegiances became badly shaken. The mass actions surrounding the defeat of the Kapp Putsch dramatized the widening gap between SPD practice and many working-class aspirations, and in the elections of June 1920 the USPD now reached 18.6 per cent of the vote against the SPD's 21.6, with another 1.7 per cent falling to the KPD. Moreover, in the labour movement's traditional industrial strongholds the trend was all the more marked. In this sense, January 1919 marked less the end of the revolution than the beginning of a fresh radicalization – and one that proceeded both outside and against the framework of SPD policies. The SPD now held an extremely partial relationship to the class whose general interest it had always claimed to represent: henceforth, it spoke mainly for the respectable trade-unionized core of the skilled male (and to a great extent middle-aged) working class, while the younger, less skilled and irregularly employed workers looked elsewhere. A permanently divided working class was not the least of the outcomes of the revolution.

According to its own lights, the SPD had accomplished a large amount. The constitutional, corporative and welfare-state advances could even form the basis for an optimistic projection in which structural reforms would pass eventually into a process of socialist transformation. The Social Democrats certainly saw themselves as progressing in that direction. But in the actual circumstances of 1918–19 their constitutionalist course had been implemented at a double expense: the social and political bases of authoritarianism in the state and the economy had been protected, indeed reconstructed, in their moment of maximum vulnerability; and the most vigorous manifestations of popular democracy had been rebuffed, not to say brutally suppressed. The real tragedy of 1918–19 was not the failure to force through a maximalist socialist revolution. The abstract merits of the latter may be endlessly debated, but it could hardly have been sustained without an extremely bloody and protracted civil war, and the view that this was too high a price is a defensible socialist position. The real tragedy was the SPD's excessively legalistic, stolidly unimaginative and wholly conservative understanding of what a democratically ordered polity could be. The SPD faced unprecedented opportunities for radically expanding the frontiers of democracy in 1918, both by dismantling the bases of authoritarianism in the discredited *ancien régime* and by harnessing the new popular energies the councils movement so dramatically released. The chances of a further-reaching reformism were squandered. It was by its own democratic standards that the SPD failed the test.

9 The Socialist Trade Unions in War and Revolution, 1914–1919

Hans-Joachim Bieber

The Decision of 4 August 1914

When the danger of a European war loomed large at the end of July 1914, the SPD and the trade unions, in accordance with the decisions of the Second International, called for mass anti-war demonstrations. Hundreds of thousands of people took part. But after war had none the less broken out on 1 August, they no longer spared a thought for campaigns for the prevention of war. In fact, three days later the SPD voted to approve the war credits in the Reichstag. That was a sensation, especially since for decades the party had granted 'not a man, not a penny' to the Imperial government and its armament projects. To this day the decision stands as a milestone, indeed a turning point, in the history of German Social Democracy. How can it be explained?

The first reason lies in the weakness of Social Democracy at that time. In 1914 the SPD had approximately a million members, while the membership of the Free Trade Unions was around 2.5 million (even that still amounted to no more than roughly 15 per cent of the German working class). Moreover, these were predominantly employees of craft-based medium-sized companies. Hardly any were workers in large-scale industry or major state concerns. At any rate, the leadership was convinced that there were far too few of them for a successful mass strike. To make matters worse, with the declaration of war, executive power had passed to the military authorities, and the suspension of constitutional rights had become possible. Strikes were punishable as high treason.

Secondly, the German government presented the outbreak of war as a Russian attack. The Social Democrats had always declared their readiness to take part in a war of defence, and the empire of the tsar, in particular, had always appeared to them to be the 'bastion of cruelty and barbarism'.

Thus, at a stroke, the Russian declaration of war brought about a complete change of mood among the leaders of the working class. In broad sections of the population it even unleashed a wave of unbridled hatred towards the outside world and an effusive sense of community at home.

The extent to which the mass of workers were affected by this mood is open to question. Nevertheless, in the estimation of its leaders, it offered an unexpected chance to lead the working class out of its political and social isolation at last. This was the third reason for their decision of 4 August. Above all, their expectations focused on the abolition of the three-class electoral system in Prussia, the recognition of the trade unions and social reforms.

As a matter of fact there were signs of this. For the first time the government received a number of Social Democrats for confidential talks. Henceforth, the doors of the ministers, senior civil servants and generals were open to them. A number of regulations which had previously restricted the activities of the SPD and the trade unions were lifted, and in October 1914 a reorientation in domestic affairs was announced – for after the war.

Nevertheless, enthusiasm for the war among the working class does not seem to have been particularly great. In any event, the possible advantages of war were soon blotted out by the horrors of life at the front.

The Working Class and the Trade Unions, 1914–16

Those who stayed at home had even less cause for rejoicing, for the war triggered off a serious economic crisis. Within four weeks unemployment rose to over 20 per cent; it was only the upturn in war industry and the growth of the army which brought a gradual decline in unemployment. Moreover, food soon became scarce, noticeably dearer and poorer in quality. Wages failed to keep pace with prices, except in a few branches of the armaments industry. Working hours were increased. Low wages or the conscription of the men forced increasing numbers of women to help support the family by taking paid employment, even in the heaviest and most hazardous occupations, such as working on building sites and in munitions factories. In all branches of industry there was a rise in the proportion of female employees. Yet their wages were, on average, a third lower than those of male workers. Undernourishment and overwork brought increased susceptibility to sickness. The number of cases of epidemic disease soared, as did the number of industrial accidents.

The trade unions were virtually powerless to improve the workers' situation. They, too, were badly affected by the war. By the end of 1914 their membership had declined to 1.5 million. By the end of 1916 it was down further still, to no more than 950,000. The local organizations fell into disuse, particularly in small towns and villages. To a large extent meetings and agitation ceased. Only the central organs emerged relatively unscathed. Their importance within the organizations thus grew, but their accountability to the membership lessened, particularly as conscription and transport problems impeded internal communication within the unions. With a few exceptions there were no national conferences or executive elections during the war – one cause of the growing alienation between the leadership of the unions and their membership.

In these circumstances there could be no prospect of mounting successful industrial action, especially since the income from union dues declined in step with the membership, while benefits for unemployed members made heavy demands on the trade unions. In mid-August 1914 the union executives therefore decided to abstain from strikes until further notice. They linked this, certainly, with the hope that other means of solving industrial disputes would be introduced, particularly arbitration boards and collective agreements. To match supply and demand in the labour market they also envisaged public labour exchanges, with equal representation.

In addition to the unemployed, they took care of the families of members who had been conscripted. Of course, it was the responsibility of the state to support them, but the Reich did little or nothing, and the help provided by the federal states and local authorities was generally inadequate. So in August 1914 most of the trade unions decided to pay out voluntary benefits to the families of servicemen. In return, they were hoping for the introduction of public unemployment benefits, which they had been demanding for years.

But they were disappointed. State benefits for the unemployed and for the families of servicemen remained extremely low. Indeed, they were often cut by the same amount as the unions contributed, so that the state was in fact taking advantage of their generosity. The government rejected a statutory unemployment benefit, as well as public employment agencies and arbitration boards. It was left to the military authorities in some industrial areas to attempt to mediate in industrial disputes.

The State, Industry and the Labour Movement, 1914–16

In the field of domestic affairs there was little change. In 1916 a reform of the law of assembly freed the unions from police surveillance and harassment and at last enabled them to recruit young people. A year later the railwaymen were permitted to join a Free Trade Union – provided they renounced strikes. But on the issue of the Prussian electoral law there was no progress at all.

Similarly, the attitude of industry towards the unions remained virtually unchanged. It still refused to hear of co-operation. In many companies trade-union members continued to be persecuted and impeded. The government did little about it. Instead, it contributed to the growth in power of large-scale industry. In countless wholly or partly state-controlled centres which had been set up to register and distribute scarce raw materials, the largest concerns and the industrial associations acquired a decisive influence.

Despite all this, the trade-union executives continued, with few exceptions, to support the conduct of the war – by investing considerable assets in war loans, by co-operating with the authorities and by tireless appeals to the workers to 'hold out'. At the same time they were at pains to find allies in the bourgeois camp for their longer-term domestic political and social objectives. Owing to the participation of England, in German eyes the strongest industrial power of the day and German industry's most dangerous competitor, the war had certainly changed its character very rapidly from the point of view of the unions – from a crusade-like defensive struggle against the empire of the tsar to a struggle between the industrial nations for sources of raw materials and markets. The working class was a child of industrialization, and the unions were convinced that its future destiny was linked, for better or for worse, with that of German industry – notwithstanding all their domestic and social differences. Hence they soon came to regard Britain, not Russia, as the chief adversary: the circumstances of the outbreak of war, even its imperialist features, became irrelevant to them. True, they clung on to the assertion that it was a war of defence. Behind the slogan of 'safeguards', however, they toyed with war aims similar to those loudly demanded by industry: colonial conquests (Equatorial Africa and Tangiers) and the extension of German power in Europe, although they preferred forms of indirect control of annexations and, unlike the industrial-agrarian war-aims movement, they were not prepared to continue the war for the sake of these goals alone.

But opposition gradually made its presence felt within the workers' own ranks, at first – leaving aside Berlin – mainly in industrial cities such as Brunswick and Stuttgart or in individual unions in which critics of the 'policy of 4 August' produced the party or trade-union newspapers. To begin with, the opposition had chiefly economic causes and was conducted above all by armaments workers, and also by many women. The union leaderships reacted by dismissing critical editors and by founding new journals to propagate their policies more effectively. Within the SPD's parliamentary group the members of the trade-union executive, particularly its chairman Carl Legien, took up the struggle against the opposition group around Karl Liebknecht, until they achieved its expulsion in 1916. The Social Democratic labour movement was now split. In 1917 the Independent Social Democratic Party (USPD) appeared alongside the SPD. If Liebknecht and his supporters had had their way in the SPD, the union leaders would have left it and formed a new, explicitly reformist party, for under no circumstances did they wish to place in jeopardy the opportunities for the political and social integration of the working class which the war still appeared to offer them.

Between the Requirement to Work and Social Reform: the Auxiliary Service Law of 1916

Until the middle of 1916 there were no major protest movements against the war. But then the situation changed. In the West the war stagnated into positional warfare; in the East, the Russians were advancing. Hindenburg and Ludendorff, the victors of the first great battle against the Russian army and as such the most popular generals of the day, took over control of the German High Command. They immediately came up with grandiose plans to increase armaments production and enlarge the army. If their aims were attainable at all, they could only be achieved by concentrating all available manpower in war industry. This was not possible without coercive measures, and these could not be pushed through without an agreement with the SPD and the trade unions. So it came down to a piece of political 'horse-trading'. With the 'Law on National Auxiliary Service' of December 1916 all men between the ages of 17 and 60 were obliged to work for firms engaged in war production. This was the end of the worker's right to choose his place of work freely; it was now mediation committees that considered applications to change jobs. These committees comprised a military chairman and equal numbers of employer and employee representatives, appointed at the suggestion of the organizations of both parties. The politically significant aspect of this was that the trade unions were recognized as the representatives of the workers and the employers were forced to co-operate with them. A similar thing happened in the individual companies: all companies engaged in war production employing more than 50 people were compelled to set up committees of workers and white-collar staff.

The new law had a number of effects which were certainly unexpected. The need was greatest for skilled workers, particularly in mining and metal processing. Most of them, however, were already employed in the armaments industry. The boost to the armaments programme exacerbated the shortage. The armaments firms, including the state-owned ones, therefore vied with one another in offering higher wages. As a result, more and more workers attempted to obtain improvements by changing jobs – either with the blessing of the mediation committee or off their own bat. Staff turnover rose sharply, and it was not until the military authorities and managements refined their counter-measures that it was gradually forced down again.

Nevertheless, production targets were not reached, and there was no return to peace and quiet among the workforce. Since the introduction of the Auxiliary Service Law the workers had been gaining in self-confidence, especially those who had hitherto held back for fear of being conscripted. Furthermore, the trade unions were making full use of their new powers. Everywhere they held meetings. The election of the workers' committees enabled them to enter the big concerns, which until now had been closed to them. On most of the committees they won a majority. Their membership figures were also on the way up again: from 950,000 at the end of 1916 to just under 1.3 million by the end of 1917, rising to 1.5 million by the end of September 1918. This development signalled a radical change in their social composition. The increase came largely from the staffs of the large concerns, and included many unskilled workers, young people and women who had hitherto generally not been organized.

In the meantime the power of their adversaries was also growing, at least economically. The armaments industry was doing good business; it managed to prevent the restriction of war profits. It used this windfall to increase capital assets, to set up new companies and to take over other enterprises. The process of concentration speeded up. By the end of the war approximately 100 new concerns had been established. The commercial middle class was particularly hard hit. Many small and medium-sized businesses were forced to close down because of shortages of materials or labour. It was in these circles that the feeling of being economically endangered and the fear of social relegation grew increasingly widespread. Loyalties to the political system and its parties were dissolved, making way for growing political disorientation and radicalization which continued to exert their influence long after the end of the war.

The Mass Protests and Domestic Political Stagnation of 1917

Discontent was also growing among the working class and the dependent middle class, for their social position was progressively worsening. Food supplies were becoming even scarcer, dearer and poorer, as were many consumer goods, particularly clothing. Wages lagged even further behind prices, not to mention the salaries of the approximately two million white-collar workers and the civil service, which was roughly equal in numbers. Both groups were still poorly organized and neither possessed a body with political clout to represent its interests. Being acutely aware of status, they often suffered from impoverishment and declassing even more intensely than the working class. The consequences were demoralization and social resentment, as well as corruption and offences against property – particularly among railway employees – on a scale hitherto unknown in Germany. In these groups, too, this eventually resulted in political disorientation and radicalization, again with after-effects extending far beyond the war years.

In the spring of 1917 this discontent first made itself felt. Hundreds of thousands of workers went on strike, chiefly in the main industrial centres, demanding better food, and in some places higher wages and shorter hours. The trade unions were surprised by the movement. Only with difficulty did they manage to take over the leadership and bring the strikes to an end after a few days.

But the potential for protest was not thereby eliminated. There was no lasting improvement in food supplies or the provision of consumer goods, nor were any political concessions made. Instead there was a regrouping of the prewar reactionary coalition of large landowners, major industrialists, sections of the middle class, the educated bourgeoisie, the civil service and the officers. As the 'Fatherland Party' they campaigned vociferously against further domestic reforms and agitated for peace through victory, which would bring Germany supremacy in Europe, a huge colonial empire and immense war reparations – partly, of course, with the intention of blunting the political demands of the working class and re-establishing the threatened power of the old elite. Under this pressure from the right the reorientation scarcely made any headway. On the contrary, the Imperial Chancellor, Bethmann Hollweg, a level-headed and remarkably perspicacious politician who considered the integration of the working class into state and society inevitable, was brought down in the summer of 1917. His successors were insignificant and feeble; political power moved largely into the hands of the High Command (its leading light politically, General Ludendorff, was able to carry on acting like a military dictator) while a smaller share devolved to the Reichstag. The parliamentary majority of SPD, the Catholic Centre Party, the tiny band of the Progressive People's Party and the left wing of the National Liberals, which was close to manufacturing and export industry, gained in importance but was too heterogeneous to embark on a firm course of reform. Thus in early 1918 only one stipulation of the *Gewerbeordnung* (the regulations governing trade and industry) was suspended – the one restricting the unions' right to strike. Although a law for preserving the workers' and mediation committees was prepared, it made but little headway. In the politically crucial questions of the Prussian electoral law and parliamentarization there continued to be no progress, despite solemn declarations from the Imperial mouth.

Peace Treaties in the East and Continuity in Trade-Union War Policy

But the state of the war changed once again. In October 1917 the Bolshevik revolution was triumphant in St Petersburg and Russia was out of the war. The defensive struggle against the tsar's empire, which had lain behind the Social Democrats' decision to support the war in August 1914, was thus over. Yet no end to the war seemed to be in sight. In the West the battles raged on undiminished. In the East, too, hundreds of thousands of soldiers were still stationed. They were intended to lend military weight to the demands the Central Powers were now presenting to a Russia in defeat at the peace negotiations of Brest-Litovsk: the surrender of Poland, Lithuania, Courland and the Ukraine. This meant the loss of roughly a quarter of the Russian territory of the time, and about 75 per cent of the Russian coal-mining and iron industries, which placed a severe strain on the young Soviet state's possibilities of economic and social development. It had, however, no choice but to accept these conditions. It was obvious from now on that Germany was no longer waging a war of defence but a war of conquest.

Nevertheless, the SPD allowed the treaty to pass through the Reichstag by abstaining in the vote. The trade unions even expressed undisguised satisfaction at its economic aspects. Their efforts were directed, as before, towards an outcome to the war which preserved the competitiveness of German industry and secured it access to foreign sources of raw materials and markets, thus not merely ensuring that the standard of living of the German working class was maintained or raised, but also improving material conditions for political emancipation. For the same reason they rejected everything that might weaken Germany's fighting strength, particularly strikes and other actions for enforcing political demands. In any case, they regarded the working class as still too weak to meet with success in this respect and feared that militancy might jeopardize the beginnings of co-operation with bourgeois forces that were prepared for reform.

This strategy appeared conclusive, and patriotic into the bargain, but it had two implications which the trade unions did not recognize – at least not in time. First, the labour organizations' restraint enabled the government to carry on procrastinating over domestic political and social reforms. The fact that they did not insist on clearly defensive war aims but at least tacitly accepted conquests relieved the political and military leadership of the need seriously to seek an understanding with the Allies while such an accommodation might still have been possible. Secondly, with their acceptance, indeed support of the government's course, the trade unions were also undermining their own position.

Mass Strikes and the Decline of Trade-Union Authority in 1918

This became apparent in January 1918, when a second wave of strikes shook the German industrial centres. This time more than one million workers took part, and now they were demanding not only better food but also political changes. In fact, these were generally given priority. The demands were, above all, for a swift peace without annexations or reparations, frequently also for a lifting of the state of siege, the restoration of freedom of association, assembly and opinion, the release of all political prisoners and the reform of the Prussian electoral system. Once again the trade unions were taken by surprise. But they managed to get the movement under control only in areas where an urban industrial proletariat was just emerging or was scattered, as in South Germany, and where it had just begun to penetrate into the large companies, as in the Ruhr district. In Berlin, Leipzig and the big ports, on the other hand, the strikes were led by commissions or councils in which the trade unions had little or no influence left. To avoid forfeiting the confidence of the workers even further they refrained from publicly denouncing the strikes. But they also withheld any assistance to the strikers, working behind the scenes for a rapid resumption of work and giving the authorities a free hand to take harsh measures to suppress the movement. So this movement, too, collapsed after a short while, having failed to achieve anything.

Still there were no radical economic improvements or political changes. Consequently the authority not only of the government, but also of the SPD and of the unions continued to be eroded. In the months that followed, strikes, both major and minor, flared up in many localities. More and more workers refused to pledge allegiance to the trade unions, finally even in such a predominantly agricultural region as Bavaria. It was only a question of time as to when a third wave of protests would swell up, and it was more than doubtful whether the authorities would be able to halt it via a combination of repression and co-operation with the organizations of labour.

November 1918: Military Collapse and Political Revolution

When the High Command was forced to admit in October 1918 that it had lost the war, the time had come. Its hitherto legendary standing collapsed at a stroke, and every politically sensitive person could feel that a spark would be enough to unleash revolution. The old power elites now attempted to form an alliance with the labour organizations. The leaders of industry performed a radical turnabout and offered to meet the trade unions' chief socio-political demands: union recognition, retention of the workers' and mediation committees, collective agreements, employment agencies with equal representation, introduction of the eight-hour day, the dropping of the so-called 'yellow unions' (the labour organizations pledged to economic peace) and, in addition to all this, a formal agreement on co-operation. Ludendorff tendered his resignation, as did the senile chancellor, and the SPD was offered a place in the government. Following the logic of its war policies, the SPD agreed to these offers. The trade unions negotiated with the most powerful industrialists, and some SPD and union leaders entered the government. In a short space of time the Prussian three-class electoral system was abolished and full parliamentarism was introduced.

Thus almost overnight domestic political and social reforms were implemented or started for which the working class had been waiting for decades. The political and social system of Bismarck's Reich was changing radically. But this scarcely made any impression on the masses, who hardly noticed the changes since for the time being their actual situation remained quite unchanged. So the revolution came along after all. A naval mutiny in Kiel in early November provided the immediate, somewhat haphazard, cause. The seamen deposed their officers and formed councils, while the workers elected a workers' council which took over control of the city. Then they took to the railway, and wherever they went the same thing happened. The monarchs, their ministers and generals resigned; the Kaiser fled into exile in Holland. Virtually nowhere did anyone raise a finger to defend the old regime: it collapsed like a house of cards.

Both the trade unions and the SPD considered a revolution to be totally unnecessary, for their most important demands had just been met. Moreover, they feared that a coup would render Germany utterly defenceless and result in most unfavourable peace conditions. But when they noticed that there was no holding back the workers, they severed the political ties with their new bourgeois coalition partners and attempted, as in the strikes of 1917–18, to get to the head of the movement and take control of it. In many areas they managed to take over leading functions in the workers' and soldiers' councils. In industrial cities like Hamburg, Bremen and Leipzig, where the USPD and the trade-union opposition dominated, they had to be content with minority positions. In Berlin the position of the trade unions had been so badly shaken that they remained completely outside the council movement. Similarly, the six-man Council of People's Commissioners – set up by the SPD and USPD on 10 November 1918 in Berlin as the revoluntionary central body – did not contain a single trade-union leader.

Co-operation with Industry or Socialization?

All the same, the unity of the labour movement seemed to have been restored now that the reason for the split had been rendered invalid with the end of the war. Yet deep-rooted feelings of animosity continued to divide the two sides, and there were soon new disagreements on the question of what course to adopt from now on, particularly over the future economic system. For decades the SPD and the trade unions had declared that their overriding objective was to abolish the private ownership of the means of production. Large sections of the working class now expected appropriate measures. Yet the leadership of the trade unions, supported by the SPD, had no such thing in mind. It clung to its newly initiated co-operation with industry and even concluded – only three days after the collapse! – a formal agreement with it. Industry confirmed thereby the fulfilment of the traditional socio-political demands of the trade unions, while the unions agreed until further notice to renounce any socialist changes in the economic system. In addition, the two sides undertook to engage in lasting co-operation. Quite rightly, industry evaluated this agreement as a 'colossal achievement'. For their concessions either confirmed changes which had already occurred (such as the introduction of workers' and mediation committees) or were inevitable anyway in view of the imminent demobilization of the army and the industrial switch from war production to peace-time production (such as the eight-hour day and a functioning system of labour exchanges).

The main reason why the union leaders allowed themselves to be party to a deal, at so cheap a price, that guaranteed the continued existence of the capitalist system was that they had no draft plan for a socialist transformation. Under the political conditions of the *Kaiserreich* this had been so unlikely that for decades nobody had bothered to give the matter any serious thought. In the face of the enormous economic problems which the sudden end to the war had entailed, and the unforeseeable economic consequences of defeat, the union leaders had scant faith in their ability to carry out a socialist reconstruction of the economy, and none at all in the individual members' capacity to do so. The disastrous effects this could have, under the given conditions, as demonstrated by the state of affairs in Bolshevik Russia, served as a warning to them; they would on no account assume responsibility for a similar development in Germany. Furthermore, they were convinced that the industrialists' attitude towards the workers and their organizations had undergone a radical change and that a new era in industrial relations had dawned in which more reforms in favour of the working class would be possible, particularly .with an SPD majority in the Reichstag, which was considered virtually certain. But there was one thing the trade unions had not reckoned with – their base.

In the industrial areas, particularly in the mines, socialization was being demanded with ever-increasing strength. In countless pits, councils were formed, independently of the unions, claiming some measure of control over management, or simply removing it. Wildcat strikes threatened to bring the economy to a standstill. This movement could probably have been appeased quite rapidly had it been offered the expropriation of the mining industry alone or rights of control and co-determination for the workers in the management and supervisory bodies of the large companies. It is likely that such measures would have been politically feasible. The mining industry itself considered expropriation a possibility, while sections of manufacturing industry even secretly desired the socialization of heavy industry. But the union leaders misinterpreted the council movement as an attack on the position of the unions in the companies and pressed for the use of military force. As the army was in a state of dissolution and what remained of it was largely unreliable, the government therefore turned to the existing commanders. The officers, who were royalists to a man, seized this unexpected opportunity. They mustered corps of volunteers and proceeded to deal with the striking workers, often with unbelievable ferocity. One of their first deeds was the murder of Karl Liebknecht and Rosa Luxemburg, the leaders of the Communist Party, which had been founded early in 1919. Conditions verging on civil war prevailed until the summer of 1919. In the end it was the troops who won; the bourgeoisie triumphed. But large sections of the working class were profoundly disappointed and embittered. The political split which had been patched over in November 1918 again gaped open, deeper and wider than before, and continued until 1933.

The trade unions were spared a split. They declared their political neutrality and recorded an immense increase in membership. True, the political conflicts also raged within their ranks, between left and right, high and low. But by und large the old executives came out on top. The Nuremberg Trade Union Congress in June 1919 professed its belief in socialism, as a distant goal, after generations of educational and reform work. In the meantime it decided to continue co-operating with the employers, and to press ahead with social reforms and the gradual transformation of state and society in a socialist direction. For the workers' councils in the individual companies it simply demanded rights of co-determination in staffing, social and safety matters, as well as close links with the trade unions, but no powers to make economic decisions. Thus the trade unions had become a reform movement within the capitalist system, both in practice and in their programme.

The Trade Unions' Successes and Failings in the November Revolution

In the second half of 1919 the revolutionary wave died away. As the Social Democrat-led government essentially followed the line drawn up by the trade unions, the economic and socio-political results of the revolution were limited to the recognition of the unions by the state and the employers, collective agreements, the establishment in law of the eight-hour day, employment agencies with equal representation, a state conciliation service, public unemployment benefits and limited rights of co-determination in the big companies. There was, however, no fundamental shift in economic power relations in industry, and even less so in agriculture; the industrialists allowed the central working community with the unions (the ZAG) to peter out the moment they no longer had any need for it politically.

Even at the time, and certainly after 1933, the trade unions were sharply critized for failing to curb or break the power of the private economy in 1918–19, particularly by the left. It is quite true that these developments contributed in no little measure to events 14 years later, when political power fell into the hands of the National Socialists and the labour organizations were smashed. Two objections may be made, however, to apportioning blame in this way. For one thing, after decades of having their freedom of action and their opportunities for learning restricted, the union leaders were not prepared either conceptually or psychologically for the socialization of the economy or for far-reaching measures to democratize regulations governing industrial relations, overtaxed as they were by immense political and economic difficulties after the lost war. For another thing, in 1918–19 they could not have reckoned with the possibility that a few years later the domestic political and social losers of the revolution would band together and launch an attack on parliamentary democracy and the organized labour movement. They themselves were convinced democrats, honestly persuaded that their opponents had also become democrats after the experiences of collapse and defeat, or would do so in the course of time. This was an error of judgement that was to have lasting consequences. In the years up to 1933 the democratic learning processes remained rudimentary or did not take place at all in big business. This was true to an even greater extent of agriculture, and also of large sections of the bourgeoisie and the intellectuals, the administration, the judiciary and the army. If anyone is to be held responsible for this fact, it is these groups, far more than the labour leaders, who must bear the responsibility.

10 The Social Democratic Women's Movement in Germany, 1914–1918

Alfred G. Meyer

The War as a Disrupter of the Organization

August 1914 brought drastic changes in the lives of German working-class women and confronted their organization within the SPD with major challenges and opportunities. As the men went off to war, women were mobilized to do the jobs their brothers and husbands had vacated. A recruitment drive to mobilize women also began within the Social Democratic party organization. Here, too, the exodus of the men into the field made itself felt, and in many local or regional organizations women were selected to replace them. That effort ran into difficulties, however, because the increasingly heavy demands on their time, due to increased wage labour activity and the difficulties of maintaining their families during war conditions, discouraged or prevented many women from becoming actively involved in party matters. Indeed, many women who in the past had been active now withdrew for lack of time. Many members now declared themselves unable to pay party dues. In time, many party activities diminished; meetings became rare; congresses and conferences ceased to be held. Perhaps as a result of this tendency, the influence of the ultra-radical wing of the women's movement, led by Clara Zetkin, appeared for a while to be increasing.

Zetkin, together with Luise Zietz, continued to have a hand in editing the weekly journal of the Social Democratic women's movement; and from the very beginning of the war, this journal, *Die Gleichheit,* took a hard line in its attitude toward the conflict, softened only by censorship and the fear of censorship. To be sure, in its first editorial after the outbreak of hostilities, the paper chimed in with the traditional Marxian argument that the war would be a good opportunity to deal a death blow to tsarist Russia, the main bastion of international reaction. Yet the prevalent attitude of its editors was anger that the party leadership had voted in favour of military appropriations and sympathy with the handful of militants within the international movement who demonstrated their international solidarity by participating in the Zimmerwald conference. This editorial line placed the official journal on the extreme left wing of the German SPD. Now that the war brought with it not only new problems but also new opportunities, the latent split within the party's women's movement deepened significantly.

Welfare Work – a Novel Task

The political truce proclaimed at the beginning of the war made it more difficult than before to express criticism of the existing system and the policies pursued by its ruling elites, but it also made possible a wide range of opportunities for Social Democrats, and especially Social Democratic women, to engage for the first time in fruitful collaboration with bourgeois women and with public authorities. There was no dearth of immediate tasks. Proletarian women and children often faced very bitter need. Their men were gone. Their jobs frequently had disappeared. Without financial reserves they often were helpless. For the most needy, food and clothing had to be secured; for expectant mothers, pregnancy counselling, medical care and infant supplies. There was a need for soup kitchens and day-care centres to be set up. Counselling centres for widows, pensioners and the unemployed were required. A host of services had to be supplied to soldiers on leave, to crippled veterans and to the men in the front line.

From the first, the Social Democratic women's movement faced the dilemma of whether or not to co-operate in any of these endeavours with bourgeois or aristocratic women. Such co-operation had hitherto been condemned as contrary to the interests of the proletariat. Now the war brought this tradition to an end. At times reluctantly, at times eagerly, Social Democratic women's organizations mobilized their members for work in the large number of agencies that sprang up in response to wartime needs.

By and large, their members seem to have responded to this challenge without hesitation and at times eagerly. In return, many middle- and upper-class women warmly welcomed their proletarian sisters in various volunteer organizations, while others found their presence discomforting. Hence in many localities fruitful working relationships were established, while in some other places this did not happen. Those latter localities seem to have been situated in some of the most conservative regions of Germany, such as Mecklenburg and East Prussia. Similar differences manifested themselves in the attitudes of regional military commanders.

The demands made by war not only changed the movement's official attitude toward collaboration with non-proletarian women; the war also brought subtle changes in other political attitudes. First, it silenced the old debate about the usefulness of 'reformism' in the struggle against capitalism. The many needs suffered by working-class women were so pressing that nobody in the movement, even among the most militant revolutionaries, questioned the efforts to provide assistance. Moreover, in their endeavours to mitigate some of the hardships of life on the home front, the Social Democratic women's organizations frequently resorted to a method they had hitherto scorned most bitterly: they developed the habit of petitioning the authorities, and they became skilful in this.

If those who spoke for the women's movement felt uncomfortable about these new habits, they justified them by arguing that they provided opportunities for furthering the cause of the working class. The Social Democratic women who worked in the many welfare organizations could seek to impress on the clients that the benefits provided for them were a legitimate claim on society rather than charity. Further, they could prevent religion from intruding into welfare work. Many of them finally regarded the wartime measures taken by the government in imposing controls over resources as a token of the growth of socialism within capitalist society, and they welcomed the opportunity to train themselves in public work through this process. On various occasions, leaders of the Social Democratic women's movement tried to promote more trenchant long-range aims. The services that women were rendering to their country in the war were used to argue for broader welfare legislation and for at last granting political rights and legal equality to women. Naturally, much agitation by the women's movement also contained hopes for a quick ending of hostilities and a lasting peace, but what kind of peace it should be was as hotly debated among the women of the movement as within Social Democracy as a whole.

Long-Term Results

In retrospect, it becomes obvious that the practical work in which the Social Democratic women's movement engaged during the war turned out to be an important school for participation in public affairs such as that which became available in the post-Wilhelmine era. Many of the welfare issues that the war had placed on the agenda remained to be dealt with during the Weimar period, and the experience of dealing with these issues in collaboration with men and women from other parties turned out to be valuable training.

Some women obviously had hoped that it would do more than that, in that the emergency measures taken during the war would serve as a transition to socialism. That, however, was an illusion. Moreover, while Gerald D. Feldman claims that the working class on the whole emerged from the war as one of the few groups or classes to benefit and to improve its over-all position in society, that cannot be said of the proletarian women. To be sure, they were to receive political rights and legal equality in the Weimar Republic. But their economic status declined relative to what it had been. During the war they were mobilized to fill essential positions temporarily vacated by men, only to be demobilized once the war as over. As usual, the women of the proletariat had been used as the ultimate reserve army of labour.

Nor did the Social Democratic women's movement make substantial gains. Instead, the war years threatened the very basis of its existence. To be sure, the movement was encouraged to deploy its active members in a wide array of public service assignments. But the pressure of work to make ends meet also decimated the organization. Although at times the movement was able to use its public service functions for the purpose of attracting new numbers, and new members into union organizations, the far more persistent trend was a rather substantial loss of members. The reasons for this may not only have been lack of time, lack of money for membership dues and declining organizational activity. The conditions of the political truce may also have made active membership in a militant opposition party irrelevant to many women; or else the strident tone of *Die Gleichheit,* which went against the grain of the political truce, may have turned many woman away from the party in patriotic indignation. The rapid loss of subscribers suffered by the journal may be taken as a demonstration of this trend.

This loss of subscribers was actively promoted by the leadership of the party and of the unions. They had responded to the relentless radicalism of *Die Gleichheit* by creating a rival trade-union women's journal, *Gewerkschaftliche Frauenzeitung,* edited by Gertrud Hanna. Once it had begun publishing, the party and the unions organized meetings in which women were urged to switch their subscription from *Die Gleichheit* to the new journal. Fifteen months after its first appearance, the new bi-weekly had 100,000 subscribers; and by the end of the war that figure had doubled.

Once the party split, with the secession of the USPD, the editors of *Die Gleichheit* sided with the secessionists, which then prompted the SPD leadership to make an effort to regain control of this publication as well. Since many leaders of the party's women's movement likewise joined the USPD, the party also needed to rebuild its entire women's organization. An SPD women's conference in 1917 demonstrated the establishment of this new branch and the appearance of an entirely new cadre of women, led by Marie Juchacz, who came to assume leadership over this organization and after the war were to emerge as the leading women within the SPD. The conference firmly endorsed the commitment to practical welfare activity, primarily on the local level, instead of the class struggle heretofore posited as the sole aim.

This turn to practical work may have won many women back to the movement and thus strengthened it. But it has also been interpreted as a voluntary step taken by the women back to playing auxiliary roles within the movement and restricting them to areas of work that were of little interest to their male comrades.

11 The Politics of Rationing versus the Politics of Subsistence: Working-Class Women in Germany, 1914–1918

Ute Daniel

In June 1915, a group of women asked rhetorically in an anonymous letter to the Senate of the City and State of Hamburg, 'So where is the government of Hamburg?' (Ullrich, 1982, 40). The letter continued with complaints about the high prices and the scarcity of food – henceforth the main problems of civil life in Imperial Germany. In posing this question the women expressed their opinion that the government was expected to solve these problems and that it was failing to fulfil its duty.

The conception of the institution of the state underlying this rhetorical question constitutes one of the most important elements of the sociology of the state as developed by Max Weber. In Weber's sociology the typology of governmental power, as well as its social reality, depends on the kind of legitimization governments adopt to proclaim their right of existence. According to Weber, legitimate authority (*legitime Herrschaft*) – that is, the type of government to which modern European states in his view belonged – is legitimized by the general belief of the members of a specific society that the state is able to proclaim rational and efficient normative rules and that it has the power to guarantee them. Empirically, this legitimization is manifested if, and only if, the meaningful actions (*sinnhaftes Handeln*) of the people are structured by this general belief in the state as initiator and guarantor of rational and efficient normative rules.

In the present essay I intend to argue, firstly, that in the First World War the bad living conditions and the way the state tried to cope with them led to a situation where in Germany the majority of the people eventually rejected the legitimate character of the Imperial government; in doing so, a great part of the population came to reject the authority of the state to set normative rules; secondly, that in this process of delegitimization, working-class women played a crucial role. I propose to exemplify my arguments by giving a rough sketch of rationing in Germany between 1914 and 1918 and by analysing the strategies of subsistence which wage-dependent women and families developed. In this context I shall ask which conceptions of government and society were manifest among working-class women.

Rationing and Price Control

When at the end of 1914 it became clear that the war would not be over by Christmas, government control of food supply and prices commenced with the establishment of price ceilings. From now until the end of the war, this price-ceiling policy constituted the principal feature of governmental food control. Its dilemma was that it had to serve two different purposes which, under German wartime conditions, proved to be irreconcilable. Food prices had to be high enough to compel a reduction in consumption. On the other hand, they had also to be low enough to give the people the impression that the state was acting in favour of an equitable distribution of scarce goods. In that way the authorities sought to stabilize the consensus between the governed and the government which was indispensable if total war was to be endured and won.

In the winter of 1914–15 it became clear that it was not possible to realize both aims at the same time. A decision had to be made as to whether high prices should be given priority as a means of stretching available reserves or whether low prices were to be preferred as a preventive measure against general discontent turning eventually into social unrest.

The governments of the German states and of the Reich opted for low prices. That is to say, they gave priority to price ceilings at a level which, for the present, would not curtail consumption. This price-ceiling policy was applied only to those kinds of food which began to show signs of acute dearness. Two problems soon arose. Firstly, the price ceilings for certain products led to a wave of high prices for as yet uncontrolled kinds of food. Secondly, the reserves of low-priced food rapidly melted away. It became clear that food and price-control policies had to be extended beyond imposing selective price ceilings. Consequently, at the end of 1914 and during the years 1915 and 1916 the states and the Reich intervened more strongly in the food market. War boards (*Kriegsgesellschaften*) for numerous kinds of food were established and the products they controlled were submitted to rationed consumption. It started with grain, followed by flour, oats, vegetables, fat, meat, butter, margarine, milk, eggs, potatoes, fish, sugar, jam, etc. The effects in all the subsequent cases proved to be very similar. Once price ceilings and rationing had been established for a certain product, consumption of and prices for other products not yet controlled began to rise. This was followed by new price ceilings and rationing for these products, too, but at an ever-increasing price level. In 1916, prices and the distribution of nearly all edible products, including acorns and horse chestnuts, were controlled. Even so, most of them remained scarce as well as expensive.

In 1915–16 this situation led to acute suffering for large sections of the population. Their discontent with the conditions of everyday life was turned not only against the agrarian population and the profiteers, but primarily against the central and local governments. From the beginning, the authorities had proclaimed their responsibility for food supply and just prices, but they had subsequently failed to meet their obligations – or so more and more people interpreted the situation. This conviction that the government had failed to fulfill its social duties was expressed initially and most dramatically by working-class women who, being responsible for the subsistence of their families, were confronted with enormous difficulties. The women did not only grumble; they developed their own method of surviving under wartime conditions, which turned out to be fatal for government supply policy, as well as for relations between the authorities and the civil population as a whole.

Subsistence Strategies

The more food control and price ceilings became general, the more consumer goods from the regulated market drained away into the black market, where an illegal barter economy was established. Money increasingly lost its function as a general medium of circulation. The rural population made their way into the towns in order to exchange butter, meat, etc. for industrial products and repair services. Shopkeepers ceased to sell for money and turned to bartering or to consuming their merchandise themselves. Moreover, there existed a third group who soon became the embodiment of the illegal consumer economy – the 'hamsterer', and that meant the urban population scouring the countryside for food. Single persons, families and crowds of hundreds of people went from farm to farm, bartering and buying in total disregard of rationing decrees and price ceilings. These 'hamsterer' practices were by no means a prerogative of the well-off: working-class families short of money fell back on their rural relations, thus compensating for lack of money with family ties. In some towns the weekends saw such a rush of working-class women preparing to scour the nearby countryside that the railway stations had to be closed from time to time and additional 'hamster trains' (*Hamsterzüge*) had to be run. In the end, many male and female workers interrupted their working hours or even quit their jobs temporarily in order to acquire food in this direct way, wage-earning having ceased to be the most effective method of providing for subsistence in the towns. The politics of rationing integrated the illegal subsistence strategies into their calculations. In some cases smaller towns, because of their more intimate connections with the rural environment, received smaller allocations of meat, and in this way their inhabitants understood that they should look for the rest themselves. Contemporary observers estimated that roughly 50 per cent of all controlled victuals reached the consumers by illegal circulation. Spot checks demonstrated the extensive character of illegal supply. Investigations into the families of 8,000 dock-workers in October 1917 revealed that 7,000 of them, in circumvention of the rationing decrees, had hoarded a stock of potatoes sufficient to guarantee their subsistence in the coming winter. And a one-day check on railway traffic in a small western German town in June 1917 brought to light roughly 36 pounds of butter, 421 eggs, 5 hundredweight of flour, nearly 30 pounds of peas, 80 pounds of potatoes, 42 pounds of veal and 12 pounds of ham – all hoarded by urban 'hamsterers'.

The criminal statistics of wartime, too – in spite of the fact that they underestimated wartime criminality because of the reduced rate of reported cases – reflect the extent to which women regarded illegal behaviour and offences as a normal way of gaining advantage in their struggle for survival: whereas in 1913 roughly 33,000 women had been convicted of offences against property, in 1917 this figure had risen to nearly 66,000 – an increase of 100 per cent. Not only did the absolute figures of convicted women rise significantly, but the percentage of first offenders also increased. Most of the women convicted of offences against property had either stolen food in shops or in the countryside or had manipulated food-ration cards or vouchers.

The authorities were confronted with the fact that a great part of the foodstuffs which they, after all, needed to run their rationing policies simply vanished in hidden channels. In this situation they faced a choice between two problematic alternatives: in order to stop the draining away of rationed goods into the illegal consumer-goods market they would have to combat, above all, the so-called 'hamster family', that is, the women with their children and relatives scouring the countryside for food; for of all the kinds of illegal supply activities it was the invasion of huge crowds of hungry city-dwellers which in the most drastic way left the rural supply districts of the bigger towns unable to fulfil their delivery quotas. As a result, the official rations, already too small to guarantee subsistence, in such cases had to be reduced even further. The vicious circle was complete: the smaller official rations became, the more extensive the illegal supply activities. Thus rationing policies could not work in the long run without combating the 'hamster family'. But on the other hand, effective prevention of illegal subsistence strategies would have meant forcing a great part of the population to starve to death, official rations lying significantly below the minimum subsistence level. Under these circumstances even the authorities did not dare to interfere seriously with hoarding and blackmarketeering. And apart from this decidedly curious fact that the authorities did not consider it expedient to prevent illegal supply activities, they did not think it to be possible either.

Short of policemen and officials in general anyway, they had also to come to terms with the fact that an increasing number of people, especially working-class women, responded to the half-hearted government sanctions against illegal self-supply with resistance and bitterness. They denied the authorities the moral legitimation to interfere with their survival strategies. And they questioned the general assumption that government laws, decrees and admonitions were to be observed. More and more people considered themselves ethically authorized to circumvent food controls. With increasing frequency they evaded railway-station checkpoints, tried to deceive policemen and officials in every possible way, and even physically attacked rationing officers. The authorities – and this I consider to be a very important development in German wartime society – in some sense accepted this popular view: whereas at the beginning of the war they had decided, with respect to public opinion, in favour of the rationing and price-ceiling policy, now they decided – in the second half of the war – again with respect to public opinion, not to enforce this policy consistently.

Privately, officials now tended to justify their own measures and their role in society less often in terms of their proclaimed power to set normative rules and to guarantee them than in terms of vindication on the basis of the so-called 'sound judgement of the population'. In the second half of the First World War politicians and officials had to reckon with factors of morale which henceforth proved to be more decisive for social stability than ever before. They had to persuade people to accept the authorities as the principal source of a just and efficient regulation of society; otherwise the people would cancel the consensus between the governed and the government (the so-called 'civic truce' or *Burgfrieden*) and would cease to support the government's efforts to win the war.

But persuading the people that this consensus had to be maintained turned out to be an impracticable task. For since 1915–16, when social tensions became acute, there came into existence a medium of subversive communication which proved to be far more decisive than official interpretations of reality. Spontaneously and uncontrolled, a system of informal communication spread among the population and propagated oppositional interpretations of reality. This communication system embraced the whole Reich, as well as the front lines, and constituted a domain of alternative publicity. Here slogans, legends, rumours and jokes depicted an image of war, state and society which proved to be most damaging to the reputation of the authorities.

The most important transfer-points for this subversive way of perceiving the situation were – besides the correspondence between family members at home and at the front, especially between women and their husbands on active service – crowds and queues caused by war conditions. In queues in front of shops, offices and notice-boards, and in railway compartments, people exchanged their views on current affairs. Here working-class women in particular, together with soldiers on leave, were observed by officials and agents propagating hearsay horror stories about foodstuffs wasted by administrative failures; about officers in the rear areas wallowing in luxury while their soldiers died of hunger; about big cities like Munich where the corpses of the starved reportedly had to be removed in furniture-vans and tramcars. Rumours circulated about German prisoners of war in Great Britain or elsewhere who allegedly encountered German flour and heaps of German eggs, exported to enemy countries by German local governments greedy for money. These channels of subversive communication – from 1916 onwards eagerly scrutinized by the authorities – not only spread rumours and complaints, but also something analogous to popular theories of war. For example, it was rumoured in 1917–18 that, although Germany had lost the war long ago, the upper classes had no interest in ending it, believing that a further decimation of the population would prevent a revolution. Other rumours maintained that Germany could have had an armistice in 1916, if the industrialists had not protested against it on the grounds of still insufficient profits.

The authorities learned to fear this informal communication as the main medium of sedition. In this, it proved to be far more effective than the oppositional propaganda of the organized left. The flood of rumours, legends and jokes – expressing as well as reinforcing popular unwillingness to endure wartime living conditions – radicalized the civil population to a point where general discontent turned into collective action. The subversive communication system not only explained, but also gave rise to, the spontaneous riots which after 1916 turned German towns into theatres of civil war. Typically, these episodes of collective action started with a rumour alleging that in a certain shop bread or some other commodity could be bought without ration cards. Very soon, a crowd would assemble and realizing that the information was incorrect, would begin pillaging or rioting in the streets, in this way frequently causing a chain-reaction of social unrest. As often as not, these riots were likely to be the source of even more rumours, further transforming public opinion for the worse. This was especially true of rumours about the numerous rioters killed by the police.

Working-class women (housewives as well as female labourers), together with juveniles, made up the group which showed the greatest inclination to participate in these spontaneous collective actions. For these women rioting, plundering and even physically attacking local officials became 'normal' means of expressing opposition. Their actions also proved to be an effective way of enforcing higher rations, for women soon discovered that in a variety of cases nervous local governments reacted to collective actions of this kind by increasing food supplies – at least temporarily. This additional food supply had to be taken either from the black market or from other geographical areas where social stability seemed to be more secure. Wherever local governments participated in the black market and failed to keep it secret, they confirmed the widespread popular view that the authorities themselves did not respect their own laws. In cases where the authorities diverted quotas from other towns, the affected people learned via the informal communications network that they had been cheated and that it was their own fault for not having rioted in time too. The subversive network thus not only made publicly known the strong connection that existed between rioting and a temporary additional food supply; it also propagated the lively suspicion that bottlenecks in supply within a certain community might be caused by social unrest in a different region – a suspicion not likely to strengthen confidence in the local government's willingness to give priority to guaranteeing the subsistence of its own people.

So rationing policies and strategies of illegal self-supply reached a deadlock. Rationing could neither be abolished nor could it be accomplished. The less rationing decrees were observed, the worse the supply situation became and the greater was criticism of rationing policies and the government in general. Finally, even the authorities ceased to lay claim to their competence to set the rules. Towards the end of the war they, too, like the majority of the population, perceived the state as an institution no longer able to enforce policy with any significant chance of its realization.

On the other hand, the resistance of the majority of the people to government decrees and against the state in general failed to develop into political alternatives to war and rationing. The capability of the population to structure its social and economic environments was rooted in, and confined to, spontaneous collective action; and collective action alone did not lead to the organized nationwide political alternatives which were indispensable if crucial changes were to take place. Meanwhile, the existing political organizations – the political parties and trade unions – almost without exception remained integrated in the society of Imperial Germany. Not until the very last weeks of the war did they return to political decision-making.

The experience of the war in Germany nevertheless undermined in a decisive way the legitimization of government power and of the state as a whole. Above all, the women of the working classes, bearing responsibility for the survival of their families, subverted the authorities by their way of thinking as well as their way of acting. This took place long before the *Kaiserreich* was formally abolished in the so-called November Revolution of 1918–19. At that time, however, the overthrow of the once seemingly omnipotent state was easily accomplished in a way that would be incomprehensible without the preceding developments outlined above.

12 Bernstein's Political Position, 1914–1920

Susanne Miller

Bernstein's Response to the Great War

In the course of the war, Bernstein made the most spectacular decision of his political life: he separated from the party to which he had belonged for more than 40 years. In the 1870s he had promoted unity between the Lassalleans and the Eisenach group, and while Bebel had considered Bernstein's exclusion at the height of the struggle over revisionism, the latter had never at the time, so it appears, had a thought of leaving the party.

Of course, Bernstein's decision in the First World War, becomes comprehensible only if perceived in the context of the whole development of the party, above all in conjunction with his relations with men such as Hugo Haase, Karl Kautsky and Emanuel Wurm, who left the party for the same reasons as Bernstein, and founded a new one. The fact that these men were part of the Marxist centre which had fought so passionately against revisionism played no part in this; their arguments against the war politics of the party majority had the same thrust as his.

Before dealing with details of Bernstein's conduct, mention should be made to provisos, so as to avoid misunderstanding. Firstly, Bernstein was always in agreement with the official party line that the distinction between aggressive and defensive wars must be the criterion for the attitude of the German Social Democrats: rejection of aggressive war, support for defensive war. He never concurred in Marx's and Engels's thesis that the decisive point had to be whether or not a war would promote proletarian revolution. Nor did he share Rosa Luxemburg's opinion that wars were a necessary consequence of imperialism and that, therefore, the distinction between aggressive and defensive wars among imperialist powers was without significance.

Secondly, like Jean Jaurès, whom he much revered, Bernstein saw no contradiction between patriotism and internationalism. To take a stand on behalf of one's own country's interests, as long as it did not damage legitimate interests of other countries, seemed to him a matter of course, indeed an ethical commandment. That is why he affirmed the defence of the fatherland, provided it really was a matter of defence.

At the outbreak of the war, Bernstein, like the overwhelming majority of the German people and of German Social Democracy, was convinced that Germany found itself in a position of defence. He considered Serbia and Russia to be those responsible for the war – Russia because of a longstanding tradition, and Serbia because of its attitude during the Peace of Bucharest after the Second Balkan War. In the SPD parliamentary group's meeting of 3 August 1914, therefore, Bernstein voted with the majority in favour of granting war credits, and again with the entire party – except for two representatives who absented themselves before the vote – in the assembly of the Reichstag on 4 August. Looking back, during the 1919 congress of the Social Democratic Party, he declared those two days to be the blackest of his entire political life. From the beginning, he and the few Germans unaffected by the national frenzy of enthusiasm regarded the war as a catastrophe for mankind. Since Bernstein knew England well and loved it, there was an additional circumstance: the news of England's entrance into the war in the evening of 4 August signified to him the coming defeat of Germany. Bernstein is reported to have spoken 'like one of the ancient prophets . . . predicting the collapse of his own people'. In two letters to Lujo Brentano, written in the middle and at the end of August, Bernstein emphasized that from all points of view it was desirable that Germany emerge from the war victorious; while its existence was under threat, the question of guilt must take second place. But even at that time he already thought that neither France nor England had wanted the war, but that Russia had. There is no evidence to show that Germany's defeat had ever been a matter of indifference to him. It was not on this question that he came into conflict with his party; it was over the assessment of the premises which had induced Bernstein early in August 1914 to agree to the war-credits legislation. These premises pertained to two areas above all else: the guilt question and war aims. In political discussion both areas were interconnected and directly touched on the problem of obligations towards the Socialist International.

It seems that the guilt question, which Bernstein orginally thought he could leave aside, provided the first impulse to the change in his attitude. As early as 3 September 1914 Eduard David confided to his diary after a conversation with Bernstein and Haase that both were convinced that the German government bore the major responsibility for the war, and that the granting of the war credits had been a mistake. This position led Bernstein to a painful decision in the following weeks: his break with the *Sozialistische Monatshefte,* to which he had been a prominent contributor for years. It meant separation from a group which had been his sole support during the revisionism discussion, and to which he had subsequently felt close personally and politically, even though critical of it on many questions. It is above all Joseph Bloch's letters in Bernstein's papers as well as David's diary entries which testify to the intensity of these men's desire not to lose Bernstein. In his discussion with Joseph Bloch there is a sentence which may stand as the principle of Bernstein's entire conduct: 'Here conscience confronts conscience, and such a contrast is not to be down-graded to a verdict about mere opportuneness'.

From October 1914 Bernstein's position was firm. Firstly, the war had *not* been forced on Germany; it was not a defensive war but, from Germany's viewpoint, a preventive one. Secondly, Bernstein sharply opposed Germany's annexation desires, which were shared, to a certain degree, by some Social Democrats. Thirdly, he openly deplored the brutality of the German conduct of the war. Fourthly, he soon pleaded for abstention during votes on war credits. He wanted to soften the caucus censure of

Karl Liebknecht by adding that Liebknecht's motivation leading him to vote against the credits in the Reichstag on 2 December 1914 'did not contradict Social Democratic principles'. From March 1915 onwards Bernstein no longer voted for war credits. Fifthly, at an early date he desired a party initiative in a peace action. Finally, this action, in his opinion, was to be started by all the parties of the Socialist International, in both belligerent and neutral countries, simultaneously and with the same programme.

Ever since taking up this position, Bernstein expressed it not only in the internal circle of comrades but also – to the extent possible, given existing censorship – in newspaper and journal articles and in lectures. He revealed himself even more strongly than through this journalistic activity when in June 1915 he wrote, together with Haase and Kautsky, the proclamation called *Das Gebot der Stunde* (*The Demand of the Hour*). Its fundamental purport was a pacifist condemnation of modern war as combining the 'cruelty of barbaric ages' with 'the most sophisticated tools of civilization' and leading all participating nations towards bankruptcy. Without directly attacking the politics of the party majority, and after citing various remarks from economic and political circles 'which brand the present war with the stamp of a war of conquest', it declared:

> Since the plans of conquest are public before all the world, Social Democracy has entire freedom to propound its opposing viewpoint most emphatically, and the current situation turns this freedom into duty. . . . A real and lasting peace is possible only on the basis of free accords. . . . The present shape of things calls upon German Social Democracy to take a decisive step towards this end. Today it faces the choice of following this commandment or dealing a fatal blow to the confidence it enjoyed hitherto among the German people and in the whole world as the champion of peace among the nations.

Within the Reichstag party caucus Bernstein was recognized, next to Haase, as the foreign policy spokesman of the minority. This became clear when, under pressure from the intra-party opposition, the party leadership resolved to formulate guidelines about party peace aims and to have them confirmed by the *Vorstand,* the party committee and the entire Reichstag membership of the party. Bernstein and David were commissioned to submit drafts. These differed not only in their substantive contents but even more in their intentions. Liebknecht defined the formulation of the two authors' aims thus: 'Bernstein calls upon us for autonomous party policy; David stands for bloc politics with bourgeois elements'. The nucleus of Bernstein's draft was 'the right to national self-determination' as 'the highest principle of relations between peoples'. He did not, however, elaborate in detail on its consequences. He renounced, apparently so as to avoid aggravating the intra-party conflict, the adoption of a position explicitly addressing the controversial question of Alsace and Lorraine, but his formulation implied provision of a plebiscite to determine the nationality of the two provinces. This was how his draft was understood and, therefore, welcomed by the French socialists. In 1917 the USPD was to take the same position in its Stockholm Memorandum. But despite Bernstein's reluctance to venture too far on such an especially sensitive subject, he encountered complete failure at the party conference in August 1915. The meeting hardly debated his draft, and David's was adopted, with a few changes, by a majority of almost two-thirds.

In March 1916 the Reichstag party split. Bernstein at once joined the Social Democratic Working Group (SAG or *Sozialdemokratische Arbeitsgemeinschaft*). He showed more hesitation in joining the Independent Social Democratic Party (USPD) founded at Easter 1917. As he wrote later, he was surprised that at the conference, which was convened to unite the opposition, there was a motion to found a new party. Like Kautsky, he voted against it, but when a large majority resolved on the foundation of a party, he joined it – with internal reservations. The common denominator of the extremely heterogeneous forces which found themselves in the USPD was opposition to the majority of the party. And it was this which, during the party's short and turbulent existence, maintained its cohesion.

To mount this opposition, Bernstein was no less determined than, say, Georg Ledebour or Rosa Luxemburg, despite everything that separated him from them. As they did, he accused the party of having betrayed its earlier principles. The notes for Bernstein's speeches of January 1916 reveal, after the enumeration of the sins of the government's war policy, the accusation: 'In earlier days we would have mounted a flaming protest against all this; today we are silent, in part because we *must* be [censorship], but in part because we are *prisoners* of our politics. From being defenders of the vote of 4 August 1914, we have become defenders of the *war policy*. A tilting plain – unconscious downward slide.'

Questions of theory were immaterial to Bernstein's attitude in the war. His arguments were built on traditional maxims of his party: rejection of wars of conquest, recognition of the right to national self-determination, avowal of adherence to proletarian internationalism. Wolfram Wette and Roger Fletcher are justified in asserting that Bernstein was not in principle a pacifist but that a pacifist tendency was prevalent in him. Here, too, it must be said, Bernstein had solid roots in democratic socialist tradition. The fact that he felt so strongly committed to this tradition explains both why he left the Majority Social Democrats and why, as the first among the prominent foundation members of the USPD, he found his way back to them.

Bernstein's Response to the Revolution of 1918

During the 1918–19 revolution Bernstein considered it to be his task to function as a mediator between the two Social Democratic parties. In the revolutionary events themselves he played only a minor part. As a co-opted official in the Treasury he exerted hardly any influence on policy. Political isolation characterized his life during that period and increased until his death.

It was Bernstein's hope that the end of the war should mean the start of the reunification of the two Social Democratic parties. He thought that membership in both parties could constitute his contribution towards its realization. But he took the organizational step in that direction at the moment when the prospect of overcoming the split had passed for good: on the day of the bloody Christmas unrest in Berlin which caused the Independents to leave the government, he petitioned for membership in the Majority Social Democracy. He remained in the USPD until its resolution of March 1919 not to tolerate dual membership rendered it impossible for him to remain. But even without this formal reason we may conjecture that he would soon have left the USPD, for he would not have gone along with the political radicalization of the Independents or with their programme of adherence to the council system (*Rätesystem*) and to the dictatorship of the proletariat. Indeed, he was in accord with many decisions of Majority Social Democracy during the revolution. The following points, above all demonstrate this concurrence:

Firstly, under the given circumstances he approved of parliamentary democracy even though, as he had written in a paper of 1916, he considered parliamentarism to be the governmental system of the capitalist social order.

Secondly, to the council movement, that most original phenomenon of the German Revolution, he conceded a merely transitory function prior to the summoning of the constitution-making National Assembly. He regarded Liebknecht's demand of 9 November, 'All power to the councils', as provocation of the counter-revolution.

Thirdly, Bernstein was among the most trenchant Social Democratic critics of Russian Bolshevism. He warned his comrades insistently against copying it: 'The Bolshevists have combined an amateurishly experimental economic policy with a system of the most brutal violence contemptuous of all civilized development, and by throttling necessary economic drives caused production to decline'. In Russia the Bolsheviks had been the counter-revolutionaries, and so they were in Germany; their system 'is in fact the death of the achievements of the revolution', Bernstein declared at the Berne International Socialist Congress.

Fourthly, on the question of socialization he, like all Social Democrats, held steps to be necessary but, in a lecture at Basel on 24 February 1919 about socialization of enterprises, he counselled very careful investigation before they were taken. Apparently, therefore, he was not opposed to the passivity in this area shown by the Majority Social Democrats, which was sharply criticized by the Independents who, on their part, took no initiative of their own.

Fifthly, Bernstein's loyalty to the governing Majority Social Democrats probably rested primarily on his acknowledgment of the difficulties in their path and on his appreciation of their readiness to shoulder responsibility. At the International Socialist Congress at Berne in February 1919 Bernstein utilized his international connections and his own high reputation so as to create sympathy for the misery of the German people and the precarious position of its government. It speaks for his standing that, without being an official delegate, he was given the floor.

Sixthly, Bernstein thought the strikes and putsches in the first half of 1919 disastrous for the young republic. Still, given his pacifist leanings, it is astonishing that, as far as is ascertainable from available evidence, he did not belong to the numerous critics of Noske's policy in the ranks of Majority Social Democracy, but he was not its apologist.

After the election defeat of the Majority Social Democrats in the summer of 1920, Bernstein was one of the few in the party who advocated participation by the Social Democrats in the government and the continuation of coalition; this points to his positive evaluation of the Weimar coalition under Social Democratic leadership.

It was not a criticism of Majority Social Democratic domestic or military policy that led Bernstein, half a year after his return to his old party, into difficulties once again: it was his statement on the war and on the Versailles Peace Treaty. At the Weimar Party Congress of the Majority Social Democrats in June 1919 he pleaded for recognition by the party of the German share of responsibility for the war so as to create a basis for an understanding with its foreign comrades. He besought the party not to turn against the peace treaty with nationalist slogans, but rather to recognize that nine-tenths of its demands, hard as they were, represented 'irrefutable necessities'. The indignation of the party congress was almost unanimous. Bernstein had remained true to himself: once again his commitment to truth and his sense of justice had driven him to remarks which encountered a wall of incomprehension and repudiation. This cannot be traced to a want of psychological empathy, for Bernstein knew the party pysche thoroughly and had shown on other occasions that he had some grasp of psychology. But for him it was more important to speak his mind on what he judged to be correct – which on occasion he did rather awkwardly – than to be considerate of his comrades' sensibilities.

Bernstein was belatedly rehabilitated when, in the following year, he was appointed to the committee for the formulation of a new basic programme for the party. In an analogy to Engels's remarks about the Erfurt Programme, one might say about the Görlitz Programme, adopted in 1921, that Bernstein's critique had 'thoroughly hit home'. But it seems an irony of history that the Görlitz Programme remained in force for four years only and, after the fusion of the rump-USPD with the mother party, had to be replaced by a new one, the Heidelberg Programme, which in turn bore the stamp of Karl Kautsky.

Differences of opinion, however, no longer disturbed the close friendship of the two old men, renewed during the war after years of estrangement. What Bernstein had to say about theory he had essentially stated at the turn of the century, and it has inspired German Social Democrats to this day. The last 30 years of his life were dedicated to immediate politics – political journalism, political history and parliamentary activity. These three decades, too, are of significance to us. They reveal to us a man who, in questions of political morality, would not falter – and that is no small thing.

Part III
Triumph and Tragedy

13 Working-Class Culture and Working-Class Politics in the Weimar Republic

Dieter Langewiesche

In Search of New Programmes

From the very beginning, the German workers' movement saw itself as being not simply an interest group for politics and trade unions, but 'the greatest cultural movement that the world had ever seen' (A. Braun, 1906, 4). However, the workers' movement seldom concretely defined what 'socialist culture' or, more specifically, 'working-class culture' was supposed to mean. Although the workers and their organizations often merely appropriated already existing cultural norms, there still existed a clear dividing line between the workers' and the bourgeoisie's understanding of culture. If the latter's goal was the cultivation of the individual, the socialist organizations' cultural goal was a striving towards the cultural ascendancy of the proletariat as a class. A steadily growing network of socialist cultural clubs had come into existence before World War I. These organizations aimed at accompanying individuals from the cradle to the grave. They served the ambitious goal of making the workers heirs to, and successors of, all culture, within the restrictions of the class state and class society of the German Empire. Among the forces that were to wean the workers and their families away from the churches was socialist children's literature, as well as socialist free-thinkers and cremation societies. In the postwar Weimar Republic, the socialist cultural clubs continued to grow. However, their functions changed radically, because the place of Social Democracy and the unions in state and society had changed.

In the German Empire, the workers' movement saw itself as confronting a hostile environment. Although the movement did collaborate with this hostile environment in many ways, it fundamentally rejected it. The labour movement viewed its socialist cultural organizations as an anticipation of future society, set against the existing German Empire. In the Weimar Republic, the SPD and the unions could not maintain this concept of a socialist counter-society within existing society because both SPD and the trade unions had taken over numerous duties in the state and in the society – even in the ministries. This change from the supposed enemies of the state, from the 'vagabonds without a fatherland', as contemporaries called them, to the most important supporters of the new parliamentary democracy demanded that the role of the socialist cultural movement be formulated anew.

The developments which took place from 1918–19 on can be described as a steady search for new programmes for the present and the future – in political, union and also cultural spheres. The cultural labour movement in the Weimar Republic split into a Social Democratic and a Communist movement, as had the political labour movement before it. Between 1919 and 1933, three major tendencies of the cultural labour movement can be recognized. Firstly, workers' educational opportunities grew and became differentiated, although at the same time education was transferred from the workers' own management to state and city educational institutions. Secondly, a cultural socialism which sought new future utopias emerged. Thirdly, the cultural labour movement had to come to terms with the new 'popular culture' disseminated by expanding leisure-time industries, in particular by the new and influential mass media of film and radio.

Working-Class Education

Let us first look at the development of working-class education. The unions, more than any other form of organization, were strongly identified with working-class education. The unions' range of activity grew enormously during the time of the Weimar Republic. In 1927, there were approximately 200,000 union functionaries, most of them volunteers. Of these, about 100,000 were members of factory committees, who had a variety of tasks in the larger companies. In the same year, the unions supplied almost 47,000 of the elected members of health insurance committees. In order to prepare this enormous army of functionaries for its duties, the individual unions and their federation, the National German Trade-Union Congress (ADGB), created countless educational opportunities. What was characteristic of this educational work was its dualistic character. The unions and the SPD ran and financed some educational institutions, and at the same time they worked closely with state and city institutions.

One example of an educational institution created by the unions was the Berlin union school. Between 1921 and 1931, it prepared more than 36,000 union members for their new tasks in the Weimar Republic. In 1926 and 1930 the German Metal Workers Association, the largest union, and the ADGB, opened their own schools. Both men and women (for whom there were special courses) were taught at these schools.

In addition to these educational institutions run by the unions there were also institutions financed by the state. Social Democratic and other unions chose and supported participants for these schools. Main topics of instruction were economics, law and social policy, but German was taught too, as the basic knowledge that the participants brought with them from elementary school proved to be quite deficient. Most of the participants in these schools went back to their old jobs after they had attended school. Many filled volunteer and sometimes even major positions in worker organizations. One such institution was the Academy of Labour in Frankfurt, which in the first 10 years of its existence educated 639 participants, of whom only 25 were women.

In contrast to these educational institutions for functionaries the Tinz Adult Education School in Thuringia saw itself as a '*Weltanschauung* school', one which deemed its mission to be the imparting of an all-round socialist 'class education'. The school held a unique position within the adult education structure of the Weimar Republic. It was owned by the state and took only participants up to the age of 30 who had an elementary-school education. Socialists provided instruction in economics, history, sociology, the humanities and the arts. For the most part, the participants were Social Democrats, about a third of them women. Most of the participants used this education for individual advancement, which, however, took place within the workers' movement.

The Social Democratic and union workers' movement in the Weimar Republic greatly expanded not only institutional opportunities for functionaries but also the 'education of the masses'. The dualistic character of the educational movement is apparent here, with increased co-operation between working class organizations and state and city institutions. In 1931, there were more than 2,000 Social Democractic workers' libraries. They no longer had the same importance in the socialist educational system that they had enjoyed in the prewar years. Still, 4 per cent of all union members to whom a workers' library was available made use of it. These workers' libraries were overshadowed by the greatly expanded city public libraries. The public libraries catered to the wishes of the labour movement, which had an influence on them through the city boards.

In addition, the Social Democrats and the unions held a great number of lectures. Here, too, they co-operated with the city adult education schools which had sprung up during the Weimar Republic. Many of these schools aimed at workers in order to integrate them into society. The *leitmotiv* of the adult education schools, 'socialization of the spirit', proved to be utopian. There were successes, however, since a large number of the participants were indeed workers. In Hamburg where special courses for members of the SPD, the unions and the young socialist workers' group were offered, about one third of all students were workers. The city-run adult education school took over the duties of an educational institution for the labour movement. The Hamburg public libraries system was complemented by the Hamburg union library of the Weimar Republic which specialized in professional literature for union functionaries. The city-state was particularly well-suited to such co-operation since Social Democrats participated in all the Weimar governments in Hamburg.

By participating in state and community educational offerings, the Social Democrats and unions 'socialized' a great deal of the education system they had inherited from the Empire. In addition, they expanded their own educational institutions in order to prepare the huge army of functionaries and approximately 50,000 (in 1931) elected city officials for their duties. The basic political philosophy of the SPD and the unions is reflected in the thematic breadth of this extensive educational work and in the co-operation with state and city institutions. In their political practices, the SPD and the unions identified themselves with the Weimar democracy: they took over a great variety of tasks both in order to keep the republic alive and to reform it into a democratic welfare state.

The German Communist Party took a completely different stand towards the Weimar Republic. Both labour parties followed a course that originated in the prewar years when the socialist labour movement was not yet a divided one. What had been united during the Empire fell apart during the world war. The Social Democrats adhered to the prewar labour movement's willingness to be integrated into state and society, while the German Communist Party radicalized the old class-war programme. Similarly the Communists' educational work, which was far less extensive than that of the Social Democrats, kept itself completely removed from other educational institutions. Characteristic of the tasks that the Communist cultural organizations set for themselves in 1930, in the service of the class war, were those outlined at the first meeting of their Marxist workers' schools. The Marxist workers' schools 'must be the representatives of a merciless fight against the system of private, community, state, union, Social Democratic and church-run adult education schools. These are breeding-grounds for future strike-breakers and murderers of workers.' (cited in Langewiesche, 1982, 381)

Cultural Socialism

Although Social Democrats and unions identified themselves with the Weimar Republic (they held celebrations every year in honour of the constitution), this did not mean that they were satisfied with what the republic had achieved. Social Democrats and unions continued to search for new models for the future. This search was evidenced in the cultural utopias that the Social Democrats planned. These models were necessary because the old class-war model no longer corresponded to the new position of the Social Democratic Party and the unions in the Weimar state. In the 1920s, a type of cultural socialism emerged that attempted to counteract the danger of a loss of utopias. A 1931 issue of the ADGB organ, *Die Arbeit* (*Labour*), asserted: 'The magic of individual danger has been taken away from organizations. Loyalty has been transformed into a matter of calculation; utilitarian considerations replaced loyalty'. Many Social Democrats and union members felt the same way. They feared that what the labour movement had won in terms of power it would have to pay by a loss of utopia. Such a loss could endanger the future of the labour movement. In order to counteract this danger, cultural socialism developed the concept of 'the new human being', who had to be realized before the socialist society of the future would be attainable. As Erich Winkler put it at the 1924 Social Democratic Cultural Week in Leipzig, 'First of all, the picture of a new order has to be strongly anchored in the minds before it is possible to erect the building. And every political influence is pointless if the acquisition of education, knowledge and culture does not take place at the same time.' (Langewiesche, 1982, p. 383)

In formulating this cultural programme for the future, cultural socialism was reacting to the bitter experiences of the Social Democratic labour movement. After the revolution of 1918–19, the movement had first experienced a storm of new members and then had to cope with a huge wave of deserters. The diagnosis arrived at was that socialist certainty about the future had been destroyed during the years of war and revolution, and that this certainty had to be recreated culturally. It was in this way that the programme of the 'socialist cultural life' of the 'new human being' came about. Valtin Hartig, director of the Leipzig Workers' Educational Institute, proclaimed the cultural-socialist creed at the 1924 Leipzig Workers' Cultural Week:

> This is the heart of the socialist crisis, which has not yet been overcome: once the party was an organization of belief and *Weltanschauung* as well. Today the party neither can nor ought to have that role. Today the party ought to be more of an organization for accomplishing political goals, an organization that is, however, directed towards great ideas, in order not to be swallowed up by the shortsightedness of daily work. A vacuum has come into the party. What is missing is that which would allow the need for belief and *Weltanschauung* to flow in. If we recognize this, this means that we have already found the solution. Right in step with the party as an organization for achieving political goals comes the socialist cultural movement, which has its own forms to create. This movement frees the party of ideologies that would otherwise hinder it from doing what is necessary. The politician ought not to be allowed to be an ideologue; as a matter of fact, ideology is the very negation of the politician. This division of the movement is a gain for the party; the party thereby gets the freedom to carry out politics politically. The division is a gain for the cultural movement; the movement can continue to hold on to a pure ideal, an ideal that would be dirtied and trampled by the exigencies of politics. (Hartig, 1925, 884)

The socialist cultural movement functioned as a 'third pillar' within the labour movement, along with the SPD and the unions. This 'pillar' had the task of realizing the necessary prerequisites for the 'new human being' and the new 'socialist way of life'. The cultural socialists repeatedly stressed that these necessary preconditions had not yet been created. Kurt Heilbut, who had been very active in the socialist cultural movement and who died in Auschwitz in 1943, made a distinction between three steps in the 'relationship of the socialist worker to the bourgeois-capitalist culture:

> Firstly, imitation of the bourgeois culture, or rather, non-culture. Secondly, rejection thereof. Thirdly, formation of a new socialist culture. Most workers are still at the first step. They are proud of the fact that they can imitate everything bourgeois. For the most part, they have petit-bourgeois ideals: drinking, trashy literature, jazz, boxing and so forth. (van der Will and Burns, 1982, 187)

There are many such diagnoses of the times. Many disappointed cultural socialists felt it a necessity to renew socialism completely by returning to socialism's roots. As a result of the major cultural ideas developed in this context, Weimar cultural socialism fully reversed prewar ideas about achieving a socialist society. Neither the overcoming of the capitalist mode of production nor the 'path of power' via elections was seen as a prerequisite for the realization of a socialist society. Rather, the prerequisites for the realization of socialism were now seen to be in the individual's way of life. First of all, individual socialists ought to adjust their individual lives, their everyday existence, from clothing to family life, according to socialist principles. The cultural socialist thus made the realization of socialism a pedagogic exercise. First the 'new human being', and then the new socialist society.

It is difficult to make a judgement about this change in policy. The cultural socialist hope for a new society created out of the spirit of pedagogy can be understood as a compensatory flight from the reality of the 'bourgeois republic'. It was a republic in which the voters did not give the SPD a parliamentary majority. And therefore the SPD and the unions had only a limited influence on the republic's social conditions and economic order. The cultural socialist hope for the 'new human being' can also be understood as a means of revising the belief in a quasi-natural 'path to power', as a way out of the fatalistic conviction that socialism would be realized in accordance with economic laws. Cultural socialists tried to motivate the individual, because responsibility for the realization of socialist ideas for the future lay with the individual worker.

It is difficult to judge whether these major ideas of the cultural socialists merely compensated for the limited possibilities for reforming the Weimar Republic or whether they indeed activated the socialists' will to change society. It is impossible to decide, since the National Socialists in 1933 violently put an end to all cultural-socialist experiments, and these were not resumed after 1945.

Culture in Everyday Life

If one wishes to test, at least hypothetically, the chances of realizing the cultural-socialist plan, one must ask if the planned 'revolutionizing of the mind' (as Kurt Löwenstein called it) included people's daily lives. More than anything, everyday life means one's working life. In his 1927 work, *Kulturlehre des Sozialismus* (*Cultural Teachings of Socialism*), Gustav Radbruch focused on the alternatives of 'culture apart from work' and 'culture of work'. For Radbruch, the answer to this question is unequivocal: for the cultural socialists, work and culture were opposites that could only be reconciled in a socialist society. In cultural-socialist writings and meetings, everyday life, when it appeared at all, was represented as a non-culture painted in the darkest of colours. In the cultural socialists' opinion, factory and work were 'Mechanized hell/Time in which you are worked to death', as Bruno Schönlank had his dramatic chorus, 'Der gespaltene Mensch' ('The Divided Person') proclaim. Or, like Gustav Radbruch, one passed over the 'most difficult problem, the problem of culture of work, of joy in one's work', with as few sentences as possible, in order to look for 'the cultural idea of socialism' in other spheres, spheres which appeared to offer better opportunities for realizing this cultural idea. According to Radbruch, 'Drama, symphonies, architecture will be the major forms of socialist culture. They are of society and for society, works of the many for the many. If we want to characterize the contrast between individualistic and socialistic culture, then we have to say that an architectonic age takes the place of a literary one.'

The cultural socialists attempted to develop alternative cultural possibilities, but working life was omitted from these as being culturally inaccessible. In a 1928 lecture broadcast by the Munich radio station, the Workers' Radio Organization declared that 'The life of the worker, aside from his life at work, must be culturally enlivened and enriched'. The cultural socialists thus retreated from a central area of life and instead attempted to draw closer to their utopia of 'socialist cultural life'.

Many cultural socialists saw in the mass festivals of the 1920s, more than in anything else, an art form created by and for the masses. The cultural socialists' fascination with these mass festivals was twofold: first, the appeal to and inclusion of the many in these performances; and second, the leap out of everyday life, the 'putting aside of the everyday person', as Valtin Hartig called it. Another celebrated these mass festivals as 'first steps in the land of socialist humanity'. Adolf Johannesson, director of the large and renowned Hamburg workers' dramatic chorus, expressed the same view when he wrote of the chorus, 'It should depict the soul of the masses; should allow their experiences, feelings and desires to appear in a visibly and intensely exaggerated form; and it should not be a depiction of how a group of people really act. The eye and the ear of a festive group do not want everyday pictures and sounds; they want to indulge themselves in spheres that are usually unattainable for them.'

With this particular concept, Weimar cultural socialism peaked in a sort of holiday culture, a culture for the rare moment. This 'culture apart from work' and beyond every life could not, however, give the worker any realizable instructions for achieving the hoped-for socialist society of the future.

It would nevertheless be incorrect merely to regard the cultural socialists' programme and practice as a means of achieving a new ideology, one removed from everyday reality. Cultural-socialist ideas influenced child-rearing, family life, home furnishing and home-building. Unfortunately, the significance of cultural-socialist forays into these areas has not been researched so far. Cultural socialism in the Weimar Republic had the same function as that of the socialist programme for the future of the pre-World War I workers' movement. Cultural socialism functioned as an integrating force, ideologically elevating political and union practice and giving the labour movement a perspective for the future. It made co-operation with state and society possible without obscuring the dividing lines between socialist and 'bourgeois society', and without giving up socialist expectations for the future. The greatly altered conditions that were to be found in the transition from Empire to Weimar Republic made these difficult tasks even more difficult. The flight of parts of cultural socialism into the culture of the elevated moment, far removed from everyday reality, was a consequence of these difficulties. At the same time, it was a sign of the great problems the Social

Democratic and union labour movement faced in coping programmatically with the changed political and social environment.

Cinema and Working-Class Culture

One can understand the retreat of cultural socialism's utopia from the everyday world only if one realizes to what extent the enormously expanded leisure-time industries permeated people's everyday lives after World War I. In the Weimar Republic, movies and radio became mass media which many saw as new and dangerous powers controlling people's emotions. These media were referred to as 'great-power film' and 'great-power radio'. Whoever controlled film and radio would rule the world – and many were fully convinced of this, Social Democrats as well as Catholics, Communists no less than Conservatives. The Social Democratic and Communist workers' movement reacted to these new media in a traditional manner. They attempted to set up similar institutions in order to make these new cultural developments a part of the labour movement. However, from the very beginning, the labour movement could compete neither with the expanding film industry nor with radio, which had existed in Germany since 1923. By the end of 1919, there were already 2,386 cinemas in Germany. In 1929, with more than 5,300 cinemas, Germany counted as the largest European market for the international film industry in Europe. In the middle of the 1920s, more than two million people went to the cinema every day, and in 1924 in Berlin alone, over 40 million movie tickets were sold. Radio developed at a yet more furious pace. Radio broadcasts began at the end of 1923, and by 1932 there were already 4.1 million subscribers. After Britain, Germany had the second highest number of radio subscribers in Europe. The percentage of working-class listeners to German radio grew to 25.6 by 1930; about three quarters of all listeners were people who were not self-employed.

The great number of organizations within the German labour movement discussed intensively how they ought to react to the challenge of these new media. In 1926, the Social Democrats founded the 'Socialist Cultural League' as a cultural umbrella organization. In 1929, the League held a conference concerning the new media in order to learn how the 'great powers' of film and radio could be tamed. Let us first consider the strategies that were discussed: the most radical suggestion was to 'socialize' the film industry completely. The SPD brought up this suggestion frequently. However, because of the film industry's international involvement and the pre-eminence of the United States in film production since World War I, this suggestion was impracticable. Most of the participants in the conference held this view. Alternative suggestions were the creation of as many city cinemas as possible, and of state funded film production companies. In 1928, such an attempt at state participation was undertaken when the government, with the help of Social Democratic ministers, acquired a majority of stock in the second largest German film company, 'Emelka'. By 1930 this experiment had already failed. One possible consequence of this failure was that the Social Democratic cultural organizations became more pessimistic in their estimation of how much the state could get involved in film production. The cultural organizations had set their hopes on the 'schooling of the masses' in order to reform the cinemas. The reform was to start with the consumer. Social Democrats and unions had first considered producing films themselves. During the Weimar Republic, however, they gave up this idea as they were deterred by high costs and financial risks. They then devoted themselves to other ways of influencing the film consumption of their members and their families. One way was through regular film critiques which were published in the Social Democratic press. In addition, films that were labelled 'recommended' by the party's cultural experts were promoted. Among such films were the famous Russian films, of which Eisenstein's *Battleship Potemkin* is the most notable. The KPD used the 'Russian films' mainly as propaganda material that depicted the superiority of Communist ideology and would help workers identify with the Soviet Union. Moreover, Soviet film production made it unnecessary for the KPD to produce its own films. The SPD had mixed feelings about Soviet films. These feelings ranged from total rejection to enthusiastic approbation. Yet the wave of 'Russian films' abated fairly soon, once the famous Soviet films had proven to be a financial success and had been run in all the large cinemas.

Because it became financially impossible for the workers' movement to produce its own films, particularly after the advent of the sound film era in 1929, and because the original attraction of the 'Russian films' waned, the labour movement was left with only two alternatives, the founding of its own cinemas or of negotiating contracts with commercial cinemas, in order to influence which films were shown. The movement tried both, but with only limited success. There appear to have been only a handful of cinemas that were founded by Social Democratic and Communist organizations in some large German cities towards the end of the Weimar Republic. These proved to be short-lived. Perhaps the Austrian experience served as a warning. The Austrian Social Democrats built up a film company that owned 13 cinemas and supplied another 25 with films by 1934. However, the public's taste and the new sound films forced the company to orient itself along the profit-and-loss lines of commercial film companies. The company could not live up to the lofty criteria of the labour movement.

The possibility of working together with the commercial cinemas seemed to offer more chances than the founding of their own cinemas. But here, too, success was small. It was not possible for the labour movement to bring its favoured films into cinemas in such numbers as to drive out undesirable films. The major cause of this lack of success was to be found in the members of the working-class organizations. The organizations had hardly any influence on their members' choice of films. For example, in a working-class district of Hamburg in 1928, films for adults and children were shown by the working-class organizations regularly over a five-month period. These films had to be suspended because the members showed little interest in them. The Hamburg Social Democrats concluded from this lack of interest that, as far as the party was concerned, films were mainly useful as propaganda devices.

The Social Democratic, trade-union, and also Communist organizations (the latter having attempted to work together with cinema owners far less than the SPD) had their greatest success with propaganda films. In using films as propaganda and instructional material, the workers' organizations were on familiar ground; here they were not subject to the rules of the capitalist marketplace. Up until 1931, the larger local Social Democratic and trade-union organizations had their own equipment for showing films; some even had their own screening rooms and automobiles that took films to various communities. Brunswick offers a good example of how films were used for propaganda purposes. In the district of Brunswick in 1928, Social Democrats set up a travelling cinema called the 'People's Red Cinema'. Set up in a truck, the cinema travelled around to smaller towns and presented film performances that always followed the same pattern. First there was a supporting film, followed by a major film, then the organizers gave a speech, and at the end came another major film. The major films were Social Democratic productions, such as *Am Anfang war das Wort* (*In the Beginning Was the Word*), *Kreuzzug des Weibes* (*Woman's Crusade*), *Freie Fahrt* (*All Clear*), *Der schwarze Sonntag* (*Black Sunday*), or the films *Brüder* (*Brothers*) and *Kinderrepublik Seekamp* (*Children's Republic of Seekamp*), an advertisement for the socialist organization, 'Children's Friend'. In 100 evenings these performances reached approximately 15,000 people, of whom 13,000 would not usually have come to SPD events – since only about 2,000 people usually took part in any 100 normal party events.

Social Democratic and union propaganda films all followed the same pattern. They contrasted the past with the present. The message which was inevitably brought out in all these films was that history was progress, brought about mainly by the labour movement. Let us consider, for example, the film, *Freie Fahrt,* shown by the 'People's Red Cinema'. The bourgeois *Braunschweigische Landeszeitung* of 1 March 1929 said of this film: 'A great four-act film, an advertisement for joining the SPD, a film that could not have been produced more cleverly. Once there was no public relief. A pregnant woman has to work in the factory up until the last moment, while her child plays in the street unwatched. She collapses at her difficult job. "It's too late," says the doctor who has been called to the scene. A sacrifice to the bourgeois society which exploits the worker! Then Social Democracy enters. Workers are shown and told how much they owe to Social Democracy's social services. Social Democracy, and Social Democracy alone, accomplished this; you may thank the Social Democrats by supporting and joining them.'

In all these films, the Weimar Republic appeared as the high-point of history and the films showed how the SPD and the unions identified themselves with the republic. Communist cultural organizations reacted completely differently to commercial films than did the SPD and the unions. The Communists had placed all their hopes on the 'Russian films'. When the public's interest in these films ebbed, the KPD called for the reduction of film to mere 'agitprop'. For the Communists, 'agitprop' meant not only production of propaganda films but also, and more importantly, the mobilization of the populace in order to boycott 'anti-proletarian films'. The KPD, with its calls for boycotts and discussions, assumed the status of a consumer organization, an organization that tried to camouflage its extremely small influence by means of radical phraseology.

In short, the KPD and the SPD had no answer to the large feature films that the international film industry produced and that found a large viewing audience among the workers. Sometimes the parties used feature films to advantage. When showings of the anti-war film, *Im Westen nichts Neues* (*All Quiet on the Western Front*), based on the novel by Erich Maria Remarque, were temporarily prohibited in 1931, the SPD, the unions and other Social Democratic groups organized closed performances for their members in commercial cinemas. Within a few weeks in Berlin alone, 400,000 members and their families had seen the film. But such successes were rare, just as were the discussions that the KPD tried to lead among cinema-goers. Both Social Democrats and Communists considered films to be one of the 'most important capitalist means for controlling people'. Films could not be integrated into the network of the workers' cultural organizations, but some other possibilities for films remained. The organizations' propaganda, educational and cultural work successfully employed films as tools, though film as a central part of the new mass 'popular culture' remained closed to the labour movement as a whole.

Radio and the Labour Movement

With regard to the new medium of radio, the Social Democrats and the trade unions attempted to learn from their experiences with the film industry. At first, there was a desire to have their own radio station, but soon another strategy was adopted. The SPD and the unions wanted the state to take over control of radio; in this way, radio would be taken away from industry, and the SPD and the unions would be able to have some sort of influence over the medium by means of state boards. The Social Democratic labour movement was therefore satisfied when a 1926 law governing radio subjected the new medium to state control. With its particular concept of radio, the socialist labour movement took on the status of one interest and consumer group among many, a group that placed its hopes on the fact that, by law, it would have some influence on the regulation of radio. The labour movement in so doing followed a path that did not lead in the same direction as had the subcultural seclusion of the prewar labour movement. The goal was not to set up a socialist radio station in competition with the bourgeois one; rather, the goal was the democratization of radio. As a result, the SPD and the ADGB turned their backs on radio's officially postulated (but unrealized) claims of being unaffiliated to any particular party. Socialist policy towards radio meant plurality of views, rather than neutrality. In the Weimar Republic, however, the intended democratization of radio under the protection of the state proved unsuccessful. The new 'great power' was not pluralistic and open, as the socialist labour movement had hoped it would be. (With the advent in 1932 of the Papen government, radio became an openly political instrument of government. It was then relatively easy for the National Socialists to enter into the already existing relationship between government and radio.)

The SPD and the trade unions participated in educational programmes, designed to increase understanding of state and society. Working conditions were addressed; for example, the SPD and the unions sponsored programmes about accident prevention in the workplace. The existing radio stations allowed the labour movement different degrees of participation and a particularly good relationship was established with the Hamburg station. In 1928, a Workers' Board of Trustees was set up, the Hamburg Social Democrats and union members took part in it. The Board of Trustees provided, apart from the '*Sonntag-Feierstunden*' ('Sunday Festive Hours'), a programme designed to compete with Sunday morning church services, the leisure-time programme '*Abend der Werktätigen*' ('Workers' Evening') and programmes in the '*Stunde der Werktätigen*' ('Workers' Hour') series. The 'Workers' Hour' series covered a wide range of topics. In 1928, it presented 26 lectures about the Weimar constitution, social work in the cities, welfare work, educational and child-rearing ideals, women in the new state, health concerns, school and home, the housing shortage, and so forth.

The successes that the labour movement achieved in participation in radio programming should not, however, be overestimated. As far as the new medium of radio was concerned, the Social Democratic labour movement found itself in a dilemma. The traditional focus and conception of socialist educational work did not come anywhere near exhausting radio's possibilities. Radio was made up mainly of entertainment programmes, which, in socialist cultural understanding, were more non-culture than culture. Socialist organizations could exert no influence on such strong points of radio. Neither working-class radio clubs nor the labour movement could prevent radio from acquiring a steadily increasing public or permeating workers' everyday lives. The SPD's pluralistic participatory concept did not function to the extent hoped for, and the labour movement neither wanted to, nor could, carry on the prewar tradition of subcultural seclusion. More than anything else, the SPD's and the unions' different place in state and society, as well as the mass media's stronger competitive position, forced the SPD and the unions to follow a different course. This course had become apparent before World War I, but it was only really implemented during the Weimar Republic. For the SPD, following a different course meant looking to the state. The KPD, however, engaged in an uncompromising battle with Weimar democracy. The KPD's attitude toward radio, accordingly, was to reject it completely. The KPD's situation regarding radio was even more desolate than it had been regarding films. While the party had at least been able to make use of the attractive 'Russian films' for quite some time, when it came to radio the KPD had nothing to offer its members. Therefore, the KPD called on its members to tune in to the Moscow programmes.

While all that remained to the KPD was watching and listening to the Soviet Union, together with hope for the future state in Germany, the SPD and the unions at least attempted to secure themselves a modest share in the new mass media by means of their radio and film policies. However, the concept of the entire labour movement ultimately foundered on the shores of both these media, media whose broad influence both the Communists and the Social Democrats assessed as being extremely powerful, as did the trade unions.

The ability of the labour movement to integrate societal innovations into its own network of cultural working-class organizations had found its limits. With the spread of 'popular culture' through radio and film, the inner disintegration of the cultural labour movement in the Weimar Republic began to take place. These experiences explain why no serious attempts were made after 1945 to recreate the old cultural labour movement in its entirety. The building of a socialist subculture no longer belonged to the politics of the SPD and the unions.

14 The SPD in German Politics and Society, 1919–1929

Detlef Lehnert

German Social Democratic political action in the 1920s was determined by three fundamental decisions, for which the most important prerequisites had been created in the year when the Weimar Republic was founded.

Firstly, without the support of a clear majority of the SPD members, parliamentary acceptance of the Versailles peace treaty on 23 June 1919 would not have been possible. No more than the right-wing parties did the majority of the liberal German Democratic Party (DDP) representatives wish to shoulder responsibility for acknowledging the consequences, unpopular among the people, of the German defeat in the First World War. True, the first SPD chancellor, Scheidemann, had resigned in dissent from the party majority and, under the initial impact of the harsh peace conditions, he pathetically exclaimed in the National Assembly, 'Any hand must wither that puts itself and us in these chains.' But such initial indignation had abated just as quickly as the protest, five years before, against the unleashing of the world war, for the practical consequences of strongly worded resolutions were rather too daunting: it was simply impossible to reject the war credits and now the Versailles treaty, thereby posing a challenge to the respective domestic or foreign adversary, while simultaneously remaining in the accustomed groove of Social Democratic party activity.

Secondly, the decision to organize the state as a parliamentary democracy had been taken as early as 19 January 1919 during the elections, made possible by the SPD, for the constituent National Assembly. The acceptance on 11 August 1919 of the Weimar constitution with the votes of the SPD, DDP and Centre Party codified the old ideals of the 1848 revolution, which had for decades remained the model of the SPD despite occasional verbal skirmishes with bourgeois democrats. The far-reaching identification of the unshakeable principle of popular sovereignty with the egalitarian ballot ('one man, one vote', and now 'one woman, one vote' as well) was so solidly anchored in Social Democratic tradition that the workers' and soldiers' councils, created during the November Revolution, were regarded merely as improvized bodies of debate and administration, not as viable state organs. The alternative of the 'pure council system', favoured by the socialist left and the Communists, which because of its explicit emphasis on factory workers as the foundation of elections could function only as the 'dictatorship of the proletariat', contained at the domestic level the same type of problem that faced every radical collision course in foreign policy: it was unthinkable politically to denaturalize, as it were, the bourgeoisie by depriving it of the vote on the one hand, while on the other to achieve the external and internal pacification which the overwhelming popular majority craved after four years of war.

Thirdly, the agreement between the leading groups of trade unionists and entrepreneurs on 15 November 1918 denoted the path of class compromise and renounced every vision of an 'expropriation of the expropriators'. Even though party and union rhetoric did not relinquish the goal of socialization of the means of production, the practical politics of the Social Democrats in the 1920s can be expressed by the motto, social policy rather than socialization. The reasons for largely rejecting direct interference in private property to promote strategies of state-socialized compensation are quite comparable to those pertaining to political realism on the basis of Versailles and parliamentary democracy: without a willingness to run the risk of civil war, of which the social ravages under the dictatorship of the Bolsheviks in Soviet Russia presented a repellent example, the implementation of far-reaching measures of expropriation did not seem feasible to the SPD, with the result that this frontal trial of strength was removed from speculation at the outset.

If we designate the Versailles treaty as the external, parliamentary democracy as the internal and the welfare state as the social conditioning factor of the Weimar Republic in its founding days, then the Social Democrats had good reason for confidently presenting themselves as the 'state party of the republic', as the editor-in-chief of *Vorwärts,* Friedrich Stampfer, called it in 1924. For no other political party so consistently and to the bitter end adhered to 'fulfilment' of the peace treaty, the letter and spirit of the constitution and a social-political class compromise as did the SPD. It would surely be wrong and resemble the creation of a legend to canonize the SPD because of this adherence to principle. The imperturbable loyalty to political principles, which appear to command consensus today just as they could claim, at the time, the persuasive force of rational argument, simultaneously demonstrated German Social Democracy's lack of flexibility. Committed to a traditional policy of organization, in a phase of crises pregnant with emotion, it perceived political mass psychology as a largely alien realm.

SPD Peace and Military Policy Between the World Wars

The radical blow which Versailles dealt to the hopes for a mild 'Wilsonian Peace' (linked to the League of Nations concept of the American president) placed severe doubts on the credibility of Social Democratic foreign policy from the outset. French policy regarding the Rhineland in particular, which under the nationalist right-wing government of Poincaré bore an expansionist character until 1923, lacked the slightest regard for the reputation of the German republican governments, thus decisively contributing to the spread of German nationalist and early fascist feelings of resentment in the middle strata.

There is general support for the thesis that, after the shattering vote loss of the SPD in the federal parliamentary elections of June 1920 (21.7 per cent, from 37.9 per cent in January 1919), the Social Democrats could participate in the government only because of agreement on foreign policy with the moderate bourgeois parties. This was as true for the renewed Weimar coalition under Chancellor Wirth of the Centre, after the London ultimatum of the Western powers in May 1921, as with regard to the Grand Coalition (with the industry-linked German People's Party or DVP) which had to be formed in August 1923 at the climax of the hyper-inflation, accelerated by the 'Ruhr struggle' against the French occupation force. Even the return of the SPD to the federal cabinet after the electoral success of May 1928 (29.8 per cent as against 20.5 per cent and 26 per cent in May and December 1924) lasted just as long as Foreign Minister Gustav Stresemann was able to induce his DVP, which was drifting to the right, to tolerate a treaty policy feasible only in concert with the Social Democrats. Once parliament had passed the Young Plan, against the bitter resistance of the 'national opposition', the break between the governing coalition and the SPD, provoked by the industrial wing of the DVP, followed without delay in March 1930.

Thus the SPD as a government party had always to shoulder 'state political responsibility' when no viable majority for an unpopular foreign policy in the shadow of Versailles could be formed without it. Yet Social Democrats like Hermann Müller, intermittently foreign minister and later chancellor, or Rudolf Breitscheid, the party spokesman known for his diplomatic skill, deserve considerable credit for pushing through an international policy designed to reduce European tensions. Even a determinedly anti-socialist right-wing liberal such as Stresemann had to keep acknowledging that neither his much-vaunted treaty policy nor occasional special missions (in talks with the French left, for example) would have been possible had not the Social Democratic workers' movement protected him on his internal flank against nationalist broadsides.

For the Weimar SPD, its multifariously handicapped relations with the military constituted an especially delicate subject. As a power instrument of the Prussian authoritarian state, the standing army in the German Empire had been until 1918 one of the foremost enemies of Social Democracy. In the days of Gustav Noske, from the January 1919 unrest in Berlin (with the assassination of Rosa Luxemburg and Karl Liebknecht) to the Kapp Putsch in March 1920, the units of a new federal army, in part created out of the Free Corps, officially operated under orders of a power-conscious SPD politician. But troop units hostile to the republic, some of which, like the putschists of the Ehrhardt Brigade in Berlin in 1920, were already marching under the swastika, had so extensively assumed independence from the political leadership and committed so many atrocities against rebellious workers that Noske's term of office caused the SPD to lose an essential part of its support to the Independents (USPD). After the resignation of its defence minister and the electoral defeat in June 1920, the SPD no longer could, or wished to, claim authoritative influence on military policy.

The consistently negative evaluation by the SPD of the domestic role of the military is to be carefully distinguished from the party's much debated attitude to national defence. To be sure, there existed above all in the USPD, whose moderate wing had returned to the majority SPD by 1922, a decidedly pacifist element which in the left-wing strongholds of the SPD, such as Saxony, showed traits of anti-militarist principles in the spirit of prewar Marxism. As a 'national' party of long standing, however, whose majority had voted for all the war-credit bills from 1914 to 1918 and maintained the '*Burgfrieden*' or internal truce, the SPD supported the 'defence of the fatherland' on principle. The aim of Social Democratic policy, therefore, was not the removal but rather the 'republicanization' of the defence force which, within the democratic constitutional state, had increasingly become a foreign element tending toward authoritarianism and restoration. The frequently postulated aversion to any contact with anything military did not exist in such a comprehensive sense, as is evident from the remarkable popularity enjoyed in large sections of the party rank and file by the *Reichsbanner* Black-Red-and-Gold, founded in 1924 and dominated by the SPD as an organization to protect the republic.

Parliamentarism Without a Democratic Political Culture

The resolute partisanship of the SPD in favour of parliamentary democracy (which in 1918–19 eliminated chances for realization of all the council models and dictatorship concepts of the radical left from the outset) failed to earn the party much kudos from the German bourgeoisie. By the time of the 1924 federal elections the Social Democrats had lost that new potential voters' block in the middle strata – predominantly employees, but lesser officials and small independent persons as well – who in 1919, together with the agricultural workers, had given the party its considerable vote-increase compared to prewar days.

The dramatically growing discontent with parliament not only led about one third of the Social Democratic workers irretrievably into the camp of the Communists (KPD) but also damaged even more strongly the loyal constitutionalist coalition-partners of the SPD in the bourgeois centre.

Given this historical background, it is open to serious doubt whether the widespread reproach directed at the Weimar parties, and not least at the SPD, that they were insufficiently ready to compromise and resolved to govern is justified. Until 1923 the consensus experiment of the democratic parties had been practised by all participants with much good will, admittedly at the excessively high cost of the loss of most of the marginal and even of many regular supporters to the radical protest parties on the extreme right and left, which were free to proclaim their slogans and promises without the burden of enforced compromises and governmental responsibility. The negative experience of coalition politics made the acceptance of opposition status easier for the SPD at the federal level from 1924 to 1928, and this role indisputably gave the party its longest and most continuous period of organizational consolidation and increasing electoral attractiveness. At the same time the Social Democrats under their Prime Minister Otto Braun continued, together with the DDP and the Centre, almost uninterruptedly to constitute the government of Prussia which, with 60 per cent of the German population, remained the most significant federal state, and in 1928 the SPD in this governing position gained vote-increases for the state parliament which were comparable to those at the federal level.

An investigation of the reasons for the dissimilar political roles in Germany and in Prussia will show the dependence of Social Democratic influence, indicated above in the realm of foreign policy, on the attitudes of possible coalition partners. Whereas in Prussia the Catholic Centre Party, traditionally distant from the right-wing parties which had been closely linked to a Protestant state church until 1918, was more readily inclined to co-operate with the SPD, and while the Weimar coalition usually gained a small majority, both these prerequisites did not obtain in the same way at the federal level. Nevertheless, even in opposition the SPD was able to make its contribution to that relative stabilization of the republic which, in the mid 1920s, created a deceptive semblance of normality after an eventful decade of war, revolution and inflation: while the nationalists and to some extent also the right-wing bourgeois DVP, in their fight against cabinets with SPD members, simultaneously opposed the democratic constitutional order, in reality they still had to make their peace with that order once they themselves held governmental office.

The task of grinding down militant right-wing anti-republicanism in the course of parliamentary routine was naturally reserved to political elites and could not become the successful prescription for popularizing the Weimar system among the people. It is justifiable, therefore, to doubt whether the SPD took the steps appropriate for solidly planting a democratic political culture in the consciousness of the masses. Despite many an authoritarian organizational practice in its own ranks frequently, and with exaggeration, imputed to it, the Social Democratic workers' movement certainly transmitted, apart from solidarity and party discipline, the values of freedom and equality to generations of its members. But at the same time the concentration of party activities, encompassing a broad spectrum of work in education and training, on its own social stratum and on the Social Democratic political subculture carried with it the danger that the party isolated itself even more from those population groups which already confronted it with hostile reserve.

At the time of their founding and rise the Social Democrats had had to develop a subculture sharply distinguished from bourgeois society, for the ruling classes and their authoritarian state had excluded them from the political community as alleged 'vagabounds without a country'. Moreover, the workers' movement, only painstakingly constituting itself with an autonomous political and social identity, could until 1918 claim credit for saving its own members and adherents from anti-democratic influence through the existing institutions and their opinion leaders. After the transition to the republic, the SPD could have relinquished this defensive attitude more forthrightly and might even have taken up the struggle for political and cultural hegemony in state and society with aggressive argumentation. That such endeavours had scant success is explained primarily by the mentality of the German middle strata, whose traditionally anti-socialist and anti-republican sentiments were difficult to change by efforts at persuasion. But given the widespread dissatisfaction with the established bourgeois parties among white-collar employees, officials and self-employed persons, the victorious march of the Nazis as a petty-bourgeois consensus movement would not have proceeded so smoothly if the SPD had first shown greater flexibility in paying attention to the specific status fears of these social groups and to their visions of the future.

Welfare-State Problems in Times of Economic Hardship

The Weimar Republic undoubtedly produced considerable advances in social legislation. The expansion of communal welfare for especially needy people such as war victims and the sick, the introduction of statutory unemployment insurance and the promotion of public housing projects in the 20s are milestones on the road to the modern welfare state. But the political symbol of the workers' advancement in the republic was the eight-hour day, whose impairment by the entrepreneurs in the crisis year of 1923 indicated the dwindling strength of Social Democracy and the union movement.

Although the most important foundations for the Weimar welfare state had been laid through laws and ordinances made as early as the revolutionary months of 1918–19, the actual realization of the more costly reform projects especially (such as social housing construction) had to wait for the period of stabilization beginning in 1924. In this regard it is instructive to note that the SPD, backed by the union revival linked to economic upsurge, was able through aggressive opposition politics during the four years to 1928 to effect greater progress in social policy than during the previous and subsequent periods of its participation in government. This fact, astonishing at first glance, is not unrelated to the circumstance that a considerable portion of social policy lay within the competence of the federal states and of local government, where the SPD, above all in Protestant industrial areas, could occupy a leading position and practised with the Centre, the DDP, or even the KPD, a co-operation that was less ideologically burdened on individual points. Moreover, as the history of the 1927 law on unemployment insurance shows, the employee members of the bourgeois parties felt particularly pressed by an active Social Democratic opposition to produce practical reform work when competing for votes.

Beyond social policy in the narrower sense, the SPD also aimed at a further substitute for unattainable socialization objectives by helping to lay the foundation for the German tradition of co-determination within the workplace through the Works Councils Act of 1920 and through the debate on economic democracy in the second half of the 20s. Apposite in principle as is the criticism that the limited rights of participation under the Works Councils Act were a mere shadow of the workers' control in the factories which had in fact existed in the revolutionary months, even this modest authority constituted progress in comparison with the prewar 'master in my own house' attitude and was, therefore, subject to massive attack by the capitalists. Similarly, compulsory state arbitration in salary questions, supported by Social Democracy, was a thorn in the flesh of employers' organizations: while it limited union freedom to strike, it was to protect employees from arbitrary employers' actions such as mass lockouts.

Increasingly it was its economic policy deficit that became the Achilles' heel of the SPD. In the crisis years of the Weimar Republic its effects were devastating. In 1923 the Social Democratic minister of finance, Hilferding, had already done much of the groundwork for the stabilization of the currency. Yet in his second tenure of office in 1928–29 he, like most of his party comrades, was still obsessed with the spectre of inflation and ready, therefore, to yield to pressure from the bourgeois side in the direction of socially painful economizing measures. Precisely because during the inflation years great captains of industry (Stinnes, above all) had accumulated enormous fortunes at the expense of the living standards of the broad masses, the SPD then felt rather sceptical about the deficit-financed state programmes of investment such as Keynes was soon to make respectable among economists.

The decisive obstacle to a prospering welfare state, however, was the burdensome legacy of war: that is, apart from reparations payments to the victors, in particular the shortage of capital in the German economy and the cost of reproducing the workforce, which had considerably increased in relation to productivity following the physical and psychic damage of those years of destruction and hunger. Thus SPD social policy had to focus primarily on the unspectacular task of alleviating the most acute misery, while the hopes of its adherents for participation in the prosperity of bourgeois circles during the 'golden twenties' were largely disappointed. Perhaps pre-1914 Social Democratic theorists had depicted the future socialist state so brilliantly as a land of milk and honey that now, after the blood, sweat, and tears of war, the workers could not condone the new republic's often putting obstacles rather than rewards in the path to their promised social emancipation.

Conclusion

The Social Democrats were truly not to be envied their political task in the 1920s. They stood for international understanding at a time when nationalism – not only in Germany – went through the period of its most aggressive form. In domestic policy the SPD argued for sensible compromises, while ever-increasing groups of its adversaries spread ideological irrationalism and claims of totalitarian absolutism. Its economic and social policy could have shown tangible successes only by peaceable and balanced distribution of growth increments, whereas the last SPD-led cabinet during the winter of crisis in 1929–30 collapsed over the fight of the interest groups about assuming the cost of the growing unemployment insurance deficit. To put it simply and briefly, the SPD finally had to run up against the limits of its influence when, during an upheaval period demanding far-reaching innovation, it tried to persist with its essentially tradition-bound policy.

Regardless of the party's inability to cope with this dilemma, many sweeping verdicts by 'left' and 'right' authors on the failure of the Weimar SPD are overdrawn and unjust because they pay insufficient attention to the objective restrictions on its action. In the Schumacher era after the Second World War the SPD was berated in the West for occasionally forgetting, in its ambitious German policy, that it was not a third world-power capable of challenging simultaneously the United States and the Soviet Union. If this criticism contains some truth, it would be improper to reproach the SPD of the Weimar Republic with having had to remain conscious of the limited possibilities open to a party which gained between 20 per cent and 30 per cent of the votes.

The excessive expectations held of the SPD in retrospect (that it might, through a more efficacious policy, have saved Weimar democracy from destruction) may be related to the fact that as parliamentary life unfolded there was a steady decline in the number of mass-based and reliably republican parties available to the SPD as possible coalition partners. This isolated, universally beleagured and increasingly powerless position of the SPD could not, in the given situation, have been reversed even by a more flexible strategy of agitation and a more forceful utilization of institutional and extra-parliamentary methods of influence. As early as the period 1916 to 1920, during the fateful process of division, German Social Democracy had forfeited the primordial dynamism of a rising class movement. Henceforth the capacity to integrate leftward was lost once and for all – in the face of the relentless rise first of the USPD and then of the KPD to competing mass parties absorbing much energy in the fratricidal struggle among the ranks of the workers' movement. An SPD thus weakened at its working-class base in the 1920s was no longer sufficiently attractive to disgruntled voters of the social and political centre, who were calling for 'strong leadership' in the whirlpool of social insecurity. The upshot was that at the beginning of the thirties it had too little with which it might oppose the National Socialists.

15 The Socialist Trade Unions in the Weimar Republic

Klaus Schönhoven

From the perspective of the Social Democratic workers' movement, the history of the Weimar Republic was a history of disappointed hopes. The democratic parliamentary system, achieved by German Social Democracy during the revolutionary months in 1918–19 against the resistance of the reactionary right and the radical left, crumbled after a decade and was eventually annihilated by the National Socialist dictatorship. The strategy of the Free Trade Unions, aiming to stabilize the social foundations of the republic through a policy for partnership with business, also failed in the 1920s, long before the fascist accession to power in 1933 and its terrorist persecution of the German workers' movement. There can thus be no doubt that the forces of democratic socialism were too weak to save the republic they had founded. Yet it would be a mistake to place the major blame for the failure of Weimar democracy on the SPD and the Free Trade Unions, which, in membership and programme, were closely linked to that party. In the crisis phrase of the republic the leverage of the political and unionized workers' movement did not suffice by itself to withstand the onslaught of the anti-democratic camp. It is proper to ask, however, whether the projected progress of the republic was badly mapped during its foundation phase, and whether the fast decline of the first German democracy points to severe innate faults which determined its fate from the beginning.

Even if one rejects the thesis of predestined decline of the Weimar Republic and judges its chances of survival to be more promising than do the adherents of deterministic interpretations, one must nevertheless stress that the will to change among the Social Democratic founders of the republic was but feebly developed. They trusted continuity too strongly and failed fully to utilize their creative possibilities during the revolutionary transition period between monarchy and democracy. This is equally and above all true of the Free Trade Unions, whose power constellation in 1918–19 was stronger than ever before or since.

When in November 1918 the German monarchist, authoritarian state finally collapsed, the trade unions did not assume the role of spokesman of the revolutionary mass movement demanding democracy and socialization; they opted instead for a policy of co-operation with the employers. The central working community (ZAG) founded a few days after the overthrow of the state, and embracing both business and union leaders, institutionalized the principle of partnership of capital and labour, although at that moment the call for socialization and for abolition of private capitalism found widespread support among workers and white-collar employees. The attitude of the union leadership was, therefore, essentially anti-revolutionary.

The Breakdown of Co-operation between Labour and Capital, 1918–24

The hopes which the unions placed in the process of social partnership were not to be fulfilled in the days to come. Employers accepted the working community merely as an alliance, unavoidable because of the revolutionary predicament, but to be jettisoned as soon as possible. Their primary concern was protection of their property interests, which in November 1918 could be achieved only by social concessions to the organized workers' movement. In return, the unions confirmed the existing economic system, blocked the impetus towards socialization in their own ranks and believed they could create the premise for reforming private enterprise step by step through the creation of co-determination committees. The reformist optimism of the union leaders and the down-to-earth pragmatism of the entrepreneurs made the foundation of the central working community possible, but it was built on shifting foundations because each side joined it with totally different aims.

The policy of the union leadership committees, aiming at participation in, but not take-over of power, encountered much criticism among workers, notably in the Ruhr area. Here a widespread protest movement formed among the miners who opposed the union path of compromise and expressed their displeasure through militant action. The increasingly visible alienation from union reformism of considerable groups of the industrial workers at first culminated in a wave of radicalization which reached its high point in the 'Ruhr war' of early 1920 but which, after the bloody suppression of this revolt, turned into resignation. The proletarian mass protest in the Ruhr and several central German areas of industrial concentration did not expand into an extensive anti-union rebellion. However, the integrative force of the Free Trade Unions in such areas, where syndicalist and Communist groups had their strongest support, had been lastingly weakened.

Nor did the strategy of social partnership enjoy the undivided approval of members even within the Free Trade Unions. Especially among the metal-workers, their largest single organization, the policy of a working community with the entrepreneurial camp was rejected, and the leadership made itself the voice of working-class groups disappointed and embittered at the rejection of socialization. But in fact the fighting spirit of the internal opposition was far stronger than its actual power. At the Nuremberg trade-union congress of July 1919, where the Free Trade Unions adopted a new constitution and a new name – ADGB – the opposition remained a clear minority unable to gain a seat on the executive committee of the umbrella organization. A few months later, in November 1919, a mass strike of the Berlin metal-workers ended with an arbitration result totally unsatisfactory to their union. One year after the revolution the position of the employers had been so well stabilized that they could successfully thwart the unions, and already the fate of the eight-hour day, which the unions had especially celebrated as the 'social achievement of the revolution', was quite uncertain.

The process of the union loss of power, beginning simultaneously with the consolidation of the post-revolutionary order in 1919, was initially overshadowed by a huge increase in union membership which seemingly promised their consolidation and expansion. Between the autumn of 1918 and the summer of 1920, membership of the ADGB rose from barely 1.5 million to 8.1 million, whereas before the war it had taken the unions almost 25 years to represent 2.5 million workers. This victorious march of the ADGB reached its pinnacle as early as the summer of 1920, after which there began a decline, slow at first, but accelerating so as to end, during the hyper-inflation of 1923, in a mass exodus from the unions: in 1924 the organizations forming the ADGB had 4 million fewer members than in 1920, their organized power having been halved in a mere four years.

This dramatic membership decline, financially disastrous to union stability, reflected the decline in the prestige of individual unions and their increasing impotence when opposing the entrepreneurs in the employment market. During the inflation, with the value of money declining and the wage-price spiral growing at an accelerating pace, the unions struggled to compensate for the loss of buying power by pay increases in a race becoming more hopeless by the month. It is true that, except for the year 1923, one cannot speak of German workers' impoverishment during the inflation, but the steady decline in real income highlighted inequalities in the face of hunger and death ever more starkly. The rise of mortality caused by deprivation and undernourishment, the rapid spread of black markets catering above all to the more comfortably off, the poor quality of food, waves of price increases and sinking real wages embittered the workers and alienated them from the trade unions, from which they had expected tangible gains and a fundamental improvement of workers' lives after war and revolution.

The unions lost the workers' respect, moreover, because strikes ended in failure with growing frequency, and because resolute union commitment on questions of wages and hours brought no measurable results. On the political stage, too, where after the SPD withdrawal into opposition in the summer of 1920 the ADGB lacked an appropriate partner, the unions remained in the background. Their demands for taxation of property, for syphoning profits, for strengthening mass purchasing power and for an active state social policy either failed in parliament or were formulated in such general terms as to appear like lip-service rather than carefully thought-out concepts. In this context the metal-workers' strike in southern Germany in early 1922 set a special mark. For the first time since the revolution, the employers again resorted to the mass lockout to force an extension of the working week. The defeat of the unions after a bitter fight of several months encouraged the employers directly to attack the eight-hour day and clearly showed that the union concept of social partnership had been built on sand.

Early in 1923, after the occupation of the Ruhr by French and Belgian troops, the trade unions took the path of 'national resistance'. In its course there arose close co-operation between the federal government, regional authorities and unions against the foreign troops, but this could not stem the process of the power shift in favour of capital. On the contrary, union hopes of being rewarded for patriotic fulfilment of duty by socio-political concessions from the state were bitterly disappointed. The inflation, exponentially accelerating during the months of passive resistance and ending with the total demise of the currency, the catastrophic erosion of the workers' social position and pervasive unemployment led the unions to the brink of bankruptcy. Accession to the national united front could not stop union decline but rather proved to be a miscalculation of dire consequences. The financially exhausted unions fell into increasing dependence on the national government which, while preventing their total collapse through contributions from the treasury, simultaneously eliminated their autonomy. When the employers, after the Ruhr struggle had been broken off in the autumn of 1923, took the favourable opportunity finally to eliminate the eight-hour day, the unions, no longer fit for struggle, had to swallow this without resistance after the relevant national labour ministry had agreed to an extension of working hours.

At the end of 1923 the leadership committees of the ADGB faced ruin. Financially, many member unions had sunk to absolute zero. Organizationally, they had been shaken to their foundations after about 1.3 million workers had left them in the final quarter of that year alone, and while almost 30 per cent of the remainder were unemployed. Politically, the unions were without influence because bourgeois forces clearly dominated the national government. The union concept of social partnership had foundered for good, as the behaviour of the employers during the Ruhr struggle and immediately after it had demonstrated. The ADGB officially resigned from the central working community in January 1924, thus acknowledging the fate of what was now a mere ghost.

The Trade Unions between Inflation and Depression, 1924–29

The stabilization of the currency and the settlement of the question of reparations by the Dawes Plan, which initiated the phase of political and economic rehabilitation of the Weimar Republic, afforded the trade unions a breathing space and the opportunity for organizational consolidation. The precipitate decline of membership numbers was stopped by 1926. Then, until 1929, there began a period of recovery when the member unions of the ADGB showed an increase of one million workers and went about stabilizing their organization and finances. In these years of trade-union regeneration, which contained, after the extremes of revolution and inflation, an element of normalization, the unions developed a feeling of relative security. The beginning of 1928 was accompanied by a reduction of unemployment and a growth of investment. This enlarged the unions' sphere of action and that of the state. The latter now increased its direct and indirect intrusion in the economic and social order.

From the viewpoint of the unions, the 1927 law for providing employment and for unemployment insurance represented a decisive socio-political step forward, the object of decades of struggle. It transferred the care for the unemployed and the organization of employment offices to a federal authority supported and financed jointly by the state, unions and employers. Although this idea was seminal in pointing to the future welfare state, it contained so many unsolved problems when enacted in 1927 that only two years later it was to engender an unsuspected explosive socio-political result, for when the bloc of the permanently unemployed, originally composed mainly of victims of rationalization, kept growing after the outbreak of the Great Depression, this insurance system moved into a severe financial crisis, which caused the fall of the last cabinet to enjoy a parliamentary majority.

The brief period of relative economic and political stability was marked by multi-faceted and contradictory currents demanding much adaptive capacity of the unions. Concentration and cartelization of industry, more intensive work and the increase of productivity through measures of rationalization posed the questions of how the unions could compete against the growing economic power of big business, and how to lead the wages levels up from the low points of the inflation. Through intense struggles, the unions did succeed, with the help of state mediation, in raising average wages and improving mass purchasing power, but their efforts to re-establish the eight-hour day failed. A law of April 1927 provided for overtime supplements, but a general reduction of hours to compensate for progress in rationalization and to relieve unemployment remained elusive. The unions could claim scant success in the area of wage and social policy through direct confrontation with the entrepreneurs, being dependent on aid through compulsory state arbitration and through legislation. When the state withheld this support, which to an economic policy founded on private capital had a merely compensating function, trade-union endeavours often remained ineffectual. This was evident in tax and tariff policy. Here the unions were able to achieve neither an increase in property taxes nor a reduction of protective tariffs which raised the cost of food and mass consumption goods.

Within the ADGB the union loss of autonomy was fully acknowledged. Hopes, linked to the revolution, to remove the authoritarian structures of capitalism having proved illusory, and the principle of equal rights of unions and employers having been infringed increasingly in the postwar years, the committees of the ADGB now discussed how to revitalize the weakened and discouraged union movement. The concept of 'economic democracy', adopted by the union congress at Hamburg in 1928, was to kindle a fresh recruitment impetus and create new perspectives. This programme demanded a gradual democratization of the capitalist economic order through public control, state administrative measures and union co-determination in the management of enterprises. Its authors thus strove to bridge the gap between the actual existence of private capitalism and its necessary transformation into a socially responsible co-operative economy while giving to the unions the outline of a perspective pointing beyond the misery of the day. The hopes which the ADGB placed in this programme, however, were not fulfilled; rank-and-file faith in progress could not be mobilized. The response to the Hamburg resolutions remained meagre even within the unions, for at the end of 1928 the acute intensification of the struggles for redistribution commanded increasing attention.

In November of that year the Ruhr iron strike, pitting the iron industry of the Rhine and Westphalia against all the metal-workers' unions, occupied the public more than any other domestic political problem. In this wage conflict, derived from union demands, the entrepreneurs from the beginning showed more concern with the principle of compulsory state arbitration than with mere bread-and-butter issues. Since the autumn of 1923 the state had interfered repeatedly in wage-rate arguments so as to defuse them through awards by the state chairman of the arbitration commission. This massive state intervention in work controversies encountered scant appreciation in the employers' camp where it was suspected that wages were thus politically dictated to support the weakened unions. The ADGB itself had strong misgivings about state regimentation, which blunted the strike weapon and considerably curtailed union autonomy. In practice, however, state arbitration was accepted because confidence in one's own strength was not strong, and extended strikes had to be avoided.

During the Ruhr iron strike the radical wing of Rhenish–Westphalian heavy industry sought confrontation with the state. It rejected the award of an arbitrator appointed by the state labour ministry, and late in October 1928 more than 200,000 workers were locked out. This provocative step was to challenge the authority of the state and to start a frontal attack on the wages agreement principle and, ultimately, on the entire social order of the Weimar Republic. At the same time the employers' offensive had political motives, for its was to be a drastic demonstration to the SPD, which had re-entered the national government in May, and to its union wing, of the limits of public influence on private enterprise. When in December this strike was finally settled through special arbitration under the chairmanship of the Social Democratic Reich labour minister, each side had won half a victory: the state was able to demonstrate its legal position only on the second try, after public opinion had taken a clear position in favour of the locked-out workers, and because special arbitration largely met the demands of the employers; in turn, the heavy-industry agitators had to cancel their attack on the arbitration principle and settle for a compromise.

Although the power struggle of the Ruhr iron strike did not totally wreck the edifice of the Weimar social order, and heavy industry's radical spokesmen were unable to realize their aims, it had become apparent that the dissociation from democracy of influential forces on the capitalist side had assumed disquieting proportions. The course and outcome of the strike marked an important stage in the debates between a highly concentrated economy and a state given to social intervention. The conflict also showed that forces were forming in the ranks of the employers which intended openly to attack the republican system and dislodge the social state. For the unions, which accepted the special award, the strike led to the depressing conclusion that they were largely dependent on state help. They could not mount any lasting resistance against the lockout of hundreds of thousands of workers. As long as the state possessed a democratic base it would be able to exercise its function of union protection. The ADGB saw quite clearly that politicization of redistribution conflicts progressively reduced the unions' spheres of activity, even if it did not yet perceive how quickly economic crises could be escalated into political crises.

The Trade-Union Road to Impotence, 1929–33

The beginning of the World Depression in the autumn of 1929, prefigured in Germany by a decline of the domestic economy since 1928, placed a new heavy burden on the unions, with which they could not cope in the long run. After the stock market crash of New York in October, scarcely any contemporary, not even among the trade unions, understood that this was an epochal event signifying the onset of a world-wide catastrophe. It was not for a year that awareness of the scope of the economic earthquake grew and that people began to grasp the extraordinary extent of this crisis, which was to dwarf every economic disaster that people had experienced since the war. The dramatic increase of unemployment, which threw millions of people into misery and despair and caused them to react with radicalism or with resignation, soon forced the unions to abandon optimism and to face the facts. The number of unemployed rose from two million in 1929 to three in 1930 and to four and a half in 1931; it reached its highest point of 6.2 million in February 1932. In the previous year, one tenth of the population had been affected by unemployment. This figure rises once the number of the welfare unemployed, who were outside the statistics, and of the part-time workers, is included. In areas of strongly concentrated industry above all, which suffered especially under the crisis, unemployment become the fate of the masses.

The impact of the crisis on the unions was devastating. Abruptly the brief phase of organizing consolidation ended and was replaced by a strong membership decline which signified the workers' constantly dwindling confidence in the concept of union commitment. Thus the ADGB lost more than a quarter of its membership between 1929 and 1932; in July 1932, two-thirds of the remnant in the ADGB were out of work or worked part-time; certain unions – construction, factory, textile – where the economic decline was even greater than elsewhere, declined by more than 40 per cent. The financial poverty of the unions reduced their activities considerably. Workers' struggles were senseless when employers could easily replace strikers by the unemployed; no effective crisis strategy was found against wage reduction when during arbitration discussion the state left the unions, which were incapable of fighting, in the lurch and placed no value on the improvement of mass purchasing power. Under such circumstances the reputation of the unions was bound to decline in the view of their members and of the public. They were largely impotent and lacked allies.

In early 1930, the rupture of the Great Coalition had brought about the failure of the last parliamentary majority government of the Weimar Republic, and the SPD had left the national government once and for all. The apparent cause of this ominous change of government was a dispute over the financing of unemployment insurance, but the fundamental subject of debate was the antagonism between capital and labour. For the unions and the wing of the SPD they controlled, it was a matter of ending the policy of dismantlement and of permanent concessions to the bourgeois coalition partners, because this policy not only endangered the unity of the ADGB and the SPD but also undermined their identity as reformist movements. For the leading groups of the army, large landholders and big industry, which now coalesced into an anti-republican united front, the declared aims were the removal of parliamentary power and the establishment of an authoritarian system of government. The prerequisite for the realization of these intentions was the elimination of the Social Democratic workers' movement from the Reich government. Thus the political right aimed resolutely at the demise of the Great Coalition. When this governmental alliance broke up in March 1930 because of a superficial quarrel about a minor increase of contributions to unemployment insurance, the anti-republican manipulators behind the stage had long cleared the way in the direction of a presidential government which was to govern without, and if need be act against, the Social Democratic workers' movement. As of April 1930, therefore, the ADGB had to struggle against a twofold threat: an historically unprecedented economic crisis and a crisis of the political system, both of which kept reducing its action scope.

After the coalition breakup and the transition to the authoritarian presidential government the unions were clearly on the defensive. Their classical function as representatives of wage-earners' economic interests had been undermined. Their parliamentary Social Democratic ally in the struggle for the maintenance of the republic had been excluded from national politics and could no longer provide state protection and support for union social policy. Even though the reactionary enemies of the republic pursued no common programme, for their concepts ranged from monarchist to fascist goals, there existed nevertheless among these power-hungry groups a fundamental consensus aiming at a far-reaching emasculation and incapacitation of the unions and at adapting them to a policy commensurate with the interests of industry. This is equally true for the moderate forces among the employers in export industry, who suggested in the summer and autumn of 1930 that the unions co-operate with them in fighting the crisis. The price of this collaboration was wage reduction, loosening of the wage agreements, and social retrenchment at the workers' cost. This price the unions thought too steep, for as junior partners of the entrepreneurs they had to fear the loss of even more esteem among their members, coupled with the adoption of a dependence threatening to turn into a deadly embrace. They also recalled their bad experience with the central working community in the early years of the republic which made a formal revival of that problematical truce appear less than advisable. From then until 1933 the forces in both camps willing to co-operate restricted themselves to informal contacts to avoid a complete rift between capital and labour.

After the catastrophic outcome of the September elections in 1930, resulting in the breakthrough of the NSDAP, which became the second strongest party in the national parliament, the threat of an openly fascist dictatorship and, therefore, the danger of the total destruction of the republic were fully apparent. In this situation the ADGB and the SPD resolved to tolerate the governing presidential cabinet of Brüning so as not to promote the anti-republican cause. After 1930 no one in the camp of democratic socialism was able to propose a practicable way out of the the dilemma of having to tolerate an authoritarian regime so as to prevent the complete abolition of the legal and social state foundations of the Weimar constitutional order. The Social Democratic workers' movement froze and lost its character as a movement. Under the twin pressures of state crisis and economic crisis there existed no scope for reformist impulses in the direction of social consolidation of the republic. At the same time the social basis for the maintenance of the democratic norms gained in 1918–19 was weakened continuously. The predicament of the workers' movement was exacerbated, moreover, by its political and ideological conflict with the KPD, for the latter hoped to exploit the economic crisis so as to mount a revolutionary offensive and did its best to destabilize the republic and to label reformism, which it considered bankrupt, as 'social fascism' and thus to defame it.

The unions had no tool with which to counteract this double lock from right and left. In 1930 and 1931 they lacked a plain strategy to tackle the economic crisis; their policy was limited to verbal protest against the progressive reduction of wages and social measures through state emergency edicts, but the national government did not respond, and hungry members remained unfed. Rapidly increasing layoffs not only wore down individual resistance of men affected by unemployment, sinking real income and growing social misery, but also reduced fighting opportunities for the unions. Demoralized members and empty strike coffers were not productive of effective mass movements. The economic crisis, weakness of organization and political isolation weighed heavily on the shoulders of union leaders who now simply lacked the strength to throw off this burden and to find a way out of the blind alley of toleration.

It was not until the winter of 1931–32 that the unions more clearly distanced themselves from the Brüning government, whose policy of reduced expenditures, dictated by the primacy of foreign policy, had led to a more and more ominous intensification of the internal crisis. The ADGB now entered the emergent debate on the possibilities of an anti-cyclical economic policy with a job-creation plan. This project demanded an active state economic policy to initiate the revival of the process of production through public works to the value of two thousand million Marks. The programme of the unions assigned absolute priority to the question of job creation, and they disregarded any apprehension that the expansion of so much credit would endanger the stability of the currency and conjure up the spectre of inflation. This misgiving also surfaced in the ranks of the SPD, but it was not only the fear of inflation which determined their reserved attitude to these union proposals. Within the party there was also a discussion, led notably by orthodox Marxists, of whether it was at all proper to appear by the sick-bed of capitalism in the role of a healer if, after the death of the patient, one hoped to be his triumphant heir. This controversy over the point of emergency aid to the beleagured capitalist order contributed to the alienation between party and unions, and late in the autumn of 1932 the latter openly considered a loosening of ties to the SPD.

It is true that the unions finally evaded a decision on principle and did not end their alliance with the SPD, but they carefully checked all the possibilities which seemed to open up a path out of political isolation and economic impotence. After Brüning's fall, and after his successor Papen's effective frontal assault on Prussia which, until July 1932, had been a bastion of democracy, things had come to such a pass that a policy of inactive waiting was no longer defensible from the union viewpoint. In its search for alternatives the ADGB leadership now followed paths pointing clearly to the right and developed corporative and corporate-state concepts. Such considerations took stronger shape under the chancellorship of General Schleicher, who succeeded Papen in November 1932 and led the last presidential cabinet before Hitler was nominated chancellor. The plan, envisaged by Schleicher himself, of a 'union axis' extending from the left wing of the NSDAP to the ADGB and furnishing an extra-parliamentary mass basis for his cabinet failed after non-committal early talks, but the movement of the unions towards the national camp left its imprint.

The incipient discussion in the union press of a possible symbiosis of nationalism and socialism signified a verbal curtsy to the anti-democratic spirit of the time and a way to edge closer to models of corporate-state constitutions. By turning away from models of reformist–socialist orientation, which for decades had been the programme stabilizing the close links with Social Democracy, the ADGB entered on the downward slope of opportunism and in effect played into the hands of the National Socialist policy of *Gleichschaltung* ('forcing into line'). This approach was to reap its bitter rewards after January 1933. Hopes for the maintenance of relative independence in Nazi Germany soon proved to be a cruel illusion. Hitler was determined to solve the union problem by force, even though in the first weeks of power he manoeuvred with care so as to minimize the risk of massive resistance by the workers' movement.

When the union leaders insisted on the policy of 'national reconciliation' in April, despite the start of nationwide persecution of their members and functionaries, and when their strategy of adaptation culminated in the surrender of their ideological foundation, the plans for the liquidation of the trade-union movement had been long completed. The attempt to prevent the death of the organization by surrender of all principles failed completely. On 1 May 1933 many union members, on the orders of their leaders, entered the ranks of the marching columns of the demonstrating Nazi participants. One day later the union offices were occupied and the leaders arrested. National Socialism taught German unionists the lesson that social emancipation of the proletariat cannot be bought through capitulation to fascism.

16 'Equal but not the Same': The Social Democratic Women's Movement in the Weimar Republic

Karen Hagemann

The shackles of millennia have burst overnight. . . .
Only yesterday German women were in bondage, an oppressed sex, to whom even an awakening democracy had little to offer. Today German women are the most free in the world. They have complete and unconditional equality with men, and they can elect and be elected to any corporate body. Whom do they have to thank for their freedom and equality? The tempest of revolution that broke over Germany with tremendous and irresistible force on 9 November . . . German women rejoice, for you have cause to do so!

With the above words in its issue of 6 December 1918 the Social Democratic women's magazine *Die Gleichheit* (*Equality*) greeted the 'equal civil status' of women accorded them by the new revolutionary government of the Council of People's Commissioners (*Rat der Volksbeauftragten*). They show clearly the great hopes cherished by the female Social Democrats, as well as by many other women, in the days of the November Revolution. At last women had gained the right to vote. Their equality was for the first time anchored in the constitution of the Weimar Republic in August 1919. With this 'civil equality' a crucial objective of the Social Democratic women's movement was attained for which they had fought for many years. The SPD had been the only party in the Empire which had demanded for both sexes universal and equal suffrage. Even the middle-class feminist movement was predominantly against this demand; it merely supported the 'lady's vote', an extension of the existing three-class suffrage. Only in the First World War, after the Imperial government itself had begun to consider suffrage reform in the face of increasing internal unrest, did the prevailing attitude of middle-class women alter. Then the Women's Suffrage Association (*Deutscher Verband für Frauenstimmrecht*) spoke out for general and equal suffrage. Towards the end of 1917 middle-class women had become as committed to this demand as were the female Social Democrats. On 19 January 1919 women in Germany were permitted to vote for the first time.

Hopes for Equality in Civil Status

To the members of the Social Democratic women's movement, the right to vote was the visible expression of the equality of status of women in the new Germany. In the opinion of the leading functionaries of this movement, the attainment of 'equality in civil status' called for a revision of the old socialist theory of emancipation. Marie Juchacz, women's secretary of the party executive after the split in the Social Democratic Party in 1917, described to the National Assembly in February 1919 the changed perception of feminist issues. Her speech, the first by a woman to this parliament, was programmatic in nature:

> Through political equality my sex has now been given the possibility to develop fully its potential. Only now may one justifiably speak of a new Germany and of the sovereignty of the whole people . . . I would like to say here that in the present climate in Germany the woman question no longer exists in its old form, that it is solved. We will no longer need to fight for our rights with demonstrations, resolutions and petitions. From now on the political struggle will take different forms. Henceforth we women have the opportunity to use our powers within the framework of freely chosen party groups sharing a similar philosophy of life. But with this we do not give up the right to be different, to be female persons. It is far from our aim to deny our womanhood merely because we have stepped into the political arena.

Leaders of the Social Democratic women's movement considered that the basic premise for female emancipation had been set by civil equality. As a further step towards their emancipation they envisaged a 'systematic extension of specifically feminine cultural influences'. It was now the task of women to oppose 'coolly rational male politics' with a political approach 'mingling reason with emotion'. Women were seen as the 'born protectors of human life'. Areas of female involvement in politics were therefore seen as social policy and welfare work, as well as child-rearing and education. In these fields, which allegedly 'matched the natural inclination of women', women might bring to bear their 'specifically feminine cultural influence'.

At the root of this sex-specific emancipatory strategy of the Social Democratic women's movement lay a polarized image of the sexes: the woman was set in juxtaposition to the man as 'equal but not the same'. Her being was defined by her motherliness, which found expression in an attitude to life dominated by humane impulses and emotions. In contrast to this altruistic woman, the male attitude to life was characterized as rational, more generally orientated and objective. A new and truly moral and humane world could develop only if the 'male culture of facts' were complemented by 'female motherliness'. This polarized image of the sexes was vindicated biologically in the alleged 'nature of woman and man'.

Such a perception of feminist issues differed only slightly from the concept of 'organized motherliness' promoted by the middle-class feminist movement. The leaders of the bourgeois Federation of German Women's Associations (*Bund Deutscher Frauenvereine*) also proceeded from the premise that the essence of every woman, even the childless ones, was governed by a 'maternal instinct' that must dominate her activity in family and society. For these women the task of the 'motherly' woman was to weave through the whole cultural fabric a thread of 'womanhood that was a mixture of specifically feminine and basically humane characteristics, in order to complement the male fighting and power principle with the feminine love principle' (Thönnessen, 1969, 131 and 162). Despite this fundamental agreement, the leaders of the Social Democratic women's movement and those of the BDF co-operated in and outside parliament only on certain points. On many women's issues they continued to champion divergent views. It was party membership or ideology rather than sex which was the ultimate decisive factor in the making of political decisions on feminist issues. Women active in parliamentary politics demonstrated this especially clearly.

With the propagation of a sex-specific emancipatory strategy, the leaders of the Social Democratic women's movement officially revised their theory of socialist emancipation at the beginning of the Weimar Republic. Admittedly, they still saw the place of women as being within the Social Democratic labour movement, for common tasks and goals would unite men and women of the working class. Yet the old principle that the 'full emancipation' of women could be achieved only under socialism was no longer valid. Economic independence based on non-domestic paid work was no longer viewed as the prerequisite for women's social equality.

Even in the labour movement of Imperial Germany these fundamental tenets of socialist emancipation theory had been called into question with growing frequency. But it was only at the beginning of the Weimar Republic, with the change of the SPD into a non-subversive (*staatstragend*) reform party, that an official revision became necessary. In accordance with party policy generally, the SPD women's movement from 1919 onwards viewed elections as an essential means of giving effect to 'specifically feminine cultural influence'. Initially only few voices in the SPD women's movement criticized this official revision, for the new emancipation strategy enhanced the status of the realm of female experience and thereby boosted the self-assurance of female comrades. The image of the sexes that lay behind this corresponded with the consciousness of most male and female party members.

Women in the SPD

After the November Revolution many working-class women hoped for more extensive social change and equal acceptance of women in all spheres of economic, social and political life. The experiences of the war years, the climactic social and political conflicts, had awakened their interest. The most striking expression of this was the extraordinary popularity of the SPD and the Free Trade Unions among women in the first years after the war.

The influx of women into the SPD and ADGB was so great that the proportion of female members in both organizations grew markedly in comparison with prewar years. Particularly sharp was the rise in the percentage of women in the Free Trade Unions. Yet this development was not to last long. In the difficult postwar years and the inflation era many of the recently recruited female members left these two organizations. The tendency to leave them set in earlier with women than with men and was more marked. As early as 1920 the proportion of female memberships in both organizations decreased rapidly. This reduction in

Table 16.1: Female membership of the SPD and the Free Trade Unions

Year	SPD Female members	Percentage of women	ADGB Female members	Percentage of women
1914	174,754	16.1%	203,648	9.9%
1919	206,354	20.4%	1,192,767	21.8%
1920	207,000	17.5%	1,710,761	31.7%
1923	130,000	10.3%	1,201,390	30.9%
1925	152,693	18.1%	720,825	17.2%
1928	198,771	21.2%	739,645	15.1%
1931	230,331	22.8%	617,968	13.9%

female members continued in the ADGB up to the end of the Weimar Republic. According to estimates of the time, a maximum of 20 per cent of women in the workforce in the 1920s belonged to a union. The proportion of women in the ADGB was not even approximately equivalent to the number of women in the workforce at that time, which was around 36 per cent in 1925. The SPD merely achieved a balancing-out of the decline after the stabilization of economic conditions. The number of members increased after 1924 so sharply that the ratio of women to men was higher in 1931 than in 1919. These trends in female membership show the response of women to economic and political developments in the Weimar Republic and to the policies of both organizations relating to women's issues.

The hopes and expectations which large segments of the women's movement had attached to political equality were soon to be dashed. The already small percentage of women in the Reichstag and in the state parliaments continued to decline until 1933. If women comprised only 9.6 per cent of the Reichstag deputies in 1919, then they were an even smaller 6.1 per cent in 1932. The decline was especially marked in middle-class party fractions. In the course of their political work, female party members and parliamentarians could not but discover how limited their influence was. Critical realism soon wiped out the hopes of the early days. Despite 'civil equality' women were and remained economically, socially and politically severely disadvantaged. Moreover, the women's policies of the Free Trade Unions and initially even of the SPD did not meet the expectations of many new members; the emancipation of women remained an issue of only secondary importance to the two organizations. In the postwar period this was clearly revealed in the attitude of the ADGB and the SPD to female wage-labour: after the war both organizations willingly opted for a demobilization policy which aimed at excluding women from the workforce to make way for returning soldiers. In contrast to the SPD which, under pressure from the Social Democratic women's movement, soon demanded equal rights of employment for women, the attitude of the ADGB remained ambivalent. Officially the national executive of the ADGB had supported this demand since the mid 1920s. As, however, the demand for the dismissal of the 'double earner' (the married woman) became publicly louder and louder in the face of mass unemployment during the years of economic crisis, the ADGB also accepted the non-employment of women as 'the lesser social evil'. This anti-women demobilization policy was not the least reason why quite a few women chose to leave the labour organizations in the early 20s after only a short membership.

In contrast to the Free Trade Unions, the SPD acted on its political experiences of the postwar years. With the coming of stability it troubled itself more about the interests of its female members and intensified its work and agitation among women. This promoted a renewed increase in female membership. The majority of female members whom the SPD was able to win after 1924 were wives of Social Democratic workers. In 1930, 67 per cent of female party members were non-income-earning housewives. This high proportion of housewives corresponded roughly to the social composition of the female populace in the 1920s, when only 36 per cent of all women were part of the workforce. Elderly housewives were especially prominent in the SPD women's movement. In 1930 56 per cent of all female members were between the ages of 30 and 60, while fewer than 19 per cent were younger than 30. This age structure suggests that even non-employed working-class women could find the time to pursue their interests only once the children were older (Thönnessen, 1969, 134). Working women were harder to win to active social commitment than were 'mere' housewives. From them, 'free evenings after work' were only a change of shift. Housework waited. Working wives and mothers with jobs were especially burdened.

Very few working-class women could expect support from their husbands in coping with housework and children. The household and family were generally considered the 'woman's domain'. Even during the Weimar Republic only a small proportion of comrades were prepared to lend practical support to the social activities of their own wives by relieving them of a share of the housework. Many Social Democrats were simply of the opinion, 'It is enough that I am active in the party. Why does my wife need to get involved, too? She has more important tasks to do at home.' These patriarchal ideas found legal sanction in the Civil Code of 1896, which applied with undiminished validity in the Weimar Republic. Clause 1354 of this code gave the husband the 'ultimate right to decide on all matters concerning his joint marital life'.

Women of the workforce could hope for support only from their own sex. Many working-class women and girls lived in an everyday solidarity with women from their family circle or female friends and neighbours who helped each other through the battle against hunger and privation. This was their form of social action, reaching beyond the boundaries of party politics. As a rule, they lacked the time to engage in more permanent organized activity. Rather their commitment was spontaneous, prompted by current everyday problems. In contrast to the men, their starting-point for action was family-oriented.

For the majority of workers' wives and daughters, including ones with paid jobs, household and family were the central points of reference of their feminine lives. At home and at school they were brought up primarily for a 'career as housewife and mother'. They were assigned by society to take responsibility for the 'woman's world' of home and family. Working-class parents still denied their daughters a career training with the 'argument', 'But you will only get married!' As a consequence, the greater number of working-class women, in contrast to men, worked in semi-skilled or unskilled jobs. Marriage appeared to many women of the workforce as 'the least of all evils', as the only tangible means of escape from long working-hours and unfulfilling work. They sought their happiness in family life. A policy of the labour organizations that would represent fairly the interests of working-class women had to be rooted in the aspects of life that were specifically feminine. In the context of agitation, the women's movement had to tackle the problems of home and family alongside those of paid work as parts of a coherent whole.

Female Agitation in the SPD

After universal suffrage was introduced, the main goal of Social Democratic feminist agitation was to secure the votes of women. The activities of the SPD women's movement were largely directed towards this goal. In order to recruit followers, they held more or less regular public meetings for women, typically taking the form of a political talk followed by discussion. Although the party advertised these meetings with posters and leaflets, the response was rarely satisfactory. Attendance dwindled steadily. The ever-falling number of female party members (decreasing since 1920) and the SPD's decreasing influence among male and female voters caused the party leadership to propose a new conception of feminist agitation during the Berlin National Women's Congress in 1924. It was elaborated by Marie Juchacz. In her paper entitled 'Women and the Polls' she claimed that it was, above all, the women who should 'naturally adhere to Social Democracy because of their class' but who had not grasped this and thought it through who would vote for conservative parties. The 'apathetic women' allowed themselves to be 'tossed from pillar to post' and succumbed to 'every propaganda ploy'. The conservative parties therefore had the greatest success in winning female votes, for they met the need for variety and relaxation in an 'overworked and anxiety-filled existence' in their methods of agitation. Juchacz challenged the functionaries present to put more energy into meeting the needs of these 'apathetic women'. As a practical expression of this new concept of agitation, the party executive produced the illustrated magazine *Woman's World* (*Frauenwelt*) in March 1924, complete with a supplement on fashion and children. The Social Democratic slant of this 'female and family magazine' was so carefully hidden under household and family tips, features and uplifting poems, paper patterns and fashion sketches that it was barely discernible as such. Above all, this magazine was intended to appeal to the housewife 'whose interest in politics was still very small'. In its presentation, the *Woman's World* did indeed match the wishes of these women. Yet the magazine could contribute very little towards their critical social enlightenment or to an awakened feminist self-consciousness. It merely reinforced uncritically the dominant middle-class stereotyped roles. In the twenties the *Woman's World* had a circulation of around 100,000 copies. Concurrently the party executive put out the informative paper *The Comrade* (*Die Genossin*) from 1924 onwards for committed female Social Democrats. By the early thirties its circulation had risen to 40,000 copies. The two publications took over from *Equality*, which had folded in 1923.

The new agitational line was received with scepticism by many female functionaries. Above all, they objected to the concept behind the *Woman's World*. As early as the Berlin Women's Congress the magazine's critics labelled it 'a mouthpiece of the middle-class housewife'. What was needed, in their view, was to 'school women in socialism'. They therefore demanded (without success) the reintroduction of *Equality*. At successive national women's congresses the number of critical voices grew ever larger. The Kiel congress of 1927 adopted unanimously a recommendation to the party executive rejecting the *Woman's World* in its existing form and demanding its conversion to a 'socialist light-entertainment paper'. In accordance with the wish of this conference the male editor-in-chief was relieved of his position in early 1928. His successor was Toni Sender, who had belonged to the Independents prior to the union of the SPD and the USPD in 1922. Under her direction the character of the *Woman's World* did change.

As a result of the new agitational line the traditional women's meetings were replaced more and more often by 'women's leisure breaks' and 'women's soirées' in all SPD districts of the nation. The focal point of these new women's meetings was generally something cultural – recitals, songs and music, occasionally interrupted by a short political address or a slide lecture. The main topics discussed at these gatherings were specifically women's issues. The response to this new kind of meeting was held by the women's secretariat to be extraordinarily favourable. From the late 1920s onwards, the SPD feminist movement, like the party in general, made increasing use of the new medium of film to promote their cause. Socially critical documentaries and feature films were shown. A constant cause of criticism from the secretariat was that only a small number of local branches utilized the resources open for agitation among women. Even in 1931, the year of the highest number of public feminist gatherings, only 25 per cent of the 9,864 existing local branches held public meetings for women and barely 12 per cent held film or slide evenings.

The new concept of feminist agitation met the need of many working-class women for more education, culture, entertainment and companionship. To a larger degree the party took up the everyday problems they faced as housewives and mothers. It may be assumed that this new concept of feminist agitation promoted the growth in numbers of female party members.

Social Work as the Area of Responsibility for Women

The main field of activity for female Social Democrats in the years of the Weimar Republic was social work, thus matching the sex-specific strategy of emancipation at the time. Admittedly, the SPD women's movement had been involved in active social work since before the First World War. After the war, however, social work was systematically upgraded by the party executive and the women's secretariat as the main field of action for the Social Democratic women's movement. On 13 December 1919 the party central committee, at the instigation of Marie Juchacz, decided to found a Workers' Welfare Organization (AWO) to provide an organizational framework for the involvement of Social Democratic men and women in welfare work. The guidelines of the new organization in 1920 did not envisage independent welfare initiatives. Rather its members were to exert influence on social legislation and to collaborate in local-government welfare activities. The declared task of the AWO was to bring together all comrades working in the welfare area for the purpose of exchanging their experience and schooling. But in practice, right from the beginning, independent social work was a part of the domain of this organization, faithful to the motto, 'Workers' welfare is self-help of the working-class'.

In 1930, after 10 years of work, the 'workers welfare' was in a position to draw up a successful balance sheet of its operations. In total, it had 2,300 local committees at work in Germany, their activities being carried out by 114,000 mostly honorary members. They provided counselling and information from 1,250 welfare counselling centres, helped in 744 sewing circles and made it possible in 600 local committees for more than 127,000 children to visit local holiday homes. Among their spheres of activity was care for unemployed youth, the feeding of the young, the aged and the unemployed, welfare for pregnant women by loaning them things for the baby, care of sick and needy housewives and mothers by the provision of home help, and, not least, by participation in public welfare. Above and beyond this, the central and local committees of the 'workers welfare' (*Arbeiterwohlfahrt*) were running 173 institutions of their own by 1930, mostly for children and youth, with the help of paid employees. The activities of honorary members were boosted by intensive training. From 1926 the central committee published its own magazine, the *Workers Welfare* (*Arbeiterwohlfahrt*). In the late 20s its circulation was around 8,300.

In the years of economic crisis the calls on AWO's aid resources increased dramatically. In October 1931, in conjunction with other central organizations of the Social Democratic labour movement, the AWO central committee therefore issued a call for 'solidarity support'. The working class was called on to intensify its self-help measures. Proposals were made for the setting up of kitchens, repair services and sewing circles by the unemployed for the unemployed.

Almost all the work of the AWO was carried out by women. They knew from personal experience the variety of privations to which working-class families were subject. Their involvement in social work seemed to them to be particularly meaningful and necessary. Male comrades gladly left the social work to the women, categorizing it as 'women's work'. They were happy to 'divert' the women into this field of activity since women were seen by many, perhaps only subconsciously, as competitors. They even allowed women to have a major role in the executive positions of the AWO. In the national executive of AWO, the administrative working committee, six of the 12 delegates were women. The chairperson from 1919 to 1933 was Marie Juchacz, and her deputy was Elfriede Ryneck. The division of labour between female and male members was systematically promoted by both the party executive and the women's secretariat. In order to maintain female support for the new social-welfare organization, the women's secretariat made social policy and welfare major points on the agenda of the National Women's Congress in 1920 and 1921. Even *Equality*, which until its discontinuation in 1923 functioned as the SPD women's magazine and as the AWO mouthpiece, repeatedly urged on its female readers the view that welfare work represented their 'natural specifically feminine' sphere of activity.

The sex-determined division of labour prevailing in the family and society at the time was carried over into politics. Here, too, the 'female area of activity', social work, was generally downgraded in value. This division of labour was ambivalent in its effect. On the one hand, it afforded women a fulfilling and meaningful form of social involvement without the competition of male colleagues which was so prominent in other areas of the labour movement. On the other hand, in practice it severely limited the social-political field of activity for women. All other areas of politics remained set aside for men. The ruling world of men used the (self) confinement of women to 'specifically feminine' areas to promote and render more permanent the social discrimination against women.

In political practice, the new sex-specific strategy of emancipation worked against women. True, it recognized the specific oppression of women as a sex. Yet the proclaimed 'otherness' of the woman degenerated in feminist work and agitation to a mere connecting-point to lure 'apathetic' women into politics. Their private and social reproductive labour was functionalized in the interests of the male labour movement. Female comrades were to raise their children as class-conscious fighters and thereby to sustain the political combative strength of the male. Welfare work was to relieve social distress only so as to ensure that the working class remained capable of action. Despite the new sex-specific strategy of emancipation, feminist policy remained only a 'secondary issue' for the SPD and the 'woman question' was subordinated to male politics. Women remained discriminated against within the party as a whole.

The Place of Women within the SPD

Female Social Democrats understood their feminist work to be part of their work for the whole party. They therefore demanded that feminist activities be supported equally by the men. But reality was a different story.

In the years of the Weimar Republic, the amount of work devoted to women's issues in the party was not proportionate to the total amount of political work carried out. In 1930 only 21 per cent of the 9,844 SPD local branches had a women's group. The existing 2,099 women's groups were indeed most active, with 86 per cent holding regular women's evenings.

But only 162 local branches offered special educational courses for women. Even at the district or regional level the choice of courses for women was inadequate. Central courses of education for women were offered in not more than 13 of the 33 regions. Traditionally, feminist action was anchored most firmly in the local branches of the larger and middle-sized industrial cities. It is noticeable that the percentage of female members was especially high in those SPD districts which were actively involved in feminist work.

It is true that clause 5 of the party constitution of 1924 stated that female members were to have representation in all executive positions and delegations in proportion to their number. But in practice this regulation was seldom acted upon, especially in the lower rungs of the party hierarchy. In 1930 only 22 per cent of all SPD local branches had a female in an executive position. Women were slightly better represented higher up in the party. At national party congresses an average of 17 per cent of delegates were women. Even one of the five party secretaries was a woman – Marie Juchacz. Apart from her, two other women belonged to the 21-strong party executive – as observers. These were Anna Nemitz, a former Independent, and Elfriede Ryneck. Thus the percentage of women in the top party leadership was around 14 per cent.

In the course of the 20s, leading female Social Democrats protested more and more frequently and volubly against anti-female discrimination within the party. In 1926 the *Comrade* (*Genossin*) published a broad discussion of the place of women in the party. Causes of discrimination within the party were described in this discussion as not only the traditional views supporting fixed roles for men and women, but also the fear of competition from women on the part of many male members. These people liked to see women undertaking the 'minor work' of the party – handing out leaflets, selling papers, taking up collections. But the male membership majority would rarely elect women to the more important positions of responsibility. Women were simply not considered to have the necessary political experience or competence.

In the later years of the Weimar Republic the Social Democratic women's movement saw the necessity, in view of the growing influence of the NSDAP, of combating the prevailing middle-class attitude to women. It officially explained the increasing influence of anti-feminist NSDAP slogans in working-class circles as being 'extremely dangerous because of an anti-feminism slumbering in huge sections of the workforce'. Officials of the SPD women's movement concluded that part of the struggle against National Socialism must take the form of struggle against the anti-feminism within their own ranks.

Content and form of Social Democratic feminist agitation changed once again in the early 1930s. The general political enlightenment of women came once again to the fore, their specific problems being discussed in the context of the whole society. Female Social Democrats became more specific in their criticism of discrimination against women, of their oppression as a 'sex'. They became more aggressive towards prevailing anti-feminism. Feminist rallies and demonstrations replaced 'women's leisure breaks' and 'women's soirées'.

Behind this development lay an altered feminist policy. In the final years of the Weimar Republic, pressured by economic crisis and the growing influence of the NSDAP, female Social Democrats did not only combat the prevailing image of women. Mindful that the experience of 'civil equality' had hardly altered discrimination against women, and realizing that the sex-specific emancipation strategy in practice only reinforced discrimination, they felt moved to re-examine the fundamental thinking behind the socialist theory of emancipation. In the face of increasingly noisy calls for dismissal of the 'double earner', they emphasized the equal right of women to a wage, and the importance of paid work for the economic independence of women and therefore for their emancipation. At the same time they spoke out for social recognition of housework and motherhood as an occupation, and sharply criticized the small value attached to this feminine career by the male-dominated world.

The take-over of power by the National Socialists quickly put an end to this new departure in Social Democratic women's policy.

17 The SPD and the Economic Depression, 1930–1933

Harold James

The history of the Weimar SPD is, despite the party's large share of the popular vote, a sad litany of mistakes, lost opportunities, misguided tactics and a confused strategy. Socialism, so went one of the famous analyses, offered by the trade-unionist Fritz Tarnow, did not know whether it was the doctor at the sickbed of capitalism or whether it was the heir waiting to inherit. The leading ideologist of the party, Rudolf Hilferding, wrote resignedly to Karl Kautsky on 2 October 1931 that 'there is no socialist solution to the crisis, and this makes the situation unprecedently difficult and allows the Communists and National Socialists to grow stronger'.

Historians' accounts only confirm this gloomy portrait of a party struggling in the end not only for existence, but also for a reason for existence. The question that in consequence has come to dominate historical approaches to the SPD is why and how did the party lose its sense of mission? There is a well-established historiography, going back to Arthur Rosenberg's brilliant and polemical *History of the German Republic*, which regards the party as trapped by a failure of the revolutionaries of 1918–19 to convert a formal democratic revolution into a genuinely socialist one. 'The two aims which the government (in 1918–19) sought to obtain – the democratization of Germany and the safeguarding of the working class in such a democracy – were never realized . . . Social reform and electoral reform were, and remained, the special objects of Social Democratic policy. Everything else was either ignored or attacked indecisively and with a lack of enthusiasm' (Rosenberg, 1936, 38). Rosenberg provided the starting point for analyses of the type given be Eberhard Kolb. 'In 1918–19 the Workers' Councils were not only the sole instrument available, but were also the most suitable one, for the conquest and consolidation of positions in the administration – and thus for giving a guarantee of the democratic character of the young republic . . . The failure to realize (the Councils) produced – sooner or later – political failure' (Kolb, 1962, 405). This was because 'the Majority SPD followed a policy which could only have been successful if supported by a broad mass basis, but which in fact only occasionally and inadequately came into contact with the movement of the masses' (S. Miller, 1974, 292). Or, to quote another historian of the SPD, Heinrich Potthoff, 'the parliamentary democratic republic desired by the People's Commissioners could only have an adequate basis if democracy had not halted at the gates of factories, barracks and offices, and if the structures and power relations in the civil service and the economy had been thoroughly broken up' (Potthoff, 1974, 77).

This rather pessimistic conclusion, that only in the immediate postwar turmoil had the political situation been 'plastic', had alternatives been possible, and that later the party had been imprisoned by the force of circumstance, is highly determinist. It is also, measured by the standard of historical analogy, peculiar. Is there in fact an example of such a state where a social revolution based on workers' councils, self-management and local democracy formed the basis of a long-lasting democratization? There were indeed such experiments after the Soviet invasion of Czechoslovakia in August 1968, but they produced economic chaos and, in any case, did not take place in an independent country. Yugoslav self-management has been, where not merely a sham, spectacularly inefficient. On the other hand, there are many examples of states where in the absence of a political revolution, democratization through electoral reform brought social reform programmes and long-run political stability.

So other historians have sought other diagnoses. The fault may have lain in an outdated ideology, in the failure to adjust to the realities of modern politics. The SPD, according to Robert Gates, for instance, 'failed to understand the primary importance of successful economic policy in a twentieth-century industrial democracy' (Gates, 1974, 358). A recent English-language history of the party concludes that the catastrophe was the result of an ideology which 'rationalized political passivity' (Breitman, 1981, 358). This sort of analysis invites discussion of what the options available to the political parties of Weimar actually were.

The war and the subsequent inflation produced dramatic changes in wealth and status. In the case of the petty bourgeoisie, such changes produced a loss of confidence in democratic politics. But there were also great upheavals which affected the SPD's potential support. In the first place, the working class changed. Large factories were established in parts of Germany scarcely touched by industrialization before. Munich, for instance, developed a large armaments industry. New technologies made it possible for unskilled workers to replace more skilled craftsmen in many factories. Then, secondly, a new army of office clerks, technicians, petty civil servants – whose ranks were swollen during and after the war as government faced new tasks – looked for political expressions. There were changes in agriculture too: the war and the revolution brought losses of labour, shortages of fertilizer and infuriating price controls. All these alterations in German society took place with a speed that increased the disturbance – and the sense of disorientation.

Socialist theory produced several responses to these changes. On the one hand, there was the option of dealing with the economic interests of labour within the context of the competitive corporatist pluralism already created during the war, when union leaders and socialist politicians had under the pressure of necessity been brought into the decision-making process and had been able to exact a price. This option – I shall call it the 'labourist' strategy – was followed with great success during the 1920s, but then came under strain as the whole corporatist system of Weimar politics faced the problems posed by shrinking national income during the depression. Another option, on the other hand, would have been to present the SPD as not exclusively working class, but rather as the proponent of 'social policy', of a way of providing rational and just solutions to social issues and social conflicts. These solutions would not be simply the expression of a rather narrowly defined labour bloc, but would represent the interests of the community – with the exception of a very small group of plutocrats – as a whole. This second option, we can establish with the benefit of historical hindsight, was to be fruitful in the years after the Second World War, and is reflected in the Godesberg Programme. But it would depend, too, on economic growth for its continuing success.

The Unions and 'Labourist' Politics

'Labourist' politics were the consequence of the war, and partly also of the collapse of more far-reaching plans for economic control. Instead of using the state to control industry from above, labour would collaborate with business if given higher wages and improved conditions of work. The two socialization commissions meeting in 1919 and 1920 produced only very limited plans for state ownership. An ambition to control the 'commanding heights' of the economy turned out to amount to no more than a wish that coal and potash prices should not be determined exclusively by the owners of those industries. The process of inflation – fuelled by the compact of unions and industrialists – in turn gave an additional significance to the trade unions. They were crucial in negotiating wage rises to compensate for higher prices. So the membership of the unions increased.

However, in the middle of the 1920s the unions, and the SPD, faced a crisis. With the stabilization of the currency in 1923–4, businessmen began to calculate wage rates precisely, and often they implemented very complicated piece-rate systems. The effect on workers was devastating: at a stroke the effect on the labour market of 10 years of rapid technical change – previously camouflaged by the price instability and also by the high rates of labour mobility in the inflationary world – became apparent. Rationalization, speed of work, Taylorism – these were the slogans of the new age. Between 1924 and 1931 10,000 time-and-motion specialists were trained to assess the performance of workers in the metal and electrical industries alone.

After the currency stabilisation, union membership fell off again rapidly. Many members no longer believed that the unions could negotiate efficiently on their behalf. Unskilled workers' wages were depressed by the sudden, unexpectedly high levels of unemployment in the stabilization crisis of 1923–4, and they joined Communist 'opposition' unions. In other trades – such as the Berlin metal industry – employers introduced skill differentials which undermined the bargaining position of unions on behalf of a solidarity of workers. Conditions of work deteriorated, too, as industry succeeded in obtaining large-scale exemptions from the eight-hour day:

This loss of confidence in the labour movement was not surprisingly reflected in the SPD's vote. Together with the USPD, in 1920 it still had 39.5 per cent, while the Communist Party (KPD) had 2.1 per cent of votes cast. In May 1924, however, the SPD's share dropped to 20.5 per cent, while the communists won 12.6 per cent. There was an openly acknowledged crisis in the party: it had associated itself with the foreign political retreat as Stresemann's Great Coalition government abandoned passive resistance in the occupied Ruhr; and it had been unable to protect the working class against the lengthened hours of work, high taxes, low wages and high unemployment of the stabilization period.

The reaction to this crisis confirmed the supremacy of the 'labourist' approach. A few weeks after the May elections, Hilferding wrote to the veteran ideologue Karl Kaustky to explain that the only solution for the present was to press for wage rises within the context of an economy rapidly growing on the basis of an 'organized capitalism':

> We should recognize the forms in which the economy will be organized much more correctly than we have done until now. And here, though I hate to come to a conclusion that is not quite concrete, it seems to me that the increasing power of the workers within the enterprise and their participation in direction would be necessary before we can seek greater state control and centralization. Otherwise, with the present level of the working class and its moral and intellectual capacity, it is to be feared that the reduction of productivity and the inefficiency in the workers' management would more than cancel out the gains made by cartels and trusts, which in vital areas of production have *reduced* the costs of free competition.

As the quotation reveals, it was absolutely essential to this conception that high rates of economic growth should be generated. The belief that this was possible in Weimar proved to be an expensive and embarrassing miscalculation.

Unions came to accept this vision, as expounded also by Hilferding's disciple Fritz Naphtali in a concept of 'economic democracy' (*Wirtschaftsdemokratie*). Control of the enterprise should be built up from below, through factory councils and union pressure, and not from above through socialization. At the centre, at the level of high politics, the party could play a role, not in formulating an economic strategy but in fixing wages and conditions of work. The most celebrated enunciation of this doctrine was Hiferding's statement to the SPD Heidelberg Congress in 1925 that the level of wages, as well as the degree of tariff protection, could be determined through the ballot box. Wages, so went the slogan, were in Weimar 'political wages'. They could be determined by the institutions created in 1923 and 1924 to deal with the chaos produced by currency stabilization. On 30 October 1923 a decree set up a state arbitration system, under the supervision of the Reich Minister of Labour, to deal with disputes over wages and conditions of work. On 29 December 1923 a further decree allowed the chairman of the arbitration committee to impose an award, even if the employers or the unions objected to its terms; and the Reich Minister of Labour could determine that the award was binding. After such a declaration, either of the parties, if they refused to accept the arbitration and continued the conflict, made themselves liable to a legal penalty.

This arbitration system gave the unions a crucial role in negotiating, and membership increased again from the low of 1924. As the economy recovered, dramatic wage rises were negotiated. In 1927 hourly nominal wages rose by 9 per cent, in 1928 by 12 per cent. Some observers even detected signs of a new inflationary development, since prices began to rise also. But in fact substantial real wage gains remained. Another major achievement of this 'stabilization period' was the introduction in 1927 of an unemployment insurance scheme.

This wage push resulted not only in worsening profitability, but also in a political radicalization of the employers, who mounted a vigorous campaign both against the extent of the wage increases and against the system that had made them possible. As the economic situation deteriorated, the scope for wage rises was reduced; and the SPD politicians recognized that labourist politics were becoming a quicksand. The issue came to a head at a time when the SPD, after four years of being in opposition in Reich politics, four years which had helped to improve its electoral performance significantly, was once again in a coalition under Hermann Müller (SPD) which included the right-wing liberals (DVP). Carl Severing, the SPD Interior Minister, by the end of 1928 thought that the wage increases had, in view of falling profitability, gone far enough. Labour Minister Rudolf Wissell (SPD) complained that he had no alternative but to block wage rises. Increases in civil service pay helped to cause a growing budget deficit and, by 1929, funding problems that eventually in December brought down the Finance Minister, Hiferding. Finally, the Great Coalition itself fell in March 1930 when the left of the SPD refused to accept cuts in the rate of benefit paid under the unemployment insurance scheme – cuts which were part of an attempt to relieve the strain on the state budget.

A Problem of Identity

How could the SPD maintain its support when the system it had been operating with such apparent initial success appeared to be collapsing? The end of the wage rises rapidly brought a new crisis of identity within the party. Here there had, in any case, always been a problem.

Many of the leading figures in the party were elderly and dull machine politicians, entirely lacking in charisma. Often they came from rather humble artisan backgrounds. Friedrich Ebert, the first President of the republic, was originally a saddler; Otto Wels, the chairman of the party, an upholsterer; and the powerful Prime Minister of Prussia, Otto Braun, a lithographer and the son of a shoemaker. Often these men were ill at ease in prominent public positions. Rudolf Wissell spent much of his time worrying about trivialities, such as how to invite cleaning ladies to ministerial parties. Sometimes they went too far in the other direction: Otto Braun was fiercely attacked for his love of hunting in the style of a grand seigneur of *ancien régime* Prussia. There were some exceptions, but the articulate and urbane SPD leaders, such as Rudolf Breitscheid, Paul Hertz and Hilferding, looked peculiar because their backgrounds were wrong, or because their education was too good. Breitscheid, for instance, had been a member of an undergraduate fraternity and was attacked for being too good a speaker.

This difficulty of political style reflected a deeper problem about identity. Before the war, everything had been much simpler. There had been an anti-democratic upper class, determined to use every stratagem to keep the workers in their place. The story of the SPD had been that of an heroic and triumphant rise in the face of petty persecution and harassment, until by 1912 it had become the largest Reichstag party with 34.8 per cent of the vote and 110 seats. There seemed no reason why the rise should not continue: industrialization was driving peasants and farm workers off the land, into the towns and into the arms of the socialist party.

After the war, the previously irresistible rise of the SPD no longer appeared as such. The war had split the labour movement, and in the 1920s there were at least three strong working-class parties. At the end of 1918, the KPD had been founded on the basis of the *Spartakus-Bund*: it represented, from the middle of the 1920s, a Stalinized alternative on the left. The KPD attracted some unskilled workers and many of the unemployed, who became disenchanted with the 'free unions'; but there was also substantial KPD support among skilled metal-workers and miners. Parallel with the KPD's attack on the SPD was the activity of the 'Revolutionary Union Opposition' (RGO) against the socialist unions. In 1929, for instance, in elections for the works council of the Bochumer Verein steel works, the RGO had 43 per cent of the votes.

But there was another party, too, with a strong working-class wing and with a trade-union organization: the Catholic Centre Party. In the aftermath of the war and of the democratization of Germany, the Centre became politically more influential. Until the formation in 1932 of the von Papen government, every Weimar cabinet included a Centre minister. In addition, the party self-consciously democratized itself, so that the prewar grip on the party leadership by Catholic lawyers was relaxed, and an important part was taken instead by figures from the Catholic labour movement such as Heinrich Brauns and Adam Stegerwald. The Catholic unionists held social beliefs very similar to those of the SPD, and like the 'free unions' they demanded in the later 1920s an 'active wage policy'. But they also set their beliefs within a Christian–nationalist framework, and they believed that social issues might better be solved by a kind of harmonious interest brokerage than by more open class conflict. This was the area in which they were most strident in the face of 'Marxism'.

In fact, in the Catholic unionists' construction of a model of society in which workers' interests were acknowledged within a more general framework, and in their creation of a people's party (*Volkspartei*) in the Centre, they came close to the new style of politics advocated by some SPD leaders. This new line was in part a reaction to the plurality of political expressions of working-class interests. By the 1920s it was clear that the SPD could not hope to achieve, on the basis of such support alone, a parliamentary majority. Therefore it was imperative to look for non-working-class support; and by the end of the 1920s some commentators were pointing out that as much as 40 per cent of the SPD vote did not come from a traditional working-class constituency. Two potential groups looked particularly promising: the 'new *Mittelstand*' (civil servants and white-collar workers); and the rural vote, land workers and small farmers.

An energetic socialist white-collar workers' union, the AfA–Bund, attracted about a fifth of German's white-collar workers, and a third of the lower civil-service grades. Its chairman, Siegfried Aufhäuser, was on the left of the SPD and tried to win his supporters over to a more militant form of struggle.

In the *Kaiserreich*, most farmers had been discouraged by the SPD's insistence on free trade and its belief that the logic of economic development doomed small farmers to extinction. In 1919, after the collapse of the Empire, there was suddenly a large rural vote; and in the mid-1920s the party tried to woo back the farmers, most of whom in the meantime it had lost either to the Conservative Party or to small peasant parties. A party commission under the chairmanship of Hilferding, and including agrarian experts such as Fritz Baade, set out to reconstruct the SPD's agrarian programme. The commission proposed to nationalize large estates (over 750 hectares), but insisted that small farms were viable and would be left untouched. Unlike in the case of industrial development, there was in agriculture no law of increasing concentration. State agricultural schools, new schemes for fire, hail and cattle insurance, and free legal advice would allow the small farmer to improve his lot. This would fit in well with the overall goals of the SPD since 'a deep solidarity of interests links the working class with working farmers'.

In fact, this solidarity was torpedoed by the insistent demand of farmers after 1925 – which became even more vociferous after the onset of a severe agricultural crisis in 1928 – for tariff protection. All the old issues of the *Kaiserreich* came alive again, and the SPD was forced to take notice. At the 1927 Congress, even Baade was forced to admit that 'for the SPD as the party of the urban masses, the agrarian question is in the first place a stomach question'. In the Reichstag elections of 1928 there was, nevertheless, a slight increase in the SPD's farm vote. Probably this represented a 'reward' for the party's non-participation in Reich government after 1924. Even in 1930 Hans Neisser still believed that one sixth of Germany's small farmers were voting socialist. But the deepening depression primarily benefited the Nazi Party, who in 1929 had already begun to score spectacular success, especially in Protestant rural areas.

Despite these setbacks for the SPD, it remained the key argument of the SPD's 'modernists' that the party would have to make more of an effort to appeal to such non-proletarian groups. This case received support from Theodor Geiger's famous article of 1930, in which the sociologist claimed that the NSDAP was gaining votes as a result of a 'panic in the *Mittelstand*'. Whereas the old *Mittelstand*, the small craftsmen and shopkeepers, were condemned to ineluctable decline, the new *Mittelstand* was only supporting the Nazis because of a 'status-inadequate ideology'. It was the SPD's task to destroy this false consciousness, and to aim particularly to catch more white-collar workers. What programme could the SPD offer as the basis of such an appeal? 'Successful social policy and the fight against unemployment are the only means to win confidence here – and among the workers. The chances for a status-correct [*standort-adäquat*] orientation of white-collar workers will improve automatically. The initial formation of that class is basically at an end: that means that the further growth of the class will be steady and gradual, because there will probably be no sudden leap of the type that has already occurred.'

The Politics of Re-employment Strategies

In the sphere of social and employment policies there might, in fact, exist a fair degree of harmony between groups with apparently rather different status and class positions. This was the more modern concept of politics as a matter of providing guarantees for continuing growth, prosperity, employment and justice that was to replace the SPD's still nominally Marxist conception which held that there was a perpetual 'antagonism of oppressing and oppressed classes'.

In the depression, re-employment policy was the most obvious part of such a strategy. It would benefit everyone, and impose no cost. In 1930 suggestions for work-creation schemes were already put forward by a few trade unionists. Such schemes were particularly popular among construction workers, who had been hit by the fall-off in public contracts.

At first, though, the re-employment projects looked less attractive than the idea of a revival of the partnership between unions and employers initiated in 1918 by the Stinnes–Legien pact and embodied in the 'central working community' (ZAG) which had in the revolutionary aftermath of the war discussed issues of wages and price determination. Such a partnership did not necessarily depend on the collaboration of the government: indeed, the 'working community' or ZAG had put terms to the government, and had been used by the employers to frustrate state schemes for increased control over the economy. In June 1930, and then again after the September elections which had brought such a large increase in the NSDAP vote, the unions had tried to draw up a joint plan with the employers' organizations for solving the economic crisis by means of cuts in wages and prices. The problem lay in agreeing what should be reduced first: the unions were reluctant to agree to wage cuts if these meant lower real wages, and they wanted action on prices first, or at least an attack on middlemen's profits. Some figures, such as Fritz Tarnow of the Woodworkers' Union, argued that it was essential to patch up 'a marriage of convenience' with the employers to stop the anti-democratic authoritarian radicalization of industry. But the employers were unwilling to begin the process by reducing prices; and the majority of the ADGB's central committee opposed the idea of negotiating since business had, in the words of a leading civil servant, 'let itself in with a horde of White Guards'.

Only with the collapse of these negotiations, and after the banking crash of the summer of 1931 had worsened the slump further, did more unionists turn to the idea of a grand work-creation plan as an alternative to the austerity course of Chancellor Brüning. From the economic viewpoint, it was unfortunate that such proposals should be drawn up at exactly the time when the instability of capital and money markets made a large government deficit highly dangerous. There was a great risk that large expenditures not covered by increased taxation (which would have countered the expansionary effect) would lead to a new round of collapses of confidence in public credit, bank crashes and thus to a new and disastrous monetary contraction.

But these objections scarcely mattered. Work-creation proposals appeared to offer a way out of the union leaders' dilemma: the schemes brought back the possibility of an agreement with industrial leaders and a co-operation of opposing interest groups, while they did not depend on an acceptance of the immensely unpopular wage cuts negotiated after 1930 or imposed by arbitration awards and binding decrees.

These calculations arose out of the political context in which the unions, and also the SPD, functioned. The party was losing votes, and the unions, members. Communist, and also to some extent Nazi, successes derived a great deal of support from unemployed workers. There were street battles, especially in Berlin and Hamburg, between the followers of the radical political parties; and the KPD had evolved its own paramilitary organization, the *Rot Frontkämpferbund*, in imitation of the Nazi SA. The violence of the unemployed appeared to undermine the legitimacy of the Weimar political system, and was often, indeed, directed against the Prussian police, which had been built up as a Social Democratic bastion. The Woodworkers' Union newspaper addressed itself to this problem, and complained that the unemployed workers were being used as 'the tools of movements directed against the working-class and trade unions'. In order to prevent a permanent split, and a consequent weakening, of the working class, the unions believed that the level of unemployment needed to be reduced quickly: or, at least, the unions needed to be seen trying to reduce the level of unemployment quickly.

A second consideration influenced figures such as Tarnow and the union economist and statistician Wladimir Woytinsky. The radical demands of some unionists for a complete overthrow of capitalism – those demands propogated so vigorously in the Metal-workers' Union (DMV), and also by the AfA-Bund, might well have a propaganda success with parts of the working class, and might even attract back some of the lost support. But they would also antagonize the traditional political establishment. Just as critical for Tarnow's new case was his old argument about the need to reach an agreement with the old order. Otherwise the establishment might turn, out of fear of a socialist transformation of society and economy, to the Nazis for help. The union programmes of 1932 – first the so-called WTB (Woytinsky–Tarnow–Baade) Plan and then the plan accepted at the Extraordinary Union Congress of 13 April 1932 – corresponded, in other words, to an urgent political necessity. They were intended as anti-fascist programmes, with the goal of bringing the working class and the unions back to the SPD and the Weimar fold, and at the same time as ways of appeasing the grass-roots membership.

Woytinsky believed that in an ideal world an international loan and a general international credit creation would be the most suitable way of relieving employment in Germany. Since this was no longer practicable in the light of the collapse of international capital markets in 1931, Germany should now go it alone. One million men, Woytinsky calculated, could be employed for a year from the expenditure of 2 billion marks. Such expenditure would not be inflationary: in fact, the additional money put into circulation might be as low as 200–300 million marks. Tarnow complemented this argument by explaining that cheap credit alone, as suggested by some non-socialist critics of Brüning's deflation, would not be sufficient to produce an economic upturn, and that the state would have to use the additional credit to create supplementary demand if it were to achieve an economic stimulus.

The WTB plan was taken up as union policy at an extraordinary congress of the ADGB on 13 April 1932. Its proposals were labour intensive and involved road building, agricultural improvements, flood protection, the construction of small dwellings and railway and post orders. They were to be financed through a general loan, and from long-term credits of the state-owned bank, the *Reichs-Kredit-Gesellschaft*, and other financial institutions.

The plan's figures over-estimated the extent of the employment that would be created because the proposed payments to each worker were lower than would have been acceptable – that is, outside the framework of an authoritarian state of the kind that the Nazis eventually built up and that allowed work-creation with workers on extremely low wages. But in the light of the fundamentally political purpose of the union plan, such criticisms are perhaps beside the point. More importantly, the plan also failed to meet the objections of union members tired of the conservatism, immobility and lack of imagination of the union leaders. It may thus not be a valid objection to the WTB plan to say that it demonstrated an exaggerated and unwarranted degree of economic imagination. But the union congress was bitterly attacked within the labour movement, and the April plan failed entirely to slow down the process of political radicalisation. Theodor Leipart, the ADGB's chairman, complained in August 1932 that the 'union radicals are now abandoning evolutionary for revolutionary socialism . . . [he believed] that the economy and the workers would be the ones to suffer most from this radicalization.'

The radicalization continued because at the local level the issue of wage reduction still appeared to be fundamental. There was a successful strike against wage cuts in the Weissenfels shoe industry; and from 3 to 7 November 1932 the Berlin transport workers went on strike, against the advice of the socialist union, the *Gesamtverband*. The strike in the *Berliner Verkehrs–Gesellschaft* was led – to the horror of Leipart and the union leaders – by both the RGO and the NSBO, the Nazi shopfloor cell movement. Communist and Nazi pickets stood side by side as they were arrested by the Berlin police.

Both the Metal-workers and the Factory Workers' Union were so frightened by the continuing radicalization that they dropped their commitment to the union work-creation programme. Even at the time of the April Congress, many unionists had only swallowed the work-creation scheme because it had been presented as part of a package, together with a more general plan for the reordering of the economy. Tarnow had had to commit himself to schemes for the extension of socialization (which he privately dismissed as 'music of the future') in order to rescue his ideas at the congress. In June the ADGB and the AfA–Bund together produced a new programme which drowned the idea of work creation in a flood of much more far-reaching proposals. At the head of the new list stood the traditional demand for an 'increase in mass purchasing power', in other words, wage rises, coupled with the complete restoration of the 40-hour week originally instituted in 1918 but then attacked as part of the stabilization measures of 1923. Then followed the nationalization of key industries – coal, iron and steel, cement, large chemical works and electricity – and of banks and insurance companies; the creation of a state trading monopoly for agricultural products, and state 'organization' of trade in general; and finally the combination of a democratization and decentralization of industry with the erection of a state central planning office.

One way of expressing the criticism that the work-creation programme represented too much of a concession to Weimar, to industry and to corporatism, was the argument that the real enemy of the working class was inflation. Inflation had always been the demand of the political right in Germany – since the 1890s when farmers had demanded bimetallism to replace the gold standard, because they believed the introduction of a silver currency would raise food prices. Inflation would strengthen the power of big business and agriculture, as it had done at the beginning of the 1920s; and inflation would be the result of a co-operation of labour unions with big business or agriculture during the depression. Max Cohen, for instance, argued that 'if it is not possible to raise new capital by the normal methods (loans), and if there is an artificial credit creation, there will be an inflation'. Hilferding's aide Naphtali believed that the 2 billion marks spending proposed in the WTB plan severely underestimated the amount of money required to find jobs for a million workers: an additional billion would be needed, and there would be inflationary consequences. In *Vorwärts* in September and October 1931 Hilferding warned against inflation as 'the most terrible indirect tax'. The English sterling devaluation of September 1931 'has made the crisis much worse and has strengthened the social-reactionary tendencies which increase anyway in a crisis'. The threat of inflation was just an additional proof of the need for a change in economic organization: 'for us socialists, this new and most pronounced appearance of capitalist anarchy, this failure of the credit organizations of the world . . . is the new proof of the necessity of another and superior form of organization.'

In the end, neither the unions nor the SPD were able to produce immediate workable alternatives to Brüning's policy. The demands that the labour movement had to respond to – on the one hand, conserving the loyalty of the grass roots; on the other, negotiating in the political world of the early 1930s – contradicted each other too severely. The consequent demoralization was already evident in December 1931, when Brüning's deflation reached its apogee with the Fourth Emergency Decree. Despite the wage reduction provisions, the SPD broadly accepted the Decree. Wilhelm Keil, one of the SPD's finance experts and someone who in 1929–30 had been bitterly critical of the party leadership for making too many concessions to the right, commented after Naphtali had attacked the Brüning measures at a meeting of the SPD Reichstag party, 'What is Naphtali's programme? I can see none. One should not overlook that the Emergency Decree contains, besides unsocial measures, also price cuts, rent cuts and an interest reduction on the 30 billion borrowed capital. Above all – would the Decree be cancelled if we vote against it? Not at all. No government today would cancel the decree.' This strange mixture of political calculation and respect for the symmetry with which Brüning had shared out the burdens of the depression was highly characteristic of a party and a labour movement resigned to failure and impotence. Hilferding himself, resigned to the crisis, had indeed been one of Brüning's closest and most influential political advisers in the critical months of 1931.

The demoralization of the union and socialist leaders, which first of all gave birth to the work-creation programme and then strangled that infant in its cradle, started *before* the political events of the summer of 1932 which effectively ended the SPD's political chances. The SPD and the unions had justified their tacit support for Brüning by the need to 'stop fascism'. Their line was known as 'toleration policy'. But in May 1932 Brüning fell. On 20 July 1932 Reich Chancellor von Papen took over the Prussian ministries ('the Papen Putsch') which had previously been controlled by an SPD coalition under Otto Braun. The union leaders advised against a general strike of the sort that in 1920 had defeated the Kapp Putsch, since the Reich and the employers were likely, given the state of the labour market, to win.

Unionists wondered about the lessons to be learnt from this defeat.

Some were prepared to consider abandoning the SPD and joining the Christian and liberal (Hirsch–Duncker) unions in an attempt to conserve what strength remained. The ADGB hesitated over the timing of such a merger, and the opportunity passed. Later, in December 1932, its chairman Leipart negotiated via intermediaries with Reich Chancellor von Schleicher about participation in government, but by the beginning of 1933 the talks had broken down.

After the appointment of Hitler as chancellor, the unions beat the retreat again. First they discussed with the Christian unions the formation of a unitary organization appropriate to the new corporative state: this, the *Einheitsgewerkschaft*, would also include representatives of the Nazi Party's labour wing. That such attempts of unionists to compromise with the Nazis were vain is demonstrated by the dissolution on 2 May 1933 of the non-Nazi unions. That attempt to compromise was, however, nothing more than a logical outcome of an attitude which since 1931 had raised the question of the political survival of unionism to a position of primacy at a time when union support was disintegrating, and the political system was becoming less and less susceptible to the influence of trade unions.

By the end of the 1920s, 'labourism' had run into crisis. In its place some figures – Neisser, Woytinsky, Tarnow – advocated a strategy which involved extending the SPD's appeal. But this new strategy failed utterly to convince the SPD's traditional base. It is a good illustration of the argument that the problem was not that the SPD had 'lost touch' with its working-class supporters, but that its obligation to keep in touch obstructed the development of other forms of support and of new strategies. Another way of stating this conclusion is that the idea of an integrative 'people's party' or *Volkspartei* failed as there was, during the Weimar Republic's brief life, too little that the working class had in common, too little that united the working class – to say nothing of the little that the working class had in common with other groups, with farmers or white-collar workers. The war had produced a social fragmentation, a division into hundreds of tiny, particularized interest groups. There was in Weimar no sign of that economic growth which might have promoted the integration of all these different social groups and interests under the mantle of a *Volkspartei*. Here there was a vicious spiral: one of the causes of Weimar's economic difficulties was the extent of political instability and of uncertainty about the future; but the economic crisis furthered the process of political fragmentation. By 1932, in place of either of the options – 'labourism' or *Volkspartei* – the SPD and the unions were impelled to take up a frothy and wordy radicalism.

18 The SPD and the Collapse of the Weimar Republic

Peter D. Stachura

The spectacularly tragic rise and fall of Germany's first experiment in modern parliamentary government, the Weimar Republic, has attracted much scholarly interest. Whether the republic is perceived as a mere interlude in Germany's authoritarian tradition or as a development worth examining on its own terms, there is a wide recognition of the major constituents that went into its flawed manufacture and ultimate collapse. The historiography of the Weimar era has undergone significant change over the years on the basis of fresh empirical information and concomitant new perspectives, which sometimes have also been shaped by political and ideological concerns. For instance, the greater weight attached in recent years to the social and economic determinants of political movements has resulted in important changes in emphasis and understanding of the issues involved (see Stachura, 1983, 1–14). What has not altered fundamentally, however, is the almost universal tendency to explain the events of 1933 in relation to the faults and weaknesses of Weimar democracy rather than predominantly in terms of the strengths, ambitions and power strategies of the political organization which finally triumphed at the expense of the republican system, National Socialism. As Martin Broszat has recently intimated, the Nazi 'seizure of power' or *Machtergreifung* needs to be assessed from the point of view of the winners instead of from that of the losers (Broszat, 1984, 218–19).

It may be asserted, on balance, that the republic has to be understood within a historical framework that encompasses more than the years 1918–33, and especially with reference to long-standing influences in German history such as extreme nationalism, imperialism, militarism, racism and an ill-developed liberal and democratic conciousness; the republic did not arrive or exist in an historical vacuum (see F. Fischer, 1986). Yet there is, at the same time, every justification for placing strong emphasis on what happened during the 1920s and early 1930s to help explain the republic's misfortunes, particularly since Hitler and the National Socialist movement, the principal destroyer of the democratic system, increasingly are seen to have been in large measure products of the First World War and its traumatic aftermath. Indeed, the victory of one particular party in 1933 has been used by historians to highlight the deficiencies of those parties which were, ostensibly at least, committed to the defence and preservation of the republic. When due account has been taken of the host of multifarious developments which within the period 1918–33 contributed to the republic's demise, it is widely appreciated that at source the German people and their political representatives held its fate in their own hands to a not inconsiderable extent. Consequently, the political and electoral preferences of different social groups, as well as the reactions and behaviour of their political leaders and parties, have been brought under stringent examination. And while the failures and achievements of all Weimar parties have been scrutinized in detail, most attention in this sphere has inevitably centred on the party commonly perceived as the 'party of state', the Social Democratic Party. If the National Socialist Party was the victor of the Weimar political battle, the SPD is often seen as the unmistakable loser, immediately giving rise to the questions: what role did the SPD play in the development of Weimar democracy, and how far should it be held responsible for the collapse of the system? Since the development of the SPD closely mirrored that of the republic itself, questions about the party's performance clearly have a wider importance, casting light on at least some of the essential reasons, from a party political standpoint, for the catastrophe of 1933.

The 'Party of State'

Despite the symbiotic relationship with the republic which party spokesmen were frequently at pains to acknowledge, the SPD displayed a somewhat ambivalent attitude to the state. The party was unable to make the transition from being in opposition, as it had been for almost half a century before 1914, to being an agency for government, as it was meant to be following the disintegration and defeat of the Empire or *Kaiserreich*. The years of hostility and persecution before the war, the virtual pariah status accorded Social Democracy and the working class in general by Bismarck and Wilhelm II, resulted in the SPD moulding an 'anti' outlook and mentality which, in the vastly changed situation of 1918–19, it was asked to abandon in favour of a positive sense of governmental responsibility. The first clear indication that such a metamorphosis would not come about easily, if at all, was provided by the SPD's response to and role in the 1918 November Revolution. The party, which before 1914 had effectively renounced the revolutionary road to socialism under the progressively pervasive influence of reformism and broader economic and social developments, evinced little inclination to take the initiative or provide the impetus for thoroughgoing change in 1918–19. By that time the party leadership had developed a cautious, restrained and pragmatic approach to the challenge of attaining a socialist order and, above all, had become convinced that its future lay within the confines of a parliamentary democratic and not a proletarian-Bolshevik state. The SPD's departure from what might loosely be termed 'full-blooded socialism' was formally confirmed a few years later, of course, when its Görlitz Programme (1921) rejected revolutionism and openly accepted a reformist ideological posture and strategy. Apprehensive of the potential for radicalization in 1918–19, the SPD leadership reacted in the only way it knew how: it strove to extirpate the extreme left, involving the infamous association with the army (*Reichswehr*) and the 'Free Corps' (*Freikorps*), and consolidation of a moderate course in almost all immediate political, social and economic matters. The outcome, a republic stamped with the imprint of a conservative Social Democracy, alienated a substantial section of the working class who had regarded the revolution as presenting a unique opportunity for a comprehensive and profound transformation of Germany. Thenceforth, these disillusioned and embittered proletarians turned their backs on the SPD and sought solace in the Independent Social Democrats and the German Communist Party.

The fact that the November Revolution left many vital areas of national and public life largely unscathed – the army, bureaucracy, universities, judiciary and churches, and the traditional conservative elites who dominated them – has earned the SPD vehement and persistent criticism. It is blamed for creating a 'lame duck', a republic gravely impaired from the outset, if not actually foredoomed. While there is no denying the circumspect vista of Ebert and other leaders, and their exaggerated fear of 'Bolshevism' and other manifestations of working-class discontent, including strikes, this line of argument perhaps overstates the popular will for radical change at that time. A majority of the Workers' and Soldiers' Councils, it has been shown, were committed to rather moderate schemes of reform (Carsten, 1972). From a different perspective, it might be argued that too little account has been taken of the strength of important national institutions.[1] The objective opportunities for radical initiatives may not have been as plentiful as is sometimes maintained, though it might also be said that the SPD could still have been more adventurous in carving out a more viable democratic infrastructure without running the risk of outright revolution. Moreover, although it was naturally important for the republic to have as solid a foundation as possible from the very beginning, the problems that persistently confronted it were not so overwhelming as to justify the argument that its collapse was a foregone conclusion. There was still some way to go after 1918–19 before that critical stage was reached. The 1920s, therefore, opened up a certain scope to the republic and its supporters, including the SPD, to make the democratic system more secure.

The early post-revolutionary period was extremely challenging for the republic. As it struggled to emerge from the shadow of Versailles it was faced by deep political and economic upheaval, while both left and right sought to establish their own totalitarian forms of government. The republic, in consequence, came close to total collapse in 1922–23, and a major reason for the avoidance of that dénouement was the conduct of the SPD and a majority of the working class which it represented. The defeat of the Kapp Putsch in 1920 by a general strike was perhaps the most salient example of their determination to defend the republic. In alliance also with the Free Trade Unions, the SPD was able to use its extensive political influence to realize, at least to an impressive degree, its concept of a 'social republic', a democratic state with a record of meaningful social-welfare achievement, chiefly for the benefit of the working class. The SPD was convinced that the long-term well-being of the democratic order, and its own position within it, was intimately linked to the material advance of the most natural supporters of such an order. The Weimar constitution had already laid the basis for social reform and progress by recognizing the right of every German to work and the duty of the state to protect its working population. A series of reforms soon after 1919 fleshed out this framework: the introduction of the eight-hour day, the establishment of factory councils, a system of collective wage-bargaining with provision for binding arbitration, better unemployment relief measures, the Old Age Pension Act (1923), the extension of the franchise to women, and a comprehensive National Youth Welfare Act (1922). These measures were supplemented during the mid-1920s by new housing programmes, improvements in adult education facilities and the provision of a range of civil amenities, including libraries, parks and swimming pools. The crowning point came in 1927 with the introduction of the Unemployment Insurance Act which gave enhanced benefit levels but, most importantly, established the legal entitlement of the jobless to state support. Even if some workers were disappointed that social reforms had not been pushed further, the SPD and its allies in the labour movement had ensured that for the first time the German state was genuinely concerned about the material condition of its lower classes.

By 1923–24, when the major political and economic threats to the republic at last subsided and Germany was on the verge of a period of relative calm and prosperity, the SPD could look with some satisfaction at the development of the republic since the war. Its own position as the principal bastion of the state was fully established, and although no longer commanding the same high level of popular support achieved in the National Assembly elections in 1919 and the Reichstag election in 1920, the SPD had also consolidated its leadership of a majority of the working class. However, the so-called 'golden years' of the mid 1920s paradoxically underlined serious deficiencies in the character and policies of the SPD which were to be cruelly exposed during the depression, to its own and the republic's detriment.

Lost Opportunities

Despite increasing its share of the vote between the Reichstag elections of December 1924 and May 1928 from 26 to 29.8 per cent (and thus its seats from 131 to 153) and maintaining party membership around the one million mark, the SPD was a failure in other fundamental respects. These had serious long-term implications for the stability of the republic. In the first instance, the electoral gains in 1928 flatter to deceive, for the SPD lost working-class votes to the KPD – the unemployment associated with the rationalization process in industry was a primary factor – and made up the shortfall by attracting 'new' middle-class voters who had become disillusioned with the traditional bourgeois parties (especially the German Democratic Party) and some Catholic workers deserting from the Centre Party. The SPD's proletarian constituency, which excluded most Catholic workers, was already displaying incipient signs of that contraction which became clearer during the early 1930s. The success of the party in winning over disgruntled bourgeois voters in 1928 should not disguise the fact that it had been unable to create a substantial non-proletarian following in the 10 years since the republic was established. Estimates of the SPD's middle-class constituency in 1930 vary, but it was probably close to 30 per cent, so that it was still an overwhelmingly working-class party. It had not succeeded in significantly broadening its basis of support – and thus support for the republic – in the style of an authentic *Volkspartei* or 'people's party'. The explanation for this has much to do with the impregnability of the nationalist-conservative ethos of the bourgeoisie which found political expression in support for the German National People's Party, the German People's Party, various splinter middle-class parties at the national and regional level, and later, the NSDAP. But the SPD did not make a serious enough or sustained endeavour to devise a personality, outlook or policy that would prove attractive to a broad spectrum of middle-class opinion. Its initiatives in forming white-collar unions and ancillary groups for the professional and academic bourgeoisie, as well as the formulation in 1927 of an agricultural programme aimed at the small peasant farmers, were all comparatively insubstantial in terms of constructing popular support. As it turned out, the SPD's non-proletarian constituency was composed almost exclusively of the lower middle class, including primary schoolteachers, lower-grade civil servants in local and national government and lower-paid white-collar employees in industry and commerce. Consequently, the description of the SPD as the 'party of state', implying a truly national profile based on electoral support cutting across many social and class boundaries, lacks conviction.

The SPD's credibility as a national party is further dented when its non-participation in central government during the mid-1920s is recalled. Having withdrawn in protest from Stresemann's coalition government in autumn 1923, the SPD spent the best years of Weimar as an opposition party operating outside the mainstream of national politics, and it did not return to power until the establishment of the 'grand coalition' in 1928. While it remained the leading coalition partner in the Prussian administration and continued to participate in other regional and local government bodies at this time, the SPD made a grave mistake in absenting itself from central government. The election to the Reich presidency in 1925 of Paul von Hindenburg made the SPD's detachment all the more regrettable, for although the aged Field Marshal did nothing directly to undermine the constitutional position of the republic before 1930, the very presence in the highest office of the democratic state of a convinced monarchist and authoritarian-conservative figure ought to have been cause for alarm. Following the relative stabilization of the republic from 1923–24, the opportunity was created for all republican and democratic forces to throw their weight behind a drive to consolidate the system. As the largest single party in Germany and the one mainly responsible for establishing the republic, the SPD ought to have been in the vanguard, leading from the very heart of the political and governmental apparatus. In declining to share office with the bourgeois parties, the SPD was guilty of blatantly placing narrow party political considerations before the national interest: it had still failed to resolve the crucial dilemma of whether it was a class or government party. Its 'flight from responsibility' (in the words of K. D. Bracher), which resulted in the SPD being in power at the centre for only five out of 14 Weimar years, was motivated by fear of the electoral implications of being associated with unpopular coalition government policies – that is, in the main, losing working-class votes to the KPD. But it was an attitude which revealed, above all, the SPD's lack of maturity, self-confidence and judgement. As an alternative, the party could have exerted its considerable influence and prestige to strike favourable compromises with the middle-class parties and thus minimize the danger of forfeiting support. In any case, the SPD's fear was grossly exaggerated, for as the depression years were to show, its loss of votes to the KPD in the most disturbed circumstances imaginable amounted to no more than about 4 per cent. The SPD underestimated the loyalty and discipline of its membership and electorate. It is most improbable that a similar loss would have been sustained in the more tranquil mid-1920s if the party had put its obligations to the republic first. It was a risk that should have been taken in view of what was at stake – the long-term strengthening of the republic's national governmental machinery. Its failure to respond at this point in Weimar's history indicates where the SPD's responsibility for the republic's collapse directly begins.

That the SPD was unable to recognize the primacy of the national interest at that time was related to the conservative, introspective character of its ageing leadership, which had without doubt been overtaken by a process of embourgeoisement (Hunt, 1970, 92ff, 103ff, 143ff; Guttsman, 1981, 156ff, 227ff, 251ff). This served to severely blunt the cutting edge of the party. Risks were to be avoided at all costs. The easy, comfortable approach was much preferred. Social Democratic leaders lacked imagination, flexibility and colour. Their slow-moving, deliberate approach was bound to produce a sleeping giant of a party. Personalities of energy and outstanding political skill were not to be found, with the possible exception of Carl Severing and the younger Otto Braun. The dead weight of the party's highly centralized, bureaucratized and oligarchic organizational apparatus underlined the problem of inertness. The phalanx of careerist officials engendered its own innate conservatism and contributed to that stultification of the party's decision-making procedure that was all too apparent by the late 1920s. But it would be misleading to say that the party machinery was divorced from the mass of its members. The fact was that many of the rank and file, who continued to be drawn largely from the skilled and semi-skilled groups of the urban industrial proletariat (the 'labour aristocracy'), had also during the 1920s been sucked into the process of embourgeoisement. They now had a stake in the Weimar system and had no inclination to rock the boat. To this extent, the party got the leadership it deserved. The dislike of dramatic reforms and dynamic policy initiatives and the unambiguous predilection for pragmatic reformism were shared by an overwhelming majority of both the leaders and the led (Guttsman, 1981, 159–62).

The nature of the leadership, membership and organization encouraged the SPD to draw increasingly into itself, to further extend that subculture of Social Democracy expressed through the existence of a large press and publishing empire, and of a rich variety of clubs, groups and associations which, with certain qualifications, made the party appear like an enormous ghetto, a supportive network nourishing a veritable 'siege mentality'. This was palpably not the ethos of national leadership of the state. Thus, even when the party came back into central government in 1928 its commitment was less than absolute. There remained a hesitancy and caution which seemed incongruous for a party of the SPD's oft-proclaimed devotion to the system of parliamentary democracy. Its Heidelberg Programme (1925) expressed it in these clear terms: 'The democratic republic is the most favourable basis for the struggle of the working class for liberation, and thereby for the realization of socialism. Therefore, the Social Democratic Party guards the republic and seeks to perfect it.' Rudolf Hilferding used similar words to express identical sentiments at the SPD congress in Kiel two years later. And yet the same party, in the form of its Reichstag caucus, could occasionally leave one of its own, Chancellor Hermann Müller, high and dry over matters of national policy. There was an uncanny self-destructive element in the SPD's character, which was bound to be transmitted to the republic at large.

The Totalitarian Challenge

The advent of the depression accentuated the unsteadiness of the Social Democrats' position. The simmering crisis over the funding of the unemployment insurance scheme, which came to a head in March 1930 when the SPD and DVP were unable to reconcile their differences, signalled only the beginning of the SPD's troubles, and it is its performance during 1930–33 that has attracted the heaviest criticism. It is possible that if the SPD had displayed a little more tactical skill and flexibility over the issue of the unemployment insurance scheme, without necessarily having to sacrifice its principles, the crisis that culminated in the downfall of the Müller administration could have been avoided. On the other hand, given the increasingly bitter divisions among the coalition partners, it must be highly questionable for how much longer the government could have been held together anyway. The extraordinarily intense pressures generated by the depression, especially in the spheres of social policy and public expenditure, made political co-operation at any level very difficult to achieve. As it happened, the SPD lost a great deal of its political clout when it was no longer in office. Its subsequent adoption of a policy of toleration towards the Brüning presidential government effectively relegated the SPD once again to the periphery of national politics. As the republic entered its most dangerous and challenging period and the whole system of parliamentary democracy was being insidiously undermined, the self-imposed banishment of the SPD to the sidelines was a monumental error which had fateful consequences for the viability of the republic. The justification adduced by the SPD leadership that it was backing in Brüning the 'lesser evil' rings hollow when the declared objective of the toleration policy – to keep Hitler from power – was such a calamitous failure. Equally reprehensible was the SPD's support for Hindenburg in the re-run presidential contest in spring 1932: the SPD in alliance with one of the principal grave-diggers of the republic was an absurdity. Even when it is duly acknowledged that its room for manoeuvre and opportunity to exert influence had been restricted by developments beyond its immediate control in 1932, the SPD's action was still supine. The passive retreat of the SPD from its national responsibilities, in a manner reminiscent of its attitude during the mid-1920s, allowed the republic's enemies, the broad range of anti-parliamentary authoritarian forces, too much latitude to conduct their campaign of destruction.[2] The SPD appeared to have run out of ideas and energy when it came to defending democracy. It formulated no clear or coherent plan of political action. The party merely drifted, and its paralysis soon became evident in a number of different areas.

To the central socio-economic theme of the depression – mass unemployment, which by mid-1932 numbered some 8 million registered and unregistered – the SPD, the major party of the working class, on whom the effects of unemployment were most keenly visited, offered no concrete answers. Subscribing to the belief that the balancing of the budget overrode all other considerations, the SPD felt able to go along with Brüning's deflationary measures, despite the deep hardship inflicted on the working class. It was left to the Free Trade Unions, therefore, to formulate realistic schemes of job creation, and even then the SPD, with bitter memories of the hyper-inflation of 1922–23, was far from enthusiastic because of the costs involved (Gates, 1974, 332–59). The party's failure to respond positively to the scourge of mass unemployment was complemented by its futile efforts to preserve the basis of social-welfare reforms it had been instrumental in constructing during the early 1920s. The Unemployment Insurance Scheme, for instance, had become by 1932 a pale shadow of its former self, and millions of unemployed workers were either thrown onto emergency relief or welfare assistance – where the level of benefits had been drastically cut – or were deprived altogether of material support from the state. The political price was plain enough to see: not merely did the unemployed industrial working class flock to the KPD, which constantly gained in popularity during the depression, but even among the majority of the working class who remained loyal to the SPD through all adversity there was mounting disappointment, bitterness and resignation *vis-à-vis* the republic. This crisis of confidence in the system of parliamentary democracy was most acutely felt among the younger proletariat.

The SPD was confronted by a generational problem even before the depression pushed young workers out of a job. The party's ageing but well-entrenched leadership cadres had an innate suspicion of youthful ebullience dating back to prewar times, and by the mid-1920s at the latest the party had no claims to being a movement of youth. Its staid, prosaic personality offered few channels for the expression of that vigour and latent craving for idealistic commitment which characterized large sections of Weimar's middle-class and working-class youth. The call to radical action was taken up by the NSDAP, on the one hand, and by the KPD on the other. The swing of working-class youth to political extremism was further initiated by the massive material deprivation they experienced in the early 1930s. By early 1932 approximately one million of the six million registered jobless were under 25 years of age, representing 24.1 per cent of total male and 38.5 per cent of female unemployment, concentrated among young workers in Germany's most heavily industrialized and urbanized centres. Mass unemployment among the young was inextricably linked to a whole catalogue of social ills, including criminality, poor health and suicide, for which the seriously depleted resources of the juvenile welfare system offered little alleviation. Such was the magnitude of youth's demoralization that many contemporary observers spoke freely of 'a lost generation', destroyed by unemployment and its crushing socio-psychological consequences (Stachura, 1986, 121–47). To these disoriented youngsters, the republic and the SPD were total failures, while the KPD at least seemed to offer the prospect of a better future. It was no coincidence that the socialist youth movement unofficially affiliated to the SPD noticeably stagnated between the late 1920s and 1933, or that exasperated young radicals should have seceded from the party in autumn 1931 to establish the Socialist Workers' Party (SAPD).

The SPD's waning capacity to defend sections of its natural constituency and the republic itself was underlined by its feeble response to the 'Prussian coup' carried out by Chancellor von Papen in July 1932. Why did the SPD not forcibly resist this brutal affront to parliamentary democracy, especially when it had in the *Reichsbanner* and Iron Front two large organizations dedicated to defending the republic? There were reasons more fundamental than those to do with the state of military preparedness of these paramilitary organizations and their capacity to stand up in a civil war to the *Reichswehr* and right-wing paramilitaries such as the SA (Stormtroopers). Moreover, it was not really a question of whether significant sections of the demoralized working class would have responded to a call for insurrection, although a repetition of the 1920 general strike in a period of mass unemployment, it was clear, was simply out of the question. The heart of the matter was that the SPD was committed to a non-violent form of resistance based on law and the constitution. The leadership, despite being divided on many other issues, could not contemplate for ideological and ethical reasons any kind of extra-parliamentary behaviour, whether armed revolt, mass street action or political strikes. Hence the resolve of the SPD to take their complaints to court (to the *Staatsgerichtshof*) and to try to reassert their position at the forthcoming Reichstag elections. The response was entirely consistent with the traditions of legalism, constitutionalism and humanitarianism nurtured for decades by the party, but it was also patently inadequate in the context of the political struggle being waged in Germany at that time: the rules were being dictated more and more by the strident propaganda methods and mass mobilization tactics of the NSDAP, KPD and DNVP. By contrast, the SPD's approach was out of date, unrealistic and inevitably useless. Its pretensions as the leading bulwark of the republic lost virtually all credibility now, and the party sank into an even deeper morass of disconsolate resignation in the six months prior to Hitler's appointment as chancellor.

The SPD's lack of realism was strikingly exemplified by its inclination to dismiss National Socialism as a temporary phenomenon of the depression-hit middle classes which would disappear as quickly as it had arisen once the economy revived. Hitler's defeat in the presidential elections in April 1932 and the losses sustained by the NSDAP in the Reichstag elections in November 1932 were seen as corroborating evidence for this view. Such misplaced optimism emerged essentially because of the SPD's intrinsic belief in its own invincibility – the conviction that, come what may, the party could weather any storm. The march towards the socialist state might be long but the attainment of that objective was inevitable, according to this outlook. In practice, however, this was an attitude which too easily became an excuse for doing little or nothing in the vexed circumstances of 1930–33, and ultimately only blinded the SPD to the true nature of Hitler's movement. It explains, together with the party's commitment to legalism and non-violence and its political isolation, its passive, indeed rather complacent reaction to the Nazi 'seizure of power'. The destruction of the SPD and the republic was the ultimate price exacted for this complacency.

Conclusion

Any assessment of the SPD's responsibility for the collapse of the republic must first of all recognize the party's achievements, not overlooking the basic premiss that had it not been for this party there would probably have been no republic to begin with. The SPD's allegiance to parliamentarism and democracy, to the sanctity of the law and the constitution, and its paramount contribution to social-welfare reform ought to have gone a long way in normal circumstances towards establishing the republic on a sure and lasting footing. But the republic did not enjoy the luxury of either economic or political normality; its brief existence was overshadowed by all kinds of calamity, producing an era of fundamental instability in which the usual rules of political conduct in a democratic state scarcely applied. In its failure to appreciate fully the inherent fragility and vulnerability of the republic lies the real culpability of the SPD. As the largest political party in Germany from 1918 to July 1932 it ought to have taken the lead in devising practical means for safeguarding the republic. But whereas the SPD made more sacrifices for the republican cause than any other party and to the end remained, in a formal sense at least, the foremost champion of parliamentary democracy, it adopted far too frequently the posture of a half-interested onlooker, putting selfish interests before the national need. By 1932/33, therefore, the SPD's mood of fatalistic resignation meant that the republic was devoid of firm support when it needed it most.

Without playing down the SPD's weaknesses and omissions, however, the entire matter of its role in the republic's demise has to be seen from a broader political perspective, for the record of the other ostensibly democratic parties in defending what they were supposed to have believed in is far more open to criticism. Too often these parties were unequal to the task of understanding their wider responsibilities to the state, and in moments of crisis, of which there were many, they failed to provide unstinting support to the republic. Their petty sectarian vision and mediocre leadership became one of the salient features of Weimar politics. By 1930 both the DDP and DVP had ceased to exercise any substantive influence in national affairs. Two years later both were barely afloat, having lost their middle-class following to the NSDAP. Furthermore, the Catholic parties had begun to distance themselves from the democratic principles of the republic as early as 1928–29, and during the early 1930s they became increasingly identified with the broadly anti-parliamentary and authoritarian mood of Weimar politics. Thus, in summer 1932 the Centre Party actually conducted negotiations with the NSDAP about forming a coalition government. Any such approximation by the SPD to the National Socialists would have been quite inconceivable. As for the DNVP, the vociferous anti-republican course it pursued under Hugenberg would appear to leave no doubt that it had a much greater part, and a frontal, direct one at that, in causing the republic's downfall than did the pro-democratic SPD. On this basis of measurement, therefore, the NSDAP and KPD bore the heaviest responsibility of all the parties for what happened in 1933 in view of their consistently violent, revolutionary and totalitarian strategies of assault on democracy.

As the second strongest working-class party, the KPD's role in Weimar politics has often been compared and contrasted with that of the SPD, and it has recently been argued that, on balance, the latter was more to blame than the former for the republic's end (Dorpalen, 1983, 107). This line of argument is unconvincing. The SPD's commitment to a parliamentary state made its staunchly anti-Communist attitude justifiable in these terms. The KPD's long-standing and consistent objective was the republic's destruction and its replacement by a proletarian-Marxist dictatorship following the Stalinist model. How could these two diametrically opposing standpoints be reconciled, particularly when the gulf between the parties was widened by the KPD's adoption of an ultra-leftist strategy in 1928–29 which identified the 'social fascist' SPD as its foremost enemy? The depression was also a crucial factor in further splitting the working class: the division between employed and unemployed grew rapidly and intensified social differences in the industrial proletariat as a whole. To cap everything, the KPD could even opportunistically join forces with the NSDAP to attack the SPD-led Prussian government in 1931–32 and to co-ordinate industrial action, as in the Berlin transport workers' stike in autumn 1932. Co-operation was impossible for the SPD in these conditions, and KPD appeals for proletarian unity in 1933 were rightly rejected as spurious. In the final analysis, the SPD's defence of the republic from the Communists and National Socialists may not have been sufficiently determined or organized, but at least it was on the side of democracy. This simple but basic fact places the SPD in a different and more honourable category than any of the other Weimar parties.

Notes

[1]These limitations are the theme of Susanne Miller (1978), *Die Bürde der Macht: Die*

deutsche Sozialdemokratie 1918–1920 (Düsseldorf), and Heinrich A. Winkler (1979), *Die Sozialdemokratie und die Revolution von 1918/19: Ein Rückblick nach sechzig Jahren* (Berlin) esp. p. 72ff.
[2]For a defence of the SPD's position, see the memoirs and accounts of some of its former leaders, for example, Friedrich Stampfer (1936), *Die 14 Jahre der ersten deutschen Republik* (Prague); and Wilhelm Hoegener (1958), *Die verratene Republik: Geschichte der deutschen Gegenrevolution* (Munich).

19 Eduard Bernstein as Critic of Weimar Social Democracy

Heinrich August Winkler

Compared with the 'father of revisionism', the Bernstein of the Weimar Republic remains an obscure figure. Although he lived almost until the end of the first German democracy, up to 18 December 1932, and constantly took sides in the great controversies of those times, the immediate effect of his inititatives was fairly modest. His public and private comments form a kind of continuing commentary on the politics of German Social Democracy, a commentary whose attraction lies in its 'counterfactual' character. In other words, whoever seeks to know what alternative policies Weimar Social Democracy might have pursued finds in Bernstein a contemporary answer. This can be illustrated by reference to three problem areas: Firstly, the chances open to Social Democracy to change from a proletarian class party to a left-wing people's party and to win and retain the support of the majority of the people; secondly, the position of the SPD on the problem of coalitions with 'bourgeois' parties; thirdly, the question of war guilt, in the resolution of which Bernstein saw a political issue of the first magnitude.

The Choice Between Sectarian Dogmatism and the Realities of Power

After the parliamentary democracy of Weimar had come into existence, the SPD had to ask itself whether it could remain what it was in its self-image and in social composition – a party of the working class. As such, in the elections for the National Assembly on 19 January 1919, it had been unable, either alone or together with the Independent Social Democrats, to secure a majority of votes or seats. In this election, as had happened before 1914, a considerable number of workers had preferred to vote for other parties, in particular for the Catholic Centre. In the new parliamentary system where the government was dependent on the confidence of the Reichstag, a lot more depended on the strength of individual parties than had been the case under the constitutional monarchy, where the Reichstag had had no influence on the appointment of the chancellor and the secretaries of state.

The debate as to whether the Social Democrats should reach out beyond their customary milieu and change from a proletarian class party into a left-wing people's party, in order to gain a lasting majority, began shortly after their second postwar party congress, which took place in Kassel in October 1920. At this time, after a crushing defeat at the Reichstag elections of June 1920, the SPD was again sitting on the opposition benches. At Kassel it was decided to work out a new party programme, which was to replace the still formally valid Erfurt Programme of 1891. No one was more influential in determining the outcome of these platform deliberations than was Eduard Bernstein, who was elected by the delegates of Kassel to the programme committee, contrary to the wishes of the party *Vorstand* (executive) and of the party's central committee.

In the discussions of the programme committee, the main bone of contention was the issue of how far the SPD should distance itself from the image of history and society associated with Erfurt. According to Kautsky's theoretical part of the 1891 programme, the class struggle between capitalists and workers steadily intensified. On one hand, the proletariat was progressively pauperized; on the other hand, it swelled considerably in numbers, due to the decline of impoverished sections of the middle class. Finally it stood facing only a handful of monopolists. Capitalism was therefore doomed to steadily worsening crises and ultimate collapse: the triumph of socialism was thus an historical necessity.

Those in the programme committee who took their orientation from Kautsky were from the beginning in the minority. They were confronted by two different schools of thought: the neo-Kantians who opposed to the deterministic Erfurt concept of history a moral decision in favour of socialist values, and the revisionists who, according to their partisan, Heinrich Cunow, proceeded 'from power-political considerations'. This third direction, to which, besides Cunow himself, the agricultural expert Eduard David and Bernstein also belonged, declared, in Cunow's words, 'that unless Social Democracy won over the peasantry, the lower and middle strata of the civil service, as well as a large part of the intelligentsia, the achievement of socialism would be impossible because things had not developed in the direction which Marx had predicted'. There could be no talk of social polarization – a shrinking class of entrepreneurs and a growing working class. On the contrary, there were large strata in-between, such as small freehold farmers and independent craftsmen. 'Should we want to attract these, we would have to respect their interests and could not introduce overselves as mere representatives of the workers (or possibly only of the industrial working class) and proclaim a general class struggle.'

The first draft of the programme, which was published by *Vorwärts* on 17 July 1921, marked for the most part a victory for the revisionists. The text edited by Cunow relied on several proposals and formulations. Among them, Bernstein's had generally carried the day in the deliberations of the sub-committee. Bernstein's draft characterized the Social Democratic Party as 'the party of the wage- and salary-earning classes of Germany and the similarly placed small farmers and tradesmen'. As the representative of these social classes, the party pursued the goal of 'replacing today's ruthlessly competitive, capitalistic economic system with a socialist commonwealth securing the welfare of all members of society, and thereby simultaneously generally raising the intellectual and moral culture of our nation'. In Cunow's tightened version the SPD presented itself simply as 'the party of the working people'. The party strove for the 'conquest of the capitalist economic system, by means of a socialist commonwealth which assured the welfare of all members of society, and at the same time the highest enhancement of the intellectual and moral culture of the nation'.

The committee's draft gave rise to a vehement debate within the SPD – not so much for its content as for its omissions. The concept of 'class struggle', literally the red rag to all bourgeois persuasions, did not appear in the proposal. Proletarianization from formerly independent livelihoods was described as the consequence of industrial concentration and war, but not, as in the Erfurt Programme, affirmed as inevitable destiny corresponding totally to socialist aims. These two most important characteristics of the draft – the renunciation of the evolutionary scenario of historical materialism and of the propagation of class struggle – were denounced as a revisionist fall from grace by sections of the 'party base', and of course stridently so by the Independent Social Democratic Party. The protest within the party was so strong that the committee felt obliged to compromise with the custodians of ideological tradition. A second draft, which was published in *Vorwärts* on 25 August 1921, included, prominently on display, the concept of 'class struggle'. In this text, too, the SPD was still described as 'the party of the working people'; but the 'basis of its action' was now identified as 'the *class struggle* of the working class and social strata in solidarity with it'. If the revisionists had prevailed in the first draft, success with the second one went to the centrists who managed to mediate between innovators and traditionalists.

But the revisionists and pragmatists still had a chance. At the Görlitz party congress, which met on 18 September 1921, the programme committee was enlarged by further members and commissioned to revise the second text and to present a draft ready for ratification. As the staunch reformists had a clear majority in the expanded committee, the final version of the draft, which the party congress accepted on 23 September 1921 with a large majority – only five votes opposing, the rest in favour – again reflected the influence of Bernstein and his friends.

The introductory words of the Görlitz Programme announced the

Social Democrats' claim to be the true party of the people more comprehensively, clearly and positively than had the previous drafts. 'The Social Democratic Party of Germany is the party of the working people in city and country. The party strives to unite all physically and mentally productive people dependent on the proceeds of their own labour in pursuit of common perceptions and goals in a collective struggle for democracy and socialism'. Socialism was therefore predominantly a question of political will, not, as in the Erfurt Programme, the result of an inevitable economic development.

The concept of 'class struggle' was not eliminated but appeared at the end of the second paragraph and in a context which read more like an historical justification than a social declaration of war. The capitalist economy had made broad masses of the workers into proletarians and had increased economic inequality. 'It thus made the class struggle for the liberation of the proletariat an historical necessity and a moral demand'. At the same time, and echoing such classic documents of party history as the Communist Manifesto and the Eisenach and Erfurt Programmes, the SPD gave assurance that it was not fighting for 'new class privileges and special rights, but for the abolition of class domination and classes themselves and for equal rights and duties of all without distinction of sex and lineage'.

For Bernstein, the Görlitz Programme came as a belated personal triumph. He had been the first – even before the turn of the century – to call for a review of the economic and social pronunciations of the Erfurt Programme in the light of actual developments. In the meantime, scarcely a single Social Democrat still believed in the thesis of the progressive immiserization of the proletariat, and the same applied to the expectation that the crises of the capitalist system would inevitably intensify until it sooner or later collapsed. But there was still disagreement as to the need to revise the Erfurt Programme's prognosis of the downfall of small business and the assertion of the growing proletarianization of the middle classes. At the end of the 1890s Bernstein had already tried to refute both predictions with an abundance of empirical data, and so let loose the revisionism debate within German Social Democracy. Actual developments proved him right. Small businesses did assert themselves, due in considerable part to those technical advancements which would allegedly bring about their downfall. There could therefore be no question of a general proletarianization of the independent middle strata. Commerical and industrial employees and officials were undeniably economically dependent, but the overwhelming majority of them did not perceive themselves as proletarians.

From all this arose a logical conclusion for the revisionists: in some ways, the times were not automatically favourable to socialism. The goal of a new society required rather a realistic strategy for winning power in the here-and-now. The Social Democrats had to make a long-term effort to secure a majority of votes, and as most electors did not count themselves as proletarians, and since the workers, moreover, distributed their votes among several parties, socialist and non-socialist, the party might legitimately aim at winning over non-proletarian elements as well. Their interests and their convictions had to be taken into consideration, their worries had to be taken seriously, their sensitivities spared.

It was not enough to assure white-collar employees and officials that they are part of the working class, as Adolf Braun, a member of the party executive and representative of the left wing, had done during the Kassel congress. As Bernstein remarked in his commentary on the Görlitz Programme in 1922, the concept of wage-earner was totally unsuited to the members of these social groups, and the concept of proletarian was appropriate only in a figurative sense (Bernstein, 1922, 20). To tell small businessmen that their days of independence were numbered was not only contrary to fact; it also was unwise politically, because it would strengthen craftsmen and small traders in the belief that the Social Democrats desired their social descent into the proletariat.

Regarding the 'class struggle', there were various views among the revisionists of 1921. Heinrich Cunow saw in the concept a relic of a past era and wanted to remove it completely from the Social Democratic vocabulary. Bernstein's position was more discriminating. In his draft for the general part of the new party programme the concept still appeared. The bedrock idea of socialism – the knowledge that the liberation of mankind would require an economic and social transformation – Bernstein described as the 'spiritual outcome of the great class struggle of the workers and of kindred social strata equally subservient to capital in modern society'. But when the abandonment of the concept in the first draft of the committee provoked lively opposition, he defended this decision. In class struggle Bernstein saw a social reality; indeed he acknowledged that this theory had a culturally educative effect, schooling the workers in collective solidarity. But at the same time he was conscious of the political dangers which arose from ostentatious use of the slogan of 'class struggle'. If the Social Democrats wanted to win over new social groups and to co-operate with bourgeois parties for the sake of the republic, they must not lapse into sectarian formalism. Rather the language of Social Democracy had to aim at 'upholding the state within the democratic republic'. A fetishizing of the concept of 'class struggle' was not compatible with this goal.

Bernstein did not mention the more important reason why the term class struggle acted as a deterrent outside the core of regular voters for the workers' parties, and it is uncertain whether he was fully aware of this factor. The concept had long involved a lively contradiction in terms. It could mean interest-group politics within a pluralistic system and the reduction of social discrimination. In practice, the Social Democrats had never done anything else. But in theory proletarian class struggle had meant, since the time of Marx, working-class struggle for class rule, and even in Görlitz the Social Democrats did not renounce this admittedly distant goal. In any case, the Communists already saw to it that the concept of 'class struggle' was not connected in the public consciousness with the idea of interest-group politics on behalf of the workers but rather evoked the thought of Bolshevik methods and 'Russian conditions'. In short, the concept of 'class struggle' had become as ideologically loaded as the concepts as 'social revolution' and 'proletarian dictatorship'. It was therefore wise to discontinue use of the 'class struggle' concept, at least as a political campaign slogan. The Görlitz Programme did not wholly fulfil the relevant wishes of the revisionists, but it went a long way towards meeting them.

The satisfaction which the revisionists and pragmatists experienced over their success at Görlitz did not last long. The party programme of September 1921 was in force for only one year. In September 1922 the Majority Social Democrats and the Independents – or to be more precise, that part of the Independent Social Democratic Party of Germany which did not unite with the Communists in autumn 1920 – got together again to form a united party, and the MSPD reform programme was sacrificed on the altar of party unity.

Bernstein, the champion of union, was of course elected to the committee which the Nuremberg unity congress commissioned to work out a new programme. But the traditionalists were at the helm in the new committee. The president was the former Independent Karl Kautsky, the father of the Erfurt Programme, and his draft of a general section stuck as closely as possible to the original one of 1891. Bernstein called the text 'a partly revised and partly enlarged new edition of the theoretical introduction to the Erfurt Programme' and found the fruit of this revision 'unsatisfactory'. Kautsky's assertion, for instance, that increased productivity was of advantage only for capitalists and owners of large estates was wrong. At least middling farmers would enjoy considerable advantage while a large proportion of small farmers and a considerable percentage of independent artisans would not go away empty-handed either. Contrary to Kautsky's opinion, the intellectuals could not be relegated in general to the 'new middle class'; neither could their increase be imputed to the expansion of big concerns. It was also untrue that a handful of financial magnates would become the rulers of an entire society. Rather they would possibly become masters of entire branches of production and therefore so placed as to bend the economy to their ends.

Bernstein rejected as scientifically untenable, in its crude formulation, Kautsky's thesis that capitalism tries more and more to oppress the working class. After all, 'capitalism' was not a subject who wills or intends something 'but an economy containing certain tendencies'. Unfortunate, finally, was the confusion of the coming resistance of the working class, described by Marx in *Capital,* with what had in fact already happened. 'Now we are no longer concerned with a perspective, but with a struggle. We stand in the midst of this struggle and must recognize its strength and forms in their present reality.'

Bernstein's intervention was as unsuccessful as other objections from the revisionist camp. Kautsky's programme draft was, however, the last service performed by the chairman of the committee. At the beginning of 1924 he moved from Berlin to Vienna, and the remaining members did not want to meet without him. At the Berlin congress of June 1924 Adolf Braun had to acknowledge that the committee had not fulfilled its commission. Only two months before the next party congress, which was convened in Heidelberg on 13 September 1925, did SPD members learn from *Vorwärts* that the programme committee had made a new start towards accomplishing their task.

The new draft edited by Rudolf Hilferding followed Kautsky's presentation closely, sometimes word for word. Protests by diehard revisionists and pragmatists like Friedrich Stampfer, the *Vorwärts* editor, and Eduard David, about the doctrinaire tone of the text hardly got a hearing. The final version of the Heidelberg Programme certainly gave a stronger commitment to a democratic republic than did the draft of the committee. But otherwise a return to Erfurt was evident. The first sentence was symptomatic of everything else which followed: 'The inner necessity of economic development has led to the strengthening of big business, which continuously drives back the small concerns within industry, business and commercial intercourse, reducing their social significance'.

The Heidelberg Programme of 1925 was the ideological price which the Majority Social Democrats paid for reunion with the Independents. Three years after the two parties had united, however, only a very few of the former Majority Socialists still believed that the direction of the new programme was entirely compatible with their own position. The Görlitz Programme aimed at winning a majority of electors. The Heidelberg Programme sought to restore the truth of theory. The programme of 1921 was an attempt to equip the Social Democrats to exert political power in a democratic state with a parliamentary system. Four years later the SPD passed a programme which corresponded more with the self-image of a notorious opposition party in a pre-parliamentary state, like that of the German Empire, than with what the Social Democrats actually were – the official party par excellence of the Weimar Republic.

It is impossible to answer definitively the question whether after 1922 the leaders of the former Majority Social Democrats would still have been able to push through a thorough programmatic revision against the traditionalists. The fact is that it was not seriously attempted. As the leadership organs of the SPD delegated to Hilferding the writing of party programmes and party ideology, not only did they give him virtually *carte blanche*; they also let it be known that they had limited interest regarding the clarification of theoretical questions. In Görlitz it had been no different. Then, too, the executive had given the party intellectuals plenty of leeway. But the architects of the 1921 programme were revisionists, while most of the authors of the Heidelberg Programme regarded themselves as Marxists. The victory achieved by the reformists at Görlitz was greatly facilitated by the fact that the Social Democratic workers' movement was still split in 1921, and the spokesmen of ideological traditionalism were based principally within the Independent SPD. The backing which the innovators had in the Social Democratic party leadership was sufficient to guarantee acceptance of the Görlitz Programme, but it was not strong enough to preserve the spirit of Görlitz within a united Social Democracy.

The consequences of this redogmatization are difficult to estimate. The Social Democrats had only a slim chance of winning over a substantial number of farmers, craftsmen, small shopkeepers and other self-employed persons. The anti-socialist feelings of resentment among these classes were deep-rooted and the SPD was unable to promise them anything which would have burdened the worker materially, such as the liquidation of consumer co-operatives, special taxation for warehouses, or protective tariffs. However, the Social Democrats could have reduced considerably the aversion of the independent middle classes against them if they had refrained from the scientifically untenable prognosis of the ruin of small business and from slogans parading class conflict. The small self-employed strata must have felt all this was directed against them. Had the SPD taken the trouble in some measure to neutralize the 'old middle class' with a more sensitive policy, it would presumably have been easier for it to penetrate the 'new middle class' – strata which distinguished themselves from the workers not so much by material interests, as by the fact that they had no wish to be 'proletarians'. To gain their votes the SPD had to make it abundantly clear that they were a 'people's party' and not merely a proletarian class movement.

The Social Democrats had only one chance to grow and again to become the deciding force in German politics: they had to break loose from that rigid Marxist class schema which condemned them to remain a political minority, which imposed on them a false appearance and entirely contradicted their routine practice. In view of the universal suffrage, the middle classes were a power factor, too. It was plain to see that with phrases about class struggle the SPD could not restrain the drift to the right by these strata, a drift which was noticeable from 1920 onwards and which culminated after 1929 in the turn to Hitler's National Socialists. It was easy to perceive that the return to doctrinaire Marxism could not but strengthen anti-Social Democratic aversions among all sections of the populace.

Yet reasons why the SPD nevertheless held on to the 'Kautskyan' variety of Marxism had to do not only with the leadership's subjective errors of judgement. Class struggle was not merely an ideological relic but also a daily experience. When, after 1918–19, a definite break with the world of the traditional authoritarian state had not been completed, it soon became very difficult for Social Democrats to view the republic as their state. Class struggle from above, class justice, class science and education: these were indeed polemical slogans, but at the same time they were social realities. The gain in power which big business was able to achieve after 1919 increasingly undermined the idea of a working community between capital and labour.

The social inequality burdening the workforce, as it developed during the period of inflation, was a serious obstacle to change from a class movement to a people's party. Presumably this obstacle would have been easier to overcome if the stabilization of the currency had initiated a long-lasting boom. But in the 1920s the German economy went through a period of relative stagnation, and the years from 1924 until 1928 were no exception to this general trend. At the same time there were high levels of unemployment due to forced rationalization of industrial plants. The years of 'relative stability' were characterized by hard struggles over the distribution of income and not by quiet balancing of social tensions, as would have been possible, perhaps, at a time of rapid growth.

The sharpening of social antagonisms made the leading Social Democrats constantly fearful of losing voters to the Communists by open revisionism in ideological matters and by being altogether too prepared to compromise in practical politics. The internal party opposition, consisting mostly of former Independents, saw to it that the SPD never lost sight of the Communist competition. With reference to the 3.7 million votes which went to the KPD in the Reichstag elections of May 1924, Robert Dissmann, president of the German Metal-workers Association, declared during the Berlin party congress in June of the same year, to shouts of approval from the plenum, 'These are the proletarian voters who must come back to us, whom we must regain by means of a policy of implacable class struggle'.

The Social Democratic Dilemma: Coalition or Opposition?

The above explains not merely why the Weimar Social Democrats found it difficult to change their programme and to open their party to wider strata. The obstacles which barred the way from a class party to a people's party were at the same time obstructions during the transition from the 'born' opposition party of the Empire to the governing coalition party of the republic. In the Reichstag elections of June 1920 the Weimar coalition parties – the SPD, the Centre and the German Democratic Party – lost their majority. Now the only possible form of parliamentary majority rule was a grand coalition including, beside the 'Weimar' parties, Gustav Stresemann's right-wing liberal German People's Party. In the SPD there was considerable hesitation about such an alliance, as the DVP acknowledged in their programme their bent towards a constitutional monarchy and had played a very ambiguous role during the Kapp-Lüttwitz Putsch in spring 1920.

After the electoral defeat of June 1920 Bernstein unsuccessfully advised his party to continue in power in the form of a minority cabinet of the Weimar coalition. He was one of the first Social Democrats to recommend co-operation with the German People's Party. During the Görlitz party congress he was one of the most committed advocates of a grand coalition. 'The republic has enormous tasks to fulfil', he announced. 'The German People's Party is a social force; it is in fact *the* party of the German bourgeoisie. It is supported by German finance, big business and the intellectuals. We must try to yoke this party to the republican chariot.'

Bernstein's lead succeeded, for in the meantime a majority of the party leadership came to favour a coalition with the DVP. Since that May in 1921 the SPD was – due to foreign-policy considerations – again participating in the government of the Reich, led by one of the Centre's politicians, Joseph Wirth, within a minority cabinet of the Weimar coalition. The attempt to rule with changing majorities meant in real terms acceptance of the support of the Independent SPD in foreign affairs and of the DVP in home affairs; and the difficulties of this were so obvious that one could no longer exclude the thought of expanding the coalition. And as a union between the USPD and the bourgeois parties was not to be expected, only a grand coalition came in consideration. The Prussian experience had the same effect: in the largest German state it was the SPD, having – against the will of its Prime Minister Otto Braun – refused to co-operate with the DVP, which went into opposition in April 1921. A return to power was possible only if the Social Democrats dropped their former misgivings against a grand coalition. Under pressure from almost the entire leadership, the delegates at Görlitz finally accepted with a large majority a resolution in which the SPD offered, under certain conditions, to work with the German People's Party.

For Bernstein the coalition problem meant more than a purely outward means to an end. At the beginning of 1922 he used all his persuasiveness to argue in *Vorwärts* the view that coalition politics were not merely a 'question of tactics' but a 'profound question of politics'. 'Tactical questions are matters of calculation with a view to immediately obtainable advantages; each can be considered and appraised separately. Politics embraces a whole complex of questions. It is the result of considerations of principle. What is decisive is not short-term advantages, but larger, far-reaching interests.' As the republic 'presented only a model for a republican commonwealth in the full sense of the word', Social Democrats were agreed that it had to be defended against its enemies and protected at all costs. 'But this safe-keeping is by no means simply a question of external resources. It also depends on the republic's capacity to live and develop instead of just vegetating. But it can survive in this sense only when it has a suitable government, because otherwise it will never achieve credibility in the eyes of the world at large and, in particular, for the mass of its own people' (Bernstein, 1922a).

Whoever endorsed democracy as a political way of life, so Bernstein argued, had to agree unconditionally to a coalition between Social Democracy and the bourgeois parties for the foreseeable future. His plea was a reply to the quite different view which Artur Crispien, the chairman of the Independent Social Democratic Party, had presented shortly before at the Leipzig party congress of the Independent party. According to him, coalition politics was an emergency measure, not the norm. Certainly, an 'occasional coalition with bourgeois parties' was absolutely consistent with a commitment to class struggle, but such temporary co-operation remained a purely tractical question. The principle of class struggle would be violated if anyone were to enter a bourgeois government as a Social Democrat, co-operating with bourgeois parties on a long-term basis in the hope and with the object of reconciling the classes. 'Whoever thinks and acts this way retreats from the class struggle and ceases to be a revolutionary socialist. He who remains convinced that no reconciliation of classes is possible, that it is only a matter of temporary coalition with bourgeois parties, such a person remains independent and master of his own decisions, and is always able and ready to resume the struggle against all bourgeois parties.'

After the reunion of both Social Democratic parties in September 1922, the view gained prevalence, even among former Majority Socialists, that coalition politics was only a question of tactics. It was thus no accident that the first practical consequence of reunion was the return of the SPD to opposition. The Centre Party and the Democrats sought to balance the gain in power by the Social Democrats, resulting from their fusion, by widening the government's position towards the right, taking in the DVP. Chancellor Wirth made his chancellorship dependent on the fulfilment of this demand. Experts from the SPD and DVP, including, on the Social Democratic side, the former Independent Rudolf Hilferding, came to terms on the hitherto disputed matters. But most of the former Independents did not under any circumstances want to enter into a coalition with the German People's Party, and the former Majority Socialists hesitated to set at risk the new reunion.

The decision by the Social Democratic Reichstag caucus to let the Wirth government fall rather than to agree to a grand coalition exposed their own ministers and representatives. A similar constellation became evident one year later in November 1923, with the ultimate collapse of the great coalition under Stresemann, and then for the last time in March 1930, again at the breakdown of a grand coalition – each instance followed by a marked shift to the right.

Certainly, the Social Democrats were not solely responsible – or even mainly to blame – when a grand coalition could not be achieved or broke up. The right wing of the German People's Party, dominated by heavy-industry interests, generally did not want co-operation with the SPD. In autumn 1923 these interests showed sympathy with a 'national dictatorship', and in the late twenties, with the transition to a presidential system. However, things were more than once simplified for them in that the Social Democrats preferred the role of the opposition to that of the governmental party.

The opposite pole to Bernstein's political approval of 'coalition politics' was formed within the SPD by those leftists on behalf of whom Paul Levi, the former president of the KPD, declared in late November 1923, 'We stand by the principle that our party is the natural opposition party. This republic has the same economic fabric as did the old authoritarian state . . . and thereby is the fundamental position of the Social Democratic movement determined. It is oppositional.'

Under pressure from the left, the party leadership decided, for the most part, to manoeuvre. The Berlin party congress in June 1924 adopted, on the proposal of party chairman Hermann Müller, exactly what Bernstein had always warned against: 'Coalition politics is not a question of principle, but of tactics'. Müller explained almost apologetically that if one contemplated the coalition formations of recent years, 'then we went into government only when we were *forced* into government. The reasons which forced us to it were almost always foreign-policy ones.' In March 1930 Chancellor Hermann Müller himself became a victim of this policy. Because the party had learned to look at coalition as merely a matter of tactics, they terminated the last cabinet which was still able to rely on a parliamentary majority. This time also the main blame probably lay with the right, who for a long time had been deliberately working towards the supposedly saving expedient, the presidential system. Nevertheless, it was a bad mistake that the SPD again took on itself the odium of running away from the consequences of parliamentary government when the going got tough. The credibility of democracy (for Bernstein, nothing less than a categorical imperative) suffered fatally.

Bernstein's Plea for a Realistic Approach to the 'War-Guilt' Question

The attempt by Eduard Bernstein to free Weimar Social Democracy from outdated dogmas and make it capable of winning majorities and maintaining alliances was one part of what one might call his double strategy. The other part was his early and frequently repeated admonition that the Social Democrats should acknowledge the truth in discussion regarding the question of who had brought about the war in 1914. This challenge was morally based, but Bernstein used it at the same time for political purposes. If the Social Democrats openly declared that the leaders of Imperial Germany bore the main responsibility for the world war, then the SPD could go onto the offensive against right-wing nationalism. That nationalism took its strength in good part from the twin legend about Germany's innocence regarding the war and the alleged Marxist stab-in-the-back of the undefeated army.

As early as September 1914 Bernstein had formed the conviction that the main responsibility for the outbreak of war lay with Germany, and that the SPD war-credits vote was therefore a mistake. When Kautsky in 1919, on the basis of the German archives, disclosed the diplomatic background of the outbreak of war, Bernstein was able to feel fully justified in his assessment (Kautsky, 1919). For foreign political and even more for domestic political reasons, he felt it to be urgently necessary that the Social Democrats should speak out; there was no point in quibbling. At the first postwar party congress of the SPD, in Weimar in June 1919, he appealed emotionally to the delegates not to remain manacled by the resolution made on 4 August 1914, in which the Social Democratic members of parliament had voted for the war credits. 'Let's get out of this bind, become free at last, in this matter, too.' It would not be unreasonable if the SPD were required to acknowledge the wrongs done by Germany. 'Let us be done with bourgeois notions of honour. Only the truth, the whole truth, can help us.' But the party congress was not in the mood for truth. An unfortunate turn of phrase of Bernstein – his thesis that nine-tenths of the Allies' peace conditions were 'unavoidable necessities' – caused a debate which resembled more the moral execution of a deviant than an objective discussion of his views. Otto Braun went so far as to maintain that the peace treaty fully vindicated the attitude which the party had adopted during the war. Adolf Braun reproached Bernstein with a 'talmudic method' and spoke of an 'absolutely untimely speech'. Hermann Müller, the party chairman designate, compared Bernstein with a trouser merchant because at first he considered nine, then eight tenths of the peace treaty to be acceptable. The delegate Kummer from Leipzig saw Bernstein on the same track as the recently murdered Bavarian PrimeMinister Kurt Eisner, on whose grave should be inscribed, 'He had a bee in his bonnet about truth' (*Er litt arg am Wahrheitsfimmel*). Wilhelm Keil called Bernstein's remark a 'dumb, unfortunate, destructive pronouncement'. Scheidemann described Bernstein as a 'devil's advocate' who in his extreme righteousness would go so far as to defend the enemy imperialists.

The only one to take sides with Bernstein was Gustav Hoch, spokesman of the left-wing Majority Socialists, who warned of 'the great danger of being swamped by a nationalistic tide which would mean untold disaster for the working class and for the socialist republic'. Hoch's warning was of prophetic perspicacity – while corresponding precisely with Bernstein's theme. 'When I assert the blame of the old regime', Bernstein told the delegates in his own defence, 'then I don't say, it is we, the German people, who are at fault; but I say that those are to blame who at the time lied to and deceived the German people. Thus I absolve the German people of blame.'

With this, Bernstein addressed the social dimension of the war-guilt question more acutely than anyone else. The Social Democrats handed their opponents of the right a dangerous weapon by leaving this problem in an historical twilight. Instead of accusing those who had led the German people into the war, they defended themselves against the reproach that they were responsible for the loss of the war. Nationalism was the most effective tie which held 'bourgeois' Germany together. Was it not therefore a paramount interest of the Social Democrats to bring out into clear daylight the misuse to which the old power elites, before and after 1914, had put the patriotism of the broad masses? Would this not have been the best means of forestalling an anti-Social Democratic consensus of the middle classes? Would not a definitive rebuttal of the politics of Imperial Germany have opened up in the longer term a real prospect of greater international solidarity with the new Germany?

The arguments for the full revelation of historical truth were not weaker but stronger than those used in favour of discretion. It was unrealistic to expect the Allies to withdraw their massive reparations demands because the Germans contested – or admitted – war guilt. As the victorious powers had no doubt about German responsibility for the outbreak of war, the discussions regarding war guilt could have had only limited immediate repercussions in foreign affairs. It was a very different matter when it came to the domestic political consequences of the dispute regarding the causes of the world war. Indeed, in 1919 it was already foreseeable that reluctance to provide enlightenment about the 1914 July crisis and German war aims would prepare the ground for a lie about war innocence. It was equally obvious that the Versailles Peace Treaty must become all the greater a source of national resentment, the less the consciousness of German guilt was made manifest. And it was not difficult to predict that from such resentment the call for revenge would arise and the danger of another world war would be conjured up.

The motives of the Social Democrats who wanted to avoid or at least postpone the full clarification of the causes of the war were complex. Compounding the fear of legitimizing the Allies' reparations demands by admitting guilt was the added anxiety about the cohesion of the coalition and one's own party, the shyness about profound self-criticism and an unreflected 'national sentiment'. A policy such as Bernstein demanded would certainly have required great courage. But in the end

Scheidemann's policy was open to still greater risks. The halfheartedness of the Social Democrats on the question of war guilt was no less consequential than their socio-political sins of omission in 1918–19.

Bernstein himself did not give up his fight for the truth about 1914. On 17 March 1921, in the face of strong protests from the right in the Reichstag, he declared that it could not be denied that the Imperial government had brought about the outbreak of war 'due to its whole policy regarding Austria. This is certain, and no one has more reason to establish this than the representatives of the German people.' He was sufficiently capable of objectivity to understand that one only obscured the situation by using the concept of 'sole blame'. But this concept did not even appear in the Versailles Peace Treaty. Imperial Germany had unloaded a guilt onto the German people from which it had to be liberated. 'It is the right and obligation of the republic to say, we have nothing to do with this policy, and to calmly acknowledge the judgement which the whole world had passed. Imperial Germany bears the responsibility for the outbreak of war.'

Before the two Social Democratic parties reunited in 1922, the party executives of the SPD and USPD came to an understanding about a draft for an action programme which contained a passage about the outbreak of the war. 'Capitalism and the class rule of proprietors unleashed the world war' was written in the text. Bernstein called this statement objectively false. Apart from the fact that 'capitalism' was a very vague concept and, moreover, by no means implied the same as 'class rule by proprietors', the thesis about specific war guilt of the capitalist economic system contradicted the historical truth. This war was the war of imperialism and militarism, or the war of general staffs. One might look up, among other things, Kautsky's documentary study of 1919 to see from which regions this disaster had been off-loaded onto the world. 'To each, his own. The capitalist system has many sins on its conscience, but to shove this crime onto anonymous capitalism amounts to excusing the real war-criminals. To avoid this is precisely in the political interest of the Social Democrats, the genuine party of the democratic republic.'

The thesis of capitalist collective guilt for the world war was a favourite protective device of the Majority Socialists. The leaders of the Independent Social Democrats knew why they had left the parent party, but they did not insist on discussing German responsibility for the outbreak and duration of the war. They adopted instead a misty and vaguely Marxist-sounding general formula which could only favour the rightist legends of innocence concerning the war and the stab-in-the-back. Most leading Majority Social Democrats recognized that the pathos of class struggle would bar their way to new voting strata and would make difficult the coalition politics which were necessary for the sake of the republic. Nevertheless, on the occasion of the reunion with the Independent Social Democratic Party they again paid homage to class struggle and other set scenes from their familiar Marxist repertoire. As independent forces, both parties had discovered different but by no means incompatible truths. At the moment of alliance these truths were already threatening to fall into oblivion: what both parties brought, above all, into the united

Social Democracy was their prejudices, and not their better insights.

The fusion of SPD and USPD was mainly induced by the activities of the extreme right, climaxed by the assassination of Walther Rathenau on 24 June 1922. But to surpass the strength of the right, the united Social Democrats would have needed precisely that double strategy which Bernstein recommended: they had to ruthlessly re-examine their traditional dogmas if they intended to become a left-wing peoples' party; and just as relentlessly they had to criticize their own part in the war if they were to be credible and effective when confronting German nationalism, that hotbed for all rightist mass movements.

Barely two years after the union of SPD and USPD, in May 1924, elections were again held for the Reichstag. The VSPD (United Social Democratic Party) suffered a severe setback. On paper they were still the strongest party. But they gained only 300,000 votes more than the German National People's Party, which emerged as the strongest bourgeois party by far, and in the Reichstag (thanks to the mandates of agrarian groups) as the strongest single parliamentary caucus. At their Berlin congress, held in June 1924, all Social Democrats agreed that the German Nationalists had the mobilization of national resentment to thank for their success in the elections. But only one speaker, the former Independent Heinrich Ströbel, called on his comrades to counteract the rightist slogans, such as the 'guilt lie' and 'November crimes', with 'the charge of the July and August crimes and the instigation of world war', a charge which had hitherto not been made sharply enough.

Bernstein was of the same opinion as Ströbel when a few weeks after the Berlin congress, in a letter to Kautsky, he regretted that there was still no Social Democratic offensive against the 'guilt-lie campaign' of the parties of the right – the German Nationalist, the People's and the National Socialist parties. 'With an easy rhetorical shift from the position that the Imperial system was not alone responsible for the war, to the position that it bore absolutely no blame, it is easy to persuade the masses that the Empire was toppled unjustly, and that the "Jewish republic" and its fulfilment policy are to blame for all of Germany's troubles today.' The nationalistic movement had an intenstity and a breadth which far surpassed that of the 'society of 10 December' – the private army of Louis Bonaparte – in the years 1849 until 1851. 'We are moving unavoidably toward a *coup d'état* of the nationalists, it seems to me, if we continue to muddle. The outcome is of course uncertain. A temporary victory of theirs is not impossible, and should they be even temporarily at the helm there will surely be terrorism such as most people would never dream of. Kapp was a doctrinaire, but the ones who will get the upper hand this time are unscrupulous, brutal scoundrels.' (Bernstein to Kautsky, 26.7.1924, KP, DV 525)

In regard to the problem of war guilt, the recipient of this letter did not differ much from his old political opponent and personal friend, Eduard Bernstein. A few days after the Marx government, under pressure from the German Nationalists, had published on 29 August 1924 an apologetic 'proclamation on the war-guilt question', Kautsky replied in *Vorwärts,* 'The greater the influence of the German Nationalists in Germany, the stronger will be the hatred and distrust of Germany in the world. An invigoration of this mood is at present the only foreign political result which can be achieved by the chancellor's protestation on the question of German war guilt.' If Germany wanted to make any headway regarding the war-guilt question, it was necessary to make a fundamental distinction, that between the German people and the government of Wilhelm II. Certainly the last emperor 'did not desire the world war, did not purposely bring it about', but he had made it possible by his policies for the 'real criminals' in Vienna to cause the war.

The proclamation with which on 25 October the Reichstag fraction and the SPD executive went into the second Reichstag elections of 1924 did not follow the advice of Bernstein and Kautsky. There was no mention of the war guilt of the German right. Bernstein was hardly surprised. He had long been of the opinion that the executive of the Social Democrats adopted a 'false position' regarding the war-guilt question. As he wrote to Kautsky in December 1925, he was angered by the 'exulting articles' published in *Vorwärts* when, according to the Social Democratic party organ, foreign utterances from the West could be interpreted so as to indicate that the victors were moving away from the 'war-guilt lie'. 'Does Social Democracy have the task of white-washing the criminals who drove the German people into the fatal world war? The innocence or, perhaps better, the non-guilt of the German people for the war can be proved more convincingly if, in the words of Fritz Adler, one gives up the innocence lie.'

But Bernstein remained in the war-guilt debate what, according to Kautsky, he had already been in his action on behalf of reunion of the Social Democrats after 1918 – a 'preacher in the wilderness'. In a letter to Kautsky on the ninth anniversary of the revolution, 9 November 1927, the 77-year-old complained that his articles were published neither by Stampfer in *Vorwärts* nor by Hilferding in *Die Gesellschaft.* Presumably it was too late. The belief that Germany bore no war guilt and that the victors in 1919 had punished it unjustly had taken root long ago. Whoever threatened this taboo was accused of anti-national sentiment. The fear that they might again be charged with being 'vagabonds without a country' explains why most Social Democrats preferred to let the war-guilt question lie.

It seems that Bernstein in Weimar's post-revolutionary period was always trying to square the circle. On the one hand, he wanted to change Social Democracy from a proletarian class party into a socially open people's party; on the other hand, he strove for reunification with the Independent Social Democrats, who stuck to the conception of class struggle and therefore resisted such a change. He faced the same dilemma when he tried to convince the SPD that it had to accept coalitions with 'bourgeois' parties in order to make Weimar a functioning parliamentary democracy. After the reunification of the two Social Democratic parties, coalition governments with Social Democratic participation became more difficult than before. One reason for this was the former Independents' view that the 'natural' role of the SPD was opposition. To the end, Bernstein demanded honesty in the war-guilt question and was at the same time the eloquent advocate of an understanding between Social Democracy and the liberal bourgeoisie – well knowing that most of the convinced liberals acquitted Germany of war guilt.

If what Bernstein wanted was contradictory, then so was reality. The chances were minimal that Social Democracy might save Weimar with a different policy. If alternatives existed at all, then they were those to which Bernstein tried to convert it. Herein lies the rationale for the attempt to save from oblivion the 'unknown Bernstein' of the years 1919–32.

20 The SPD in Emigration and Resistance, 1933–45

Anthony Glees

The SPD in 1933: A Party without Power – Confusion, Appeasement, Resistance and Exile

The picture presented by the SPD in 1933 can only be described as a dismal one, revealing a confusion of positions. Its leaders appeared initially to be passive towards the Nazis: some tried to appease them, some opted for 'internal exile' (keeping their mouths shut and waiting for better days). But for others there was only one route to follow – that of outright opposition, whether covertly within Germany or openly in exile. Why did the party's leadership behave in this way? The answer is complex and, as we shall see, it inevitably entails consideration of further questions which go far beyond the events of 1933 themselves, reaching to the heart of the SPD's exile history, and touching upon the very nature not only of German socialism but of German fascism as well.

The first of these questions concerns the party's inability to resist Nazism to any significant degree despite its numerical strength, its impressive organization and its clear ideological stance. The second is whether what crippled the SPD in 1933 was but another example of its classic difficulty in reconciling the rhetoric of action with action itself. After all, 1933 was, on the face of it, a counter-revolution against the Weimar Republic to which German socialism had committed itself in 1918 and whose destruction was therefore something against which the party might be expected to fight. The third question to consider is whether the gulf that appears to have yawned from 1933 until 1945 between the leadership of the mass party and the masses it sought to represent really did exist. Finally, it must be asked whether the decision to go into exile was a wise one. For although the SPD thus avoided one danger (its complete destruction by the Nazis) it risked another no less harmful – its alienation from the German people.

It should not be forgotten that the SPD had won seven and a quarter million votes (representing one-fifth of all German electors) in the last free elections of the Weimar Republic in November 1932. From the election of September 1930 (which had first revealed the strength of National Socialism) through to the November 1932, the Social Democrats and the Communists together gained more Reichstag seats than the Nazis (a point not lost on either party and one which was destined to play a major role for the SPD in exile). Even in the election of March 1933, when the Nazis received 43.9 per cent of the vote, the socialists could still muster 18.2 per cent and the Communists 12.2 per cent, despite a campaign of terror waged by the Nazis against both parties in the aftermath of the Reichstag fire on 28 February.

Yet Hitler's appointment as chancellor in January 1933 found the leadership of the SPD divided over strategy, even if they all shared the common goal of seeking in some way to preserve Social Democracy in Germany. There were those like Otto Wels, the chairman of the executive, who believed that the success of the Nazis meant that the SPD would have to leave Germany, using a base outside the Reich to inspire its members within it. Wels was supported by some of the most senior figures in the party including Hans Vogel (later to replace him), the two Rudolfs (Hilferding and Breitscheid) and Friedrich Stampfer. Others led by Paul Löbe argued that it would be possible to appease Hitler in order to get him to 'tolerate' the SPD until a change in German politics had taken place. In addition, he claimed, by going into exile the Nazis would be helped rather than hindered, and that the Nazis' cry that the socialists were anti-German (which echoed the diatribes of Bismarck and the Kaiser) would seem proven. At least part of this argument was accepted, for the SPD voted in favour of Hitler's foreign-policy declaration of May 1933.

Finally, there was a third group with whom Julius Leber, Carlo Mierendorff, Karl Höltermann (the leader of the paramilitary *Reichsbanner*) and the young Kurt Schumacher were associated. They wanted to see German socialists wage a campaign of armed resistance against the Nazis, and they stated that, given the party's legendary organization and the fact that the *Reichsbanner* had a quarter of a million members itching to fight, they stood a good chance of winning.

The most absurd option was in fact that put forward by Löbe, who completely misread Hitler's intentions. The Führer did not want to be appeased: on 19 June 1933 Löbe had called a 'Reich congress of the SPD' whose main purpose was to disown Wels and his supporters and gain approval for his own platform. At great personal risk, Vogel and Stampfer had returned to the Reich from the Saar in the vain hope of stopping Löbe. They failed, and all that Löbe achieved was the complete humiliation of himself and his associates for, on 22 June 1933, they were all arrested and the remnants of the SPD within the Reich were summarily banned.

As far as those urging armed resistance were concerned, it does seem hard to see how they could have won through. There was, throughout the history of the Third Reich, a resounding dearth of organized, armed German resistance to the Nazis, whether from the left or from the right: there was no German maquis, there were no socialist partisans (although there were individuals like the courageous Marxist artisan Elser who realized long before 1944 that bombs and bullets were the only appropriate means of dealing with National Socialism). Of course, if the *Reichsbanner* had staged a revolt in 1933, it might have established a tradition of armed resistance to the Nazis, which, even if initially unsuccessful, might eventually have borne fruit. Clearly the attitude of the German army would be the critical factor here, but as the events of 1934 showed, Hitler's hold on power was not as secure as it sometimes seemed and civil war might have led to Hitler's departure.

Why, then, was the SPD so impotent in 1933? One view is that because its leaders failed to mobilize the membership they must be blamed for their inaction since they were wrong to assume they had already been beaten by the Nazis. Recent research has suggested that grass-roots support for the party did not evaporate in 1933. It might therefore have been incorrect to argue that the party could not muster sufficient forces to put up a credible (and creditable) fight against the Nazis. To be sure, it has proved very hard indeed to measure either the extent or the effectiveness of socialist resistance to the Nazis. Whilst some authors have stressed the obvious truth that the Nazis were never overthrown by any German oppositional forces (and that it was the right and not the left who provided the best show), others have said that German workers did sabotage Hitler's war effort, for example, by working less hard than non-German workers. For them, what is remarkable is that even despite the consistent brutality of the Nazi police state, there was socialist opposition to Nazism, and as soon as Nazism had disappeared, socialism re-emerged speedily and spontaneously and with greater support than before 1933.

So did the Social Democratic leaders fail both their supporters and German democracy? A show of force would undoubtedly have saved some of Germany's honour. Of that there can be no question. But it would have been a futile gesture: the strategy of armed resistance contained far too many 'ifs' to be put forward by responsible political leaders anxious to avoid loss of life; and the ruthlessness of Nazi oppression ensured that people like Schumacher were kept under tight control and Höltermann forced to flee for his life. Gestapo surveillance, usually extraordinarily effective, would have soon smashed any socialist-led insurrection.

It is important to recall that a great deal of what the Nazis did was done against German Social Democracy. Indeed, the very term National Socialism was probably intended to be a conscious alternative to international socialism. Hitler and his cronies were quite ready to use every means they possessed to extirpate socialism from Germany. When viewed in this light, then, the activities of the SPD do not merit any blanket indictment.

To criticize the exiles for their alleged cowardice or simply for their 'pessimism' is unfair. They took the view that the SPD had fought political extremism both on the left and on the right for far longer than any one else and that by 1933 there was no longer anything that could be done to keep Hitler from power. He had won, and only a very major upheaval (which the SPD could not manufacture) would get rid of him. It was not pessimism to think in this way: since 1918 the SPD had deserved its reputation as the 'state party' of Weimar (one reason why it was singled out for attack by the Nazis and the Communists), and if the Weimar state had now ceased to exist the primary responsibility for this did indeed lie elsewhere.

The policy of exile therefore seems to have been the wisest option, and it would be quite wrong to minimize the importance of the role that the exiled leaders played in keeping alive the ideals of German Social Democracy and the real contribution they made in the fight against the Third Reich. The party was able to follow its own earlier example (from 1879 until 1890) when exile had, if anything, sharpened the party's fighting spirit and, perhaps surprisingly, kept it in business as far as German politics was concerned. It was not foolish to expect it to do so again. At any rate, the Nazis themselves were furious that active Social Democrats had managed to slip out of their grasp whilst at the same time seeming pleased they had gone. In the mid and late 1930s, Hitler repeatedly threatened Czechoslovakia and France for having given the SPD shelter. The Nazis wanted the SPD leaders where they could control them, but they also wanted to be rid of them (curiously mirroring the ambiguous Nazi stance towards Jewish emigration).

Four Prague Winters: Penetrating the Reich, Ideological Debates and Relations with the German Communists

The history of the SPD (or Sopade, as it now termed itself) in exile can be seen to possess several phases. Underpinning each of them there were similar problems concerning the need to gain legitimation as the representative of German Social Democracy as well as the obligations of strategic thinking about the best means of combating Nazism and, not least, of the ideological debate which seems to define all socialist parties.

As early as February 1933, many leading Social Democrats had secretly made their way out of Germany. They included Philipp Scheidemann (who died in Copenhagen in 1939), Albert Grzesinski (former Prussian Minister of the Interior), Erich Ollenhauer and Fritz Heine. Karl Kautsky, the SPD's premier ideologue, had lived in Vienna ever since 1924 (he died in Amsterdam in 1938; his wife Luise was gassed in Auschwitz in 1944).

It was decided to move the headquarters of the party executive to Prague, a city with a long German-speaking tradition and the capital of a country sympathetic to Social Democracy. Indeed, the Prime Minister, Eduard Benes, was to suffer in 1938 for his generosity towards the SPD.

The party (whose assets inside Germany had been seized by the Nazis) was financially vulnerable, and it set about trying to earn money. Its biggest coup took place in 1938 with the sale of the Marx and Engels papers to the International Institute for Social History in Amsterdam, which provided most of its income until 1940. (Earlier, it had turned down a more generous offer from Moscow, who had asked the SPD to name its price for the archive.)

Exile, it was thought, would sustain the SPD by permitting the leaders to do things which would be impossible were they still in the Reich. The first of these was to produce and disseminate Social Democratic literature inside Germany. For this purpose, a network of 16 'border secretariats' was established to transmit written and verbal material. The methods used to avoid the Gestapo were highly risky but most ingenious: innocuous covers (*The Art of Shaving Oneself: New Methods of Male Cosmetics*) concealed rallying cries to the faithful; other ruses involved the production of minuscule leaflets, no bigger than a postage stamp. It is hard to estimate the impact of such labours, but had they really been as ineffective as has sometimes been alleged, there would have been no need for the Gestapo to take such vicious measures against the Social Democrats they were able to unearth. Furthermore, the party executive produced a regular newspaper, the *Neuer Vorwärts*, as well as news reports on the Third Reich, called the *Sopade Berichte*, which were among the few reliable sources of information about Nazi domestic and economic policies and were very widely read, not least in the British Foreign Office.

At the same time, Prague gave the leadership (the executive now consisted of nine members) the opportunity to address itself to two other issues. The first of these was the party's response to the ideological challenge presented by Hitler's success. Here it undoubtedly took the wrong turning: it decided to portray the triumph of National Socialism as the victory of big business over the working class. Whilst this may have constituted a reasonable battle-cry to many former members, its corollary, namely a strategy of waiting for the 'inevitable' economic collapse of Nazism, diverted attention from the need to encourage opposition and revolt.

The second issue concerned relations with the German Communists. The programmatic emphasis on class struggle (embodied in the Prague Manifesto of 1934) provided an obvious bridge to the KPD, and the advantages of crossing that bridge were, for a number of exiled leaders, beyond question. The matter became acute in 1935 and 1936 when, after its Seventh Conference, the Comintern strongly supported the so-called popular-front concept. Socialists and Communists, it held, ought to join forces against fascism. The outbreak of the Spanish Civil War and the formation of a popular-front government led by Blum in France proved that it was something on which the SPD had to have a policy.

In November 1935 Walter Ulbricht (later to become East German Communist leader) approached the SPD seeking co-operation. The latter was divided in its response. Stampfer, Vogel, Hilferding, Hertz and Crummenerl urged a meeting with the KPD; Wels and Ollenhauer argued against it. As they were in the minority, one took place. The Social

Democrats refused, however, to support any joint initiative on the grounds that the Communists continued to abjure the SPD's historical role as the legitimate representative of the German working class, and further contacts were avoided. At the time, this apparently high-handed attitude of the leadership aggravated the fissiparousness of the German socialist exiles. Two members of the executive (who wanted to see a 'united Socialist Party which looked to Moscow as its natural ally') were forced to resign, and the various splinter groups, of whom the most important were the *Neubeginnen* and the International Socialist Fighting factions (ISK), continued to lambast men like Wels and Ollenhauer for what they saw as their mindless anti-Communism. They held that a call to revolution, supported by all those on the left, would rally the German workers and produce armed resistance.

Superficially, this line had something to commend it: after all, other German oppositional groups like the Kreisau Circle specifically called in 1943 for the inclusion of German Communists in their hoped-for revolt against Hitler, and there was no doubt that the commitment of many Communists produced many acts of resistance (that is, revolutionary acts) displaying extraordinary courage.

The real sticking-point for men like Wels and Ollenhauer, however, had less to do with history than with the Communists' fundamental opposition to democratic politics, experienced at first hand during the birth, life and death of Weimar, and the stark truth that all Communists, even German ones, took their orders from Moscow. Once Hitler had been disposed of, they believed, it would be more important than ever to rebuild German political life on a democratic basis and also on a national one, for it seemed to a number of Social Democratic exile leaders that the SPD's failure to identify itself properly with the German nation had been at least partly responsible for its defeat by the right both before 1914 and before 1933.

By the end of 1937, the Wels–Ollenhauer line was firmly established (not least because of the clear failings of Comintern policy in France and Spain). The Communists continued to propose co-operative ventures and to capitalize on the SPD's reluctance to consider them. Yet the executive had a more pressing problem to deal with: Benes had informed them privately that Nazi pressure upon him to expel them had become irresistible. There was a real danger that their presence in Prague might be seen, particularly in London, as justification for a German attack on Czechoslovakia. Leon Blum, however, had let it be understood that he was prepared to accept them in France.

On 3 December 1937 the *Neuer Vorwärts* ceased publication (thus preempting its banning), and in early 1938 plans were made to move the party's headquarters to Paris. The leadership travelled via Copenhagen where Wels, already seriously ill, had to remain. Erich Ollenhauer was increasingly taking over his activities even though on Wels's death Hans Vogel assumed the chairmanship of the party.

Down and Out in Paris: Links with British Labour and the Escape from the Gestapo's Clutches

Paris did not constitute a new beginning for the exiled Social Democrats. Hitler was busy converting his radical policies towards Germany into policies for Europe and the world. This placed the SPD leaders in a far more complex position. In one sense it effectively increased their powerlessness: dealing with the Nazis had become an issue which affected all nations, and the exiled German socialists would inevitably be swept aside in the maelstrom which was about to break loose upon Europe.

On the other hand, Hitler's attack on Czechoslovakia, on Poland and then on the Low Countries and France, whilst certainly constituting a caesura in the SPD's fortunes, can be seen as marking the beginning of a more realistic, and hence more significant, phase in the party's exile history. For one thing, the outbreak of war in Europe meant that the SPD's political tasks became much clearer: it no longer had to wait upon the Marxist hoofbeat of history, but could actually do something concrete to help bring down the Third Reich. For another, now that the opposing fronts had been made quite explicit, the German Social Democrats could become part of a wider and far more powerful alliance of exiled political leaders, supported by Britain. There were, indeed, some indications that this would be so: in the winter of 1939 a delegation of Social Democrats had been invited to London to meet leading members of the Labour Party and Gladwyn Jebb of the Foreign Office, and had been assured that there would be a role for them to play in Britain should they be forced to leave Paris. War might bring about Hitler's victory, but it might also bring about his defeat.

In June 1940 the French government capitulated. As part of the armistice agreement signed at Compiègne it committed itself to handing over any political exiles that the Germans requested. Once again, the German Social Democrats were faced with the prospect of physical extinction. They decided to close their Paris office and, like thousands of others, made for the south in the hope of winning time to escape. Those who could not do so received no mercy. Breitscheid and Hilferding were both handed over to the Gestapo and disappeared into the charnel houses of Hitler's Germany. Many of those who did reach the south were in for a cruel shock: they were rounded up and interned in conditions of great hardship, and many of them died.

The SPD's chief duty now was to try to rescue fellow German socialists: Fritz Heine (later to become aide to Schumacher and Ollenhauer and press chief of the SPD) seized the initiative here and led the party's efforts, begging for financial help, often from Jewish organizations in America. At this time, the party leadership began to disperse: Stampfer and Gotthelf went to America, while Vogel (by now chairman), Ollenhauer and others decided to hazard the dangerous trek across the Pyrenees to the neutrality of Portugal.

The winter of 1940 saw the SPD at the nadir of its fortunes. It had become scarcely more than a name with a history attached to it. But within a few months its position was to be transformed. For, true to its earlier promise, the Labour Party, now in government as part of Churchill's great wartime coalition, arranged for Vogel, Ollenhauer, Geyer and Heine to be flown to Britain. The specific instruction for this emanated from Hugh Dalton, Minister for Economic Warfare and the Special Operations Executive: he had determined that the SPD was to play a part in the secret struggle against the Third Reich which he was to direct. In effect, the SPD became the ally of the most resolute opponent of Hitler, committed to his destruction by force of arms.

London and Survival: The Secret War against Hitler, British Hostility towards the SPD, New Plans for Postwar Germany, and Communist Tokens of Affection

In the event, the potential opportunities offered by Britain never materialized for reasons which, even today, are not entirely clear. If the basis for truly productive exile work was to be a clearly defined role within a triangular relationship (SPD, Labour Party and Foreign Office), the collapse of this relationship within a few months of the SPD's arrival in Britain set the seal on the chances of any spectacular achievements in the final stages of exile, even if this period did see real successes.

A number of factors contributed to the decline in the party's fortunes. In June 1940 the Foreign Office had seen the exiles as being part of 'our present military plan to create, at an appropriate stage, widespread revolt in the territories ruled by the enemy'. Exactly one year later, the Foreign Office considered them politically redundant: 'far from looking abroad for leadership and encouragement', Germans inside the Reich would see the exiles as 'traitors in enemy pay'. The British would be seen to be 'advancing the political fortunes' of Germans with 'little or no following' who had 'earned the active distrust of the population'.

Why had the British viewpoint altered? It could be argued that the changes in the presentation of the war, from a struggle against fascism to a fight against Germany (and, of course, Italy and Japan), had turned the exiles, however honourable their own role, into enemy aliens, and that the British public would not have tolerated the existence of 'German anti-Nazi allies'. Yet since the exiles were to be involved in the highly secret side of the war, about which the public would know nothing, this explanation cannot be the complete one. As individuals, however, a number of socialist exiles did play a part in the secret war, Heine and von Knoeringen being the chief examples of this: it was the existence of German Social Democracy as a German anti-Nazi grouping that was not exploited. This was undoubtedly a serious error since socialists inside the Reich might well have done more to oppose the Nazis had they been aware of an SPD executive in London, treated as an ally by the British, leading them 'against Hitler, for Germany'. Nor should it be forgotten that resistance did not simply consist of armed resistance: there was a propaganda war to be fought as well, and had the British not prevented them from participating in it, the SPD leaders could have scored successes here too.

Other explanations must take on board the implications of Operation Barbarossa (although the change in British policy predated the attack on the USSR) and also the personal animosity that came to exist between Dalton on the one hand and Eden and ultimately Churchill on the other, which resulted in Dalton's dismissal from the MEW and SOE in early 1942. Lastly, there is some evidence to suggest that Stalin's own agents within British Intelligence were under orders to neutralize the influence of German socialists, who were virulently anti-Communist. At any rate, the SPD exiles soon found that their status as the trustees of German Social Democracy could find no political input into British policy, whether on Germany's future political shape or on broadcasting and subversion against the Third Reich.

And yet the idea of the party did not die and, internally, things were done which ensured it would be sufficiently robust to gain re-entry into German political life once the war was over. Perhaps the most important was the clear line of differentiation drawn by Vogel and Ollenhauer between German Social Democracy and German Communism, despite the pressure upon the leaders to overcome what many saw as the damaging division within the German left. The persistence of the KPD (bolstered by the valiant efforts of the Red Army) was but one indication of the critical significance of this issue (and, indeed, of the weight that the Communists attached to exile work). Agreement on a single left-wing party for Germany in exile would have made Communist plans for the takeover of the German left far easier to execute in 1945; the SPD's outright refusal made its democratic commitment plain and strengthened its hand in the turbulence of the postwar years.

The SPD leaders were also, as one of their first acts in London, able to overcome the divisions within exiled Social Democracy which had so weakened its position in Prague and Paris. On 6 March 1941, the ISK, the *Neubeginnen* and the Socialist Workers' groups all agreed to merge back into the SPD, thus presenting a united face to the British authorities (not that it did them much good) and bringing together the considerable strengths of men like Willi Eichler (who later wrote the Godesberg Programme) from the ISK, Richard Löwenthal from the *Neubeginnen* and Erich Ollenhauer, whose own exceptional political skills made him the undoubted leader of the SPD in exile in all but name. Their deliberations on the future of democracy in Germany and their complete and fundamental opposition to totalitarianism, whether Nazi or Communist, were of considerable usefulness to the SPD in the Bonn Republic.

Thus the final period of the SPD's second exile demonstrates a number of positive features, particularly with regard to the internal development of Social Democratic ideas. It seems hard to doubt that the British Labour movement was seen as a model for postwar German Social Democracy, both in programmatic terms and because it was a party able to reconcile socialism with national self-awareness and clear political leadership. The SPD's internal papers provide ample evidence of its comprehension of Labour's successes here, of its willingness to produce a single party leader, its ability to move from opposition to government, both innovative concepts for German politics and both taken back to Germany by the SPD, and of Labour's readiness to address itself seriously to foreign-policy issues.

Exile had indeed kept alive the concept of German Social Democracy. It would not be unreasonable to argue that exile gave the postwar party a particular face and special strengths which it could not have possessed otherwise. That the SPD was prevented from playing a more active role in the fight against National Socialism was hardly its fault. Above all, the transfer of trusteeship from Erich Ollenhauer (Vogel lay dying in London) to Kurt Schumacher, which took place at the 1945 Kloster Wennigsen meeting in Hanover, proved that the SPD had truly established a tradition of resistance to the Nazis emanating from the left which could look beyond the bravery of individuals within the Reich to the courage of the party executive as a whole.

Part IV
Renewal and Rebirth

21 German Social Democracy since 1945

William Carr

The history of German Social Democracy in the 40 years since the end of the Second World War falls naturally into four periods – the crisis years (1945–9) when two German states emerged, fatally dividing the socialist movement; the Adenauer years (1949–63) when the newly formed SPD wandered in the political wilderness; the transitional years (1963–9) when the ice-floes started to break up and the SPD at last joined in a national coalition; and, finally, the years 1969–82, when the socialists were the dominant partner in an SPD–FDP coalition led first by Willy Brandt and after 1974 by Helmut Schmidt.

A New Beginning

In 1945 socialists in all European lands lived in high hopes of a new dawn of freedom. The old order was discredited by its association with fascism, and German socialists were not alone in supposing that Europe would adopt socialist policies to overcome the problems of postwar reconstruction. Like other European socialists, the Germans were heartened by the victory of British Labour in 1945. Moreover, the heroic struggle of the Russian people had aroused widespread admiration for the Soviet Union in the West, temporarily blurring the distinction between democratic socialism and Communism and encouraging Social Democrats to believe that the feuds between SPD and KPD which had emasculated the working-class movement in interwar Germany were buried for ever. The SPD, the first party to re-emerge when parties were licensed in all occupation zones in Germany in 1945, was supremely confident that it would become the dominant political force in Germany, as the beneficiary of the anti-capitalist mood which gripped Europe in the immediate postwar years. Even the newly founded Christian Democratic Union or CDU declared as late as 1947 in the Ahlen programme that the days of unbridled capitalism were over and that a semi-public economy had come to stay.

Disillusionment

Socialist illusions were rudely shattered by the Russians. A group of German Communists led by the intransigent Walter Ulbricht, who returned from Russian exile early in 1945, were quickly installed in key positions in the Russian zone. Early in 1946 the Russian authorities decided to fuse KPD and SPD into a new party, the Socialist Unity Party or SED, ostensibly to strengthen the working class in an ongoing fight against the remnants of fascism. While socialists in the East such as Otto Grotewohl, leader of the Berlin SPD, approved of a merger, Western socialists (already deeply suspicious of Russian intentions) were universally opposed to it. The tough and abrasive Kurt Schumacher, a bitter opponent of Communism who had quickly emerged as the natural leader of the SPD in the Western zones, denounced the proposed merger as a crude attempt by a 'foreign power' to take over the SPD. He was instrumental in persuading the Berlin socialists to hold a referendum to test party opinion. The referendum showed that while Berlin Social Democrats were anxious to co-operate with their Communist comrades in building a socialist society, 82 per cent of them opposed a merger of the parties. With characteristic insouciance the Russians, who had prohibited the referendum in East Berlin, went ahead with the merger in April 1946 and banned the SPD. As the Cold War deepened in 1948–9 with the Communists' take-over in Czechoslovakia and the traumatic experience of the Berlin Blockade, zonal frontiers hardened and all co-operation between Western and Eastern socialists ceased. By 1948 Stalinist elements had imposed democratic centralism on the SED, turning it into a Russian-style party, and expelled many Social Democrats.

The SPD Re-emerges

In the Western zones the SPD took up life again where it had ended in 1933. Much new thinking had been going on in Social Democratic circles outside Germany during the war, but those who re-established the party at grass-roots level were heavily recruited from the old bureaucracy which controlled the party in the 1920s. Schumacher, who soon established complete ascendancy over the party and largely determined its policies up to his death in 1952, regarded the SPD primarily as a working-class party, although he expected the broad middle class to purge itself of its guilt by association with Nazism, and help the SPD create a socialist society. But there was little hope of turning the SPD into a people's party as long as it relied so heavily on working-class loyalties and remained mistrustful of the state, of industry and of the churches. Under Schumacher, the party slid all too easily into the oppositional stance of the Weimar days, supremely confident that it could spurn co-operation with bourgeois parties and win power effortlessly through the logic of history.

The 1949 Election

Contrary to expectations, the first federal elections held in 1949 after the establishment of the German Federal Republic (GFR) did not give the SPD an overall majority in the new Bundestag. Schumacher must bear his share of responsibility for this outcome. He was an heroic and charismatic figure whose devotion to socialism verged on fanaticism. His 10-year incarceration in Nazi concentration camps helped to transform him into an intransigent, intolerant and embittered politician who seriously misjudged the mood of the electorate. His violent attacks on conservatism, capitalism and the Catholic Church – which he denounced as 'the fifth occupying power' because of its active support for his opponents – offended the maximum number of potential voters in the shortest possible time. Equally disastrous for the party was his refusal to co-operate with others except on his own terms. Thus when the Economic Council was formed in 1947 to run the combined British and US zones (now known as Bizonia), although SPD and CDU were given parity of representation reflecting their strength in recent *Land* or state elections, Schumacher's adamant refusal to work with the CDU allowed the latter, with the support of smaller right-wing parties, to dominate the Council and secure the appointment of Erhard as Economics Director. The latter's abolition of rationing and commitment to free enterprise – though it did little to reduce unemployment in the short term – proved more appealing to the voters in 1949 than Schumacher's demand for a planned economy.

Structural changes also militated against a Social Democratic victory in 1949. The SPD had lost its Prussian hinterland where its prewar strength lay. And whereas only one third of prewar Germany was Catholic, in the GFR 45 per cent were Catholics, and Catholics were being actively encouraged by the Church authorities to support the CDU–CSU (the Bavarian wing, the so-called Christian Social Union) as a bulwark against the advancing tide of 'godless socialism'. Even so, the SPD polled 6.9 million votes (29.9 per cent) and gained 131 seats in the Bundestag – only 400,000 votes behind the CDU–CSU with 7.3 million votes (31 per cent) and 139 seats. Adenauer, whose sympathies lay firmly on the right, formed his first coalition with the Free Democratic Party or FDP and the German Party or DP, for he had no more wish than Schumacher for a Grand Coalition.

The SPD and Europe

For the next 17 years the SPD remained in the wilderness at Bonn, although it participated in several *Land* governments in Bremen, Hamburg, Lower Saxony and West Berlin. Konrad Adenauer, a Rhinelander, staunch Catholic and bitter anti-Communist, believed that the existence of two separate German states effectively excluded the possibility of reunification. He therefore concentrated his efforts on making the GFR a significant power inside the Western alliance, regardless of Russian reactions. Thus he embraced the idea of a united Europe with alacrity and sponsored the GFR's entry into the Council of Europe (1950) and the Coal and Steel Community (1952). While supporting international co-operation in principle, Schumacher argued that it was a violation of the principle of self-determination to invite the GFR to join a Council which was also inviting the Saarland – a territory which the French had unilaterally separated from the rest of Germany – to join. Similarly, after initially welcoming the Schuman Plan, Schumacher eventually opposed it because the refusal of Britain to join would, he believed, make the French – whom he cordially detested – the dominant power, and also because there were doubts whether the GFR would be allowed to take industries into public ownership. When Adenauer gave strong support to the idea of a German defence contribution integrated in the so-called European Defence Community, Schumacher and his successor Erich Ollenhauer were once again in opposition. Whilst Adenauer argued that a rearmed West Germany would eventually force the Russians to negotiate on reunification, the SPD argued that it would have precisely the reverse effect. When the EDC collapsed through last-minute French opposition and the GFR was invited to join NATO in 1955, the SPD opposed the legislation in the Bundestag. Electorally their nationalistic stance proved a liability at a time when reunification was losing its appeal for many Germans. Furthermore, the brutal suppression of the East German uprising in June 1953 and of the Hungarian uprising in 1956 seemed to dispel all hope of Russia making genuine concessions to the Western powers. Unscrupulous CDU propaganda had little difficulty in depicting the SPD as a stalking-horse for Communism when it pressed for talks with Russia. That the SPD was still advocating public ownership of basic industries despite the disastrous economic situation in the German Democratic Republic (GDR) seemed to clinch the case. Consequently the party suffered severe setbacks at the 1953 and 1957 elections. Although the Social Democratic vote increased from 6.9 million in 1949 to 7.9 million (28.8 per cent) in 1953, 9.4 million (31.8 per cent) in 1957 and 11.4 million (32.7 per cent) in 1961, nevertheless the CDU–CSU surged ahead with 12.4 million votes (45.2 per cent) in 1953, rising to 15.0 million (50.2 per cent) in 1957. In effect, as the smaller parties were squeezed by the 5 per cent clause, their total falling from 27.9 per cent in 1949 to 5.6 per cent by 1961, the CDU–CSU was the main beneficiary. An ominous sign of dissatisfaction inside the SPD was a steady decline in membership from a peak of 875,479 in 1947 to 534,254 in 1959.

The Change of Course at Bad Godesberg

At the close of the 1950s the SPD changed course. The continued failure to supplant the CDU encouraged the revisionists in the party, led by Carlo Schmid, Herbert Wehner and Fritz Erler, to redouble their efforts to rid the party of what they regarded as its old-fashioned Marxist image, which in their opinion alienated middle-class support. Electoral considerations were not the only ones. The disastrous state of the economy in the GDR and its merciless treatment of all opponents convinced many Social Democrats that a controlled economy was perhaps, after all, inimical to human freedom.

Ever since its foundation in 1875 the SPD, like other Western Marxist parties, had been racked by the tension between revolutionary idealism and reformist pragmatism. For whilst the party remained committed to the radical transformation of capitalist society into a classless socialist society, it had to offer those who voted for it immediate and tangible gains within the framework of existing society. At the 1957 election the SPD was already trying to woo the voters by playing down socialization and Marxism, but without tangible success. At Bad Godesberg the revisionists finally won the day. The new programme jettisoned Marxism once and for all, declaring that democratic socialism was rooted in 'Christian ethics, humanism and classical philosophy'. In economic matters socialism was pragmatic, combining a belief in essential planning with a belief in the market economy which Erhard had popularized in the 1950s: 'as much competition as possible, as much planning as necessary' was the new slogan. All thought of remaining a narrow class party was abandoned. The SPD now aspired to become the party of the whole people. For good measure, old-fashioned anti-clericalism went out of the window as well. And at last the party accepted the principle of national defence. Herbert Wehner, the SPD defence spokesman, came out in 1960 in support of NATO, and a bipartisan defence policy became a reality at last. These changes were not effected without vigorous opposition on the left wing of the party where 'me-tooism' was denounced as a betrayal of socialist principle. As events in the 1970s demonstrated, the SPD succeeded in becoming a major factor in German politics, but the price it paid was the acceptance of the economic status quo in the GFR so that when the oil crises ended the 'economic miracle' and large-scale unemployment reappeared, the SPD had lost its visionary gleam as well as its belief in large-scale state intervention in the economy.

The End of the Adenauer Era

The electoral fortunes of the SPD recovered after Bad Godesberg largely because the ideological face-lift coincided with the death throes of Adenauer's 'chancellor democracy'. The old man's autocratic style was beginning at last to pall. And when the Second Berlin Crisis erupted in 1961 with the building of the Berlin Wall it was Willy Brandt, mayor of Berlin and SPD candidate for the chancellorship in the coming election, who captured the mood of defiance in that city in contrast to Adenauer's lethargic response. However, though the CDU–CSU lost its absolute majority at the 1961 election, securing only 45.3 per cent of the vote compared with 36.2 per cent for the SPD, Adenauer was able to hang on with support from the FDP. The last straw was the *Spiegel* Affair in 1962. An article in that magazine drew attention to the discrepancy between NATO strategy and Defence Minister Franz-Josef Strauss's talk of a pre-emptive strike with atomic weapons to prevent a Russian attack in Europe. Strauss ordered the arrest of the author and several editors on charges of treason after a midnight raid on the offices of *Der Spiegel*. The explosion of public feeling forced Strauss out of office and the coalition was patched up only on condition that Adenauer resigned in 1963. His successor Erhard was beset by difficulties at home and abroad. Nevertheless, largely because of his popularity as the father of the 'economic miracle' – due in fact more to the Korean war boom than to his free-enterprise formula – he increased the CDU–CSU vote to 47.6 per cent at the 1965 election whilst the SPD secured 39.3 per cent. Many Social Democrats were depressed by this, the fifth electoral defeat in a row, and Willy Brandt, now party leader, resigned his seat and returned to Berlin as mayor.

The Grand Coalition

A few months later the darkening domestic scene brought the SPD to office. The economic miracle was now fading; growth rates were falling, unemployment rising, and prices edging upwards. In October 1966 the CDU–FDP coalition fell apart over taxation policy; the FDP ministers (wanting cuts in public expenditure) resigned, leaving the GFR with a minority government for the first time in its history. A new problem now emerged when the National Democratic Party (NPD) gained eight per cent of the vote in the Hesse *Land* election and 7.4 per cent in Bavaria. Stridently anti-American and anti-Russian and bitterly critical of Bonn politicians, this extreme right-wing party with its neo-Nazi overtones also specialized in attacks on foreign workers, who were attracted in growing numbers to Germany by the prospect of higher living standards. For the first time since 1945 contemporaries began to wonder whether Bonn, like Weimar, might be the prelude to the collapse of parliamentary democracy. As the crisis deepened, Erhard was supplanted as CDU–CSU leader by Kurt Kiesinger. The differences with the FDP could not be patched up. This time it did not matter, for the parliamentary socialist party, tired of exclusion from office, was ready to form a Grand Coalition with the CDU to deal with the pressing problems suddenly facing German democracy. In December 1966 Kiesinger became chancellor with Willy Brandt as vice-chancellor and foreign minister and Herbert Wehner as minister for all-German affairs. The fact that socialists were members of a German cabinet for the first time since 1930 was not, however, greeted with equal enthusiasm by all party members. Though the party executive and the parliamentary party endorsed the coalition, there were indignant protests from many disgruntled socialists and young voters dismayed by the prospect of Butskellism or what was dubbed the Kiesebrandt cabinet. Even in March 1968 the continuation of the coalition was approved by only a narrow majority at the party congress.

The Black–Red coalition of 1966–9 did better than many expected. By 1967 it had succeeded in getting the economy moving again, largely through the adoption of Keynesian techniques. The government injected 27,000 million DM into the economy. And under the Stability and Growth Act of 1967 formal consultative machinery was at last set up to help in the battle to keep prices stable and employment high. Public spending plans at federal, *Land* and local level were carefully co-ordinated while at the same time trade unions and employers were encouraged to reach agreement on moderate wage settlements. The mixture worked; price rises were halted and unemployment fell from 500,000 to 200,000 by 1969.

By 1968 the coalition faced a more serious challenge – the student protest movement which culminated in the serious riots in West Berlin in April 1968 when police and members of the *ausserparlamentarische Opposition* (extra-parliamentary opposition or APO) clashed in a manner reminiscent of the early 1930s. The movement was part of a wider movement of protest in the late 1960s in the Western world against the values of 'bourgeois democracy' and American involvement in Vietnam. There was a specifically German colouration as well: this included demands for the long overdue reform of the archaic and autocratic university system, and also a sense of mounting frustration on the left at the extent to which the Grand Coalition had emasculated opposition in the Bundestag. Fortunately, a student generation is a short one; the protest movement, failing to win popular support, burnt itself out in the early 1970s. It was fortunate, too, that the NPD did not break through the 5 per cent barrier at the 1969 election and declined rapidly thereafter.

The SPD–FDP Coalition

By March 1969 the Black–Red coalition was falling apart. Serious differences had developed, not least over a CDU–CSU proposal to reform the electoral system by abolishing second preferences, a proposal which would have eliminated the FDP as a political factor and had in the end caused the SPD to have second thoughts. At the election in September the CDU vote fell to 46.1 per cent the SPD rose to 42.7 per cent. As the influence of the Church over the political preferences of the faithful declined, the SPD had at last made inroads into Catholic urban strongholds in North Rhine-Westphalia, although in the main the CDU retained its support in rural areas. Ten years after Bad Godesberg the SPD was becoming a people's party; in 1952 45 per cent of the membership were manual workers, 17 per cent white-collar employees, 3.9 per cent civil servants and 4.6 per cent retired people, compared with 34.5 per cent, 19 per cent, 8 per cent and 18 per cent for these groups in 1968. Significantly, membership was rising from 778,000 in 1969 to 954,119 by 1981 as young people were again attracted to the party. In October, Willy Brandt was appointed chancellor and with FDP support formed a coalition government which, renewed after elections in 1972, 1976 and 1980, remained in office for 13 years.

Foreign Affairs

Possibly the most significant achievement of this government lay in the field of foreign affairs, where the SPD and Willy Brandt in particular can claim rightly to have made a real contribution to the improvement of East–West relations. Ideological conflict, once a prominent feature of the contest between CDU and SPD, had died away in the 1960s as party programmes converged and socialists and conservatives offered the electorate not dissimilar fare. The situation was reversed during the controversy over Brandt's *Ostpolitik.* Throughout the 1950s Adenauer pursued an intransigent policy towards the GDR, not only refusing it recognition as a sovereign state but severing relations with states such as Yugoslavia which did. But after the Berlin Crisis of 1961 and the Cuban Missile Crisis of 1962, when the superpowers had seemed to be on the very brink of war, international tension relaxed perceptibly. It seemed to many Germans that Adenauer's policy of negotiating (one day) with Russia from a position of strength had manifestly failed. Surely the time had come to recognize that reunification was a pipe-dream and to work for an agreement with the East Germans to try to improve the lot of fellow countrymen in the GDR? Erhard made a half-hearted gesture in this direction in March 1966, proposing *inter alia* that NATO members should join with the GDR in renouncing the use of force to settle disputes. But as long as Adenauer and Strauss – both of whom fiercely opposed any concessions to the East – remained in key positions in the parliamentary party, Erhard's initiative ran into the sand.

By this time the SPD had committed itself publicly to work for a policy of peaceful co-existence with the GDR. Initial attempts to interest the SED in exchanges to improve relations came to nothing. When the Grand Coalition was formed, however, the SPD insisted that Kiesinger adopt a more positive policy. Accordingly, he proposed in 1967 that the two Germanies try to improve relations in respect of trade and cultural exchanges. Nothing came of this, nor of Kiesinger's offer to negotiate in 1968 with Chairman of the Council of Ministers in the GDR, Willi Stoph. But once the Soviet Union forced the intransigent Ulbricht to resign, a major obstacle to better relations was removed. Coupled with this, the SPD success at the 1969 election gave Brandt a clear mandate for full co-operation with the GDR at all levels short of formal recognition.

In a series of agreements between 1970 and 1972 the GFR normalized relations with Eastern Europe. Brandt commenced in Moscow where in August 1970 the GFR and the USSR signed an agreement promising to respect the territorial integrity of all states in Europe within their existing frontiers, which included the Oder–Neisse line between the GDR and Poland and the frontier between the GFR and the GDR. In December, in a separate treaty with Poland, the GFR recognized the Oder–Neisse line. Finally, in December 1972 the two Germanies signed the Basic Treaty governing their present relationship. In it they promised to develop normal relations, settle all differences without resorting to force and to respect each other's independence.

The CDU–CSU, which upheld the old discredited Hallstein Non-Recognition Doctrine at the polls in 1969 – partly out of fear of being outflanked by the NPD – continued their opposition in the Bundestag. This reached a peak in 1972 when Rainer Barzel, the CDU leader, attempted unsuccessfully to replace Brandt as chancellor through a 'constructive no-confidence motion'. Brandt then forced an election which resulted in the SPD share of the poll increasing to 45.8 per cent while the CDU share fell to 44.9 per cent. After this the CDU–CSU abstained and the Basic Treaty was approved. If the results in terms of improved relations between the two Germanies have been meagre and disappointing – which

led to CDU accusations that too much had been conceded and t
– relations have been placed nevertheless on a more realistic
impossibilist dreams of recovering the 1937 frontiers have beer
last.

Law and Order

At home the coalition was confronted in the 1970s with the problem of urban terrorism. Bank hold-ups, bomb outrages and murders of leading citizens obliged Social Democratic ministers to become rigorous upholders of law and order. The greatly extended powers granted to the police under the anti-terrorist measures of 1972 enabled the authorities to curb violence but worried many (not only socialists) who disliked the deepening authoritarianism of the state. There was sharp criticism, too, of the so-called *Berufsverbote* which the *Länder* or state governments introduced in 1972 with Brandt's approval. Applicants for civil-service posts had to submit to a political scrutiny which by the late 1970s had disqualified many thousands of young people because of left-wing politics or association with extremists. Alarmed by what had happened, the SPD tried to amend the legislation so that mere membership of subversive organizations should not constitute a ground for disqualification. But the Federal Court rejected this amendment.

Economic Policy

The second even more intractable problem facing the coalition was the state of the economy. The first Middle Eastern oil crisis trebled oil prices in 1973, the second in 1979 doubled them. The resulting economic crisis was infinitely more serious than the mild recession of 1966–7. Structural defects (such as a failure to adapt to changing market patterns) were accentuated and unemployment grew rapidly, reaching 1.1 million by 1975. The coalition alternated between Keynesianism and monetarism in desperate attempts to contain the crisis. After 1972 increasing emphasis was laid on the second element. Crisis management, at which Helmut Schmidt excelled (Schmidt replaced Brandt as chancellor in 1974), and increasing reliance on the Bundesbank (Federal Reserve Bank) with its belief in high interest rates to stabilize the economy, became more important than long-term economic strategy. Certainly unemployment was stabilized in the late 1970s, but at a significantly higher level than in the past decade.

Reform Programme

Despite major problems, Brandt and Schmidt embarked upon an ambitious reform programme to revitalize and democratize a society fossilized in the Adenauer era into a stifling conformism and authoritarianism. Much was achieved. Marriage and family law were modernized in the 1970s though a bill to legalize abortion fell foul of the Federal Court. Social welfare was extended with a reform of family allowances and improvements in sickness benefits. Major educational reforms restructuring all institutions from schools to universities were started. Finally, the co-determination system was extended in industry. In 1951 a law gave workers in the coal, iron and steel industries parity with employers on boards of management and one-third representation on boards in other industries. After considerable internal struggle with their FDP partner – but with CDU support – the SPD government agreed to give workers equal representation on boards of all large companies, though shareholders were still to have a decisive voice in the event of conflict.

The End of the Coalition and the Future

In 1982 the coalition collapsed when the partners failed to agree on a budget. The FDP, now moving to the right, supported a CDU–CSU constructive no-confidence motion and Helmut Kohl replaced Schmidt as chancellor. At the 1983 election – engineered by Kohl – the CDU–CSU staged a recovery, obtaining 48.8 per cent of the vote while the SPD fell back to 38.2 per cent. There were probably several reasons for this setback. Some reaction against a party which had held office for 16 years was inevitable. Inside the party there had been much criticism of Schmidt's economic policy, especially of his failure to restore full employment, as well as a sense of frustration on the left that the complexities of the modern world cannot be solved by simple socialist nostrums, and that Keynesianism, which for 40 years had been the mainstay of most European governments, could no longer deliver the goods. An additional factor for many young supporters was the failure of the Schmidt government to respond to mounting pressure from environmentalists critical of the government's commitment to nuclear energy and of the decision to station Pershing missiles on German soil. That the Green Party campaigning on these environmental issues obtained 5.6 per cent of the vote in 1983 was due at least in part to support from disaffected SPD voters. This phenomenon was repeated at the 1987 election which was another great disappointment for the SPD. Although the CDU–CSU lost two million votes and its percentage of the total poll fell to 44.3, Kohl remained in power by renewing the coalition with the FDP. This time the SPD polled only 37 per cent, a decline of 1.2 per cent on the 1983 vote. Once again the Socialists had failed to break through the mood of complacency in the GFR where despite unemployment over the two-million mark inflation was virtually at zero and the DM was riding high on the foreign exchanges. Nor was the uncommitted voter attracted by the SPD demand for the removal of all nuclear weaponry from the GFR (albeit by negotiation). The beneficiaries of the election were the Greens and the FDP. The Greens, campaigning for an immediate ban on nuclear energy – unlike the SPD which proposed to phase it out over ten years – attracted many first-time voters and obtained 8.3 per cent of the poll. The FDP obtained 9.1 per cent, a reassuring sign that many voters preferred the moderate détente policies of Foreign Minister Hans-Dietrich Genscher to the alternative scenario offered by Franz-Josef Strauss. In March Willy Brandt resigned as party chairman after twenty-three years, the first victim of the renewed internal struggle between left and right triggered off by electoral defeat. The election of Hans-Jochen Vogel, chancellor-candidate in 1983, as the new chairman represented a (possibly temporary) victory for the right and centre. But at the end of the 1980s, whether left or right prevails inside the party, the unanswered questions hanging over the SPD must be whether, having proved itself as capable of governing as the CDU–CSU, the SPD can recover some of the old idealism which sustained thousands of socialists throughout the century of the party's existence and whether it can produce a distinctively socialist answer to the economic problems peculiar to the last years of the twentieth century.

22 Democratic Socialism in the Contemporary World

Neil Elder

Democratic socialism, as a third force between the ideological poles of capitalism and Communism, shows many different national mutations in the contemporary world. These different national varieties range along a left–right spectrum, towards the leftward end more clearly socialist in character, towards the right shading off in the direction of liberalism. Whatever the variety, democratic socialists have a common loyalty to the institutions and the spirit of parliamentary government. They belong to a movement seeking incremental reforms which are humanitarian in inspiration and which are directed to the improvement of the lot of society's underdogs. Thus the chief constituency of democratic socialism, so to speak, remains that of the wage-earners in advanced industrial societies – initially blue-collar workers only, but expanding more and more into the white-collar area since the Second World War with the increasing salience of the tertiary sector in advanced industrial societies. This being so, it is not surprising that the movement has by and large maintained its strength and resilience in the face of economic recession. It remains a movement moderate in temper, seeing itself as distanced from the harshnesses of the systems to its left and right and refraining from driving principles to a logical extreme. Hence its acceptance of a significant role for private enterprise and private property alongside a stress on comprehensive welfare provision and also on state action to secure a significant measure of wealth redistribution in the interests of social justice. Precisely where the balance falls as between these components depends on the national context.

Germany

Germany, the birthplace and heartland of democratic socialism, has been divided since 1949 into two states – and, increasingly, two peoples – with the democratic socialist current walled into the Federal Republic in the west. Here that current finds expression in the SPD, the Social Democratic Party, and here 'socialist' has been an electorally damaging label because of the presence of the Communist alternative fatherland next door. This lesson, as has often been remarked, was drawn at the watershed conference held by the SPD at Bad Godesberg in 1959. Since then the SPD has been located towards the right-hand end of the democratic socialist continuum, and this has been the precondition of its advance towards governmental power. It has adopted the 'social market economy' brought into being by the CDU, its main rival – an adjustment made easier by the fact that this system included a very extensive welfare provision – and reached power-sharing in the Grand Coalition of 1966–69. It then went on to become the senior partner in successive coalitions with the FDP from 1969–82. Since 1982 it has returned into opposition, the FDP having reverted to its earlier alignment with the CDU. Here it has been developing a fresh nuance of differentiation from the CDU, namely a somewhat greater readiness – building on the earlier *Ostpolitik* – to accept the division of Germany as final. This acceptance would entail the abandonment of the position reflected in the Federal Republic's Basic Law (*Grundgesetz*) that all West German political arrangments are provisional in character – the reason, indeed, why the GFR has a Basic Law in the first place and not a constitution.

Scandinavia

By way of contrast, the exceptionally powerful Swedish Social Democratic Workers' Party (SAP) occupied a position towards the leftward end of the democratic socialist continuum between the mid-1960s and the assassination of Olof Palme, Prime Minister and party leader, which traumatized the country in 1986. During this period the Swedish labour movement worked steadily towards a blue-collar/white collar alliance with a distinctly anti-capitalist edge. Already in the years of 1946–60 Sweden had become the most comprehensively unionized of 16 advanced industrial countries in the western world; in the 1961–76 period she consolidated her position in this respect. From this power-base the Swedish union movement successfully pressed the Social Democratic government for a whole series of reforms from 1971 to 1976 which made many of the powers of management subject to collective bargaining: these culminated in the Co-Determination Act of 1976 (*medbestämmandelagen* – MBL for short) and were hailed by Olof Palme as the greatest diffusion of power in Sweden since the advent of universal suffrage. The SPD in West Germany also got a co-determination measure on the statute-book in that same year. It sought to alter and extend the long-established principle of co-determination in the FRG so as to shift power to the unions (which incidentally had less than half the Swedish degree of coverage of the workforce at the time). However, not only was the measure as originally conceived less far-reaching than its Swedish counterpart, but it was also greatly diluted before enactment by the action of the SPD's Liberal coalition partners.

More far-reaching still was the scheme for 'worker funds' foreshadowed at a Swedish TUC congress in 1961, picked up by the Metal-workers' Union in 1971, and elaborated by Rudolf Meidner, a TUC economist, before being ratified by another TUC congress in 1976. Briefly, the original scheme envisaged the transfer of a percentage of private company profits annually to union-managed collective funds for the purpose of buying company shares. This was designed to be an ongoing process which would, in the space of a generation or so, result in the unions acquiring a majority holding in Swedish enterprises. Had the measure gone through in this form, it would have meant the creation by parliamentary means of a socialist production system. Not surprisingly, the issue polarized public opinion sharply along left–right lines – or, perhaps more accurately, it polarized elite opinion sharply, since the plan was so involved as to befog the average elector. More particularly, it went too far for the SAP leadership. Successive party-union committees eventually produced an agreed draft in 1981 and a bill reached the statute-book in December 1983. This put an upper limit of 8 per cent on the shares that could be bought by the new funds in any one company; provided that the funds should be used in some small measure for financing the state supplementary pensions scheme; and was described by Olof Palme as not the first step – but *the* step. Nevertheless, the whole episode provided only the latest of a series of illustrations of the ability of the Swedish trade-union movement to generate original policy initiatives in a socialist spirit. It also showed that although Palme could be classified as being on the left of the parliamentary SAP, he was reluctant to push a principle to a logical conclusion.

Scandinavia – specifically here Denmark, Norway and Sweden – was where the principles of democratic socialism were most effectively translated into political practice during the period from the early 1930s to the mid 1960s, although the UK during the six years of Labour rule beginning in 1945 also experienced an effective reforming burst (though of a different kind) and attracted more international attention. In Scandinavia the disunity of the non-socialist parties opened the way to uniquely lengthy periods of Social Democratic (Denmark, Sweden) and Labour (Norway) rule. The extreme case here is that of Sweden, where the party held office almost without a break from 1932 to 1976 and then returned again in 1982. Even in Denmark, where the Social Democrats are weakest, they have been in government for two-thirds of the time since the Second World War – and, before that, from 1929 until the German invasion in 1940.

The power thus acquired has been used in large measure to remedy the discrepancy between private affluence and public squalor by increasingly stringent taxation policies and by the rapid expansion of welfare services. This prompts the reflection that, although the entrepreneurial ethos of American political culture has prevented democratic socialism from taking root there, American radical thinking – and not least that of J. K. Galbraith, who criticized the imbalance between the private and the public sectors in the US – has had an influence on democratic socialism in Scandinavia. This has been strongest, probably, in Sweden, not least in the case of Olof Palme himself. However, the impact of extremely high marginal tax rates combined with inflationary tendencies in the economy has been a significant factor in ousting democratic socialist parties from office latterly in both Norway (1981–86) and Denmark (1982). Here they were succeeded by Conservative-led coalitions, the Conservatives being the leading advocates of public expenditure retrenchment and cuts in marginal tax rates. In Sweden, on the other hand, inept economic management by successive non-socialist governments between 1976 and 1982, combined with Social Democratic claims to be the more effective defenders of the welfare state, enabled the forces of democratic socialism to win the general elections of 1982 and 1985. Finally, before leaving Scandinavia, it is worth noting that in Finland the Social Democrats have been advancing since the mid-1960s to become the leading party in the political system. They captured the potentially powerful office of President with the election of Mauno Koivisto in 1981 and they have provided the premier in successive coalition governments since then in the person of Kalevi Sorsa. Part of the explanation for their success lies in the concurrent deepening of the split between Euro-Communists and hardliners in the once powerful Finnish Communist Party. Social Democratic evolution in Finland has now reached the point at which the party is beginning to approximate to the position of being the natural party of government, in much the same way as its sister parties in the core countries of Scandinavia from the 1930s to the 1980s.

Britain

In Britain the Labour Party was and is the major representative of the democratic socialist current. In 1981, however, it suffered the secession of the so-called 'Gang of Four' – Roy Jenkins, David Owen, Shirley Williams and Bill Rodgers – who announced their intentions in the Limehouse Declaration of January 25 and two months later set up a new Social Democratic Party. More will be said of this shortly.

Labour first achieved real power in Britain in 1945 and briefly believed that it could act as a third force in international affairs between Washington and Moscow. Events in Germany and Poland soon disabused it of this idea, and with Ernest Bevin as Foreign Secretary the country was by 1949 firmly aligned with the US in a bipolar world. On the domestic front the Attlee governments of 1945–51 were the most energetic of Britain's postwar democratic socialist administrations. They greatly expanded welfare provision, most notably perhaps by the introduction of

Aneurin Bevan's National Health Service, and they brought much of the country's heavy industry and public utilities (including transport) into state ownership, thus creating a mixed economy. Nationalization programmes, it may be noted in passing, have never featured as prominently with Scandinavian democratic socialist parties, unless one excepts the debatable case of the Swedish worker funds scheme alluded to earlier. Here these parties have been content to leave the generation of wealth in private hands while exerting a major influence over the distribution of the product.

Neither in Britain nor in Scandinavia has the party mainly representative of democratic socialism faced a serious external challenge from the radical left; in both, however – and especially in Britain and Sweden – markedly socialist pressures have been exerted upon the party from the trade-union movement since the mid 1960s. In Scandinavia these pressures have themselves been exerted within the democratic socialist tradition and in conformity with the usages and the spirit of parliamentary democracy: indeed, even the relatively weak radical left – in the shape of what might be called the national Marxist Socialist People's parties – operates within this tradition. In Britain, however, the growth of union militancy since the Wilson Labour administrations of 1964–66 and 1966–70 has been partly the cause of and partly paralleled by a growth in militancy at the constituency party level: this has led to increased tension between the party's parliamentary leadership and its extra-parliamentary apparatus. This tension began to show during the Wilson administration of 1974–76 and the Callaghan one immediately following (1976–79): it was exacerbated when Callaghan's attempts to work in tandem with the unions broke down in the health service, gravediggers' and other strikes of the 'winter of discontent' (1978–79) which did more than anything else to lose Labour its wider electoral support and to oust it from power.

The immediate cause of the Social Democratic breakaway in 1981 was the change that was made in the rules for the election of the Labour Party leader at the special conference at Wembley on 24 January that year: briefly, this gave the unions and the constituency organizations the preponderant say. Underlying this was a distaste felt by some on the right wing of the party for the tendency of these sections of the party – or, more precisely, some sections of them – to drive socialist principles to a logical extreme. Even more, the rebels were sensitive to the anti-parliamentary edge that had become increasingly apparent in many of the militants: by no means could these be counted within the democratic socialist tradition. The point being made here could be put at its sharpest by saying that, whereas the Swedish Social Democrats have recently expelled Trotskyists from their youth organizations, the National Executive Committee of the British Labour Party voted by 15 to 12 to appoint a Trotskyist as the party's youth leader.

One crucial question was whether it was better to fight entryist elements, with their skills in using the letter of democratic procedures to pervert the spirit, from within or from without the Labour Party. The cost of severance for the Social Democrats has been the loss of union support so that, being on the right-hand end of the democratic socialist spectrum, they have drawn together with the Liberals in an alliance which would appear to need an access of wage-earner strength if it is to win success under the British electoral system. Meanwhile wider electoral considerations are a powerful factor strengthening the democratic socialist leadership within the Labour Party in the continuing struggle against the troublesome minorities, fired by a quasi-religious zeal, within its ranks.

The Mediterranean Countries

In France and the Mediterranean countries – Italy, Spain, Portugal and Greece – democratic socialist fortunes have, on the whole, taken a decided upturn in the past two decades. In all of these countries the parties representative of democratic socialism have had to face severe competition on their left from Communist parties of varying shades of redness, and this competition has been felt both at the parliamentary level and within the trade-union movement where cleavages occur along ideological lines.

The most striking success story is perhaps provided by the French case. Here the role of M. François Mitterand, who was elected leader of the Socialist Party in 1971, has been crucial. Over the past 16 years he has welded together the various factions within his modernized party – in which the professional middle-class, not least schoolteachers, have always played an unusually prominent part – into an effective and coherent force. In the process, the originally much larger Communist Party has been first enlisted as an ally, then eventually overhauled in strength and now relegated to the margins of the French political scene. From an average 20–25 per cent of the vote in the postwar years under the Fourth Republic (1946–58), the Communists have declined to 15 per cent in the presidential election of 1981 and under 10 per cent in the parliamentary elections of March 1986 – their worst figure since 1932. At the same time, Mitterand became the first socialist to capture the powerful presidency of the Fifth Republic in 1981 – this for a seven-year term – and, with Communist support at the second ballot, the left also won their first ever majority in the parliamentary elections of that year. Subsequently the Communists withdrew from the coalition government then formed; Mitterand introduced proportional representation for the March 1986 elections to the National Assembly, and the Socialists, fighting on their own, narrowly lost office. But they emerged with 31.8 per cent of the votes and have become virtually synonymous with 'the left' in the perceptions of the French electorate. Indeed, they have become the opposition, and an opposition with an ingenious politician as an ally in the Elysée Palace.

These developments signify the acceptance by French socialists of the institutional framework of the Fifth Republic and the end of a long-standing basic cleavage between left and right in France on the relative merits of parliamentary sovereignty and executive power. Quite simply, the excutive power instituted by de Gaulle in 1958, and more particularly in 1962 (direct presidential elections), has proved of too much practical utility to give up. Along with this, the Socialist Party under Mitterand has shed its old Marxist intransigence and its tendency to see political conflict with the right in zero-sum terms. It quickly put through the promised nationalization of six large industrial groups on winning power in 1981 but has stopped well short of reorganizing the entire economy along socialist lines and veered away from a radical weakening of the Catholic sector of the educational system – another long-standing basic left–right cleavage in French political life. Many of its reforms, such as the devolution of power to directly elected regional authorities, are not likely to be overturned in the period of 'cohabitation' that is now beginning between a Socialist President and the right-wing government of M. Chirac. In short, the old fundamentalist socialism of the party has softened into a clear new variant of the democratic socialist tradition.

In Italy, Spain, Portugal and Greece various parties compete with one another for the moderate left centre-ground, with those which called themselves Social Democratic (Italy, Spain, Portugal) or Democratic Socialist (Greece) being in general smaller than, and to the right of, the Socialist parties which are the main representatives of the democratic socialist tradition. (In Portugal, however, the Social Democrats came out the stronger in the October 1985 parliamentary elections and now provide the prime minister, Cavaco Silva). In Italy the massive Communist Party has in the past caused splintering to take place in the left centre-ground on the question of whether or not parties located there should co-operate in government under a Christian Democratic prime minister: this happened during the period of the 'opening to the left' (1963–72). More recently, however, the Socialist Party has provided the country with the first President to come from its own ranks in the person of the aged but energetic Sandro Pertini (1978–85). It has also provided the premier, Bettino Craxi, of the longest-lived coalition in postwar Italian history (elected 1983, in office until March 1987: Social Democrats, Liberals, Republicans and, of course, Christian Democrats also participated). Italy, and to a lesser extent Spain, raised the intriguing question of whether or not the Communist Party ought to be counted as a democratic socialist force on the grounds that it is 'Euro-Communist', more pink than red, supportive of the principles of parliamentary democracy, and (in the Italian case only) in favour of NATO membership. These arguments have considerable force, but perhaps the case is best treated as an open question in view of the ambivalent aspects of the party membership's attitudes to Moscow. Again, to confine the scope of democratic socialism in the contemporary world to those parties which are affiliated to the Socialist International has the obvious merit of providing a clear-cut criterion, but it appears too restrictive in view, for example, of the arrival upon the scene of the British SDP.

In Portugal, Spain and Greece the 1970s saw the revival of liberal democratic regimes after periods of military or other right-wing dictatorship. In each case the change of system came in good time to pave the way for the country's accession to the European Community. In Portugal the Social Democrats have been in government more often than any other party since the overthrow of Caetano in 1974, but the Socialist Mario Soares captured the Presidency in February 1986 on a 51.2 per cent vote with the backing of left-wing groups generally. In Greece the Pasok

(Socialist) Party, which can be reckoned as being towards the left-hand end of the democratic socialist spectrum on several counts, came to power after an electoral victory in 1981 and has since consolidated its position after another election in June 1985. In Spain the Socialists reached government for the first time since the civil war with a resounding win under Felipe Gonzalez in the elections of 1982: they have also triumphed with a 52.5 per cent vote in the referendum of March 1986 to ensure that Spain stays in the NATO organization. Their general position has been further strengthened by a three-way split in the ranks of the Spanish Communists.

Elsewhere

Elsewhere in Europe, the Social Democrats have put up a particularly strong showing in Austria – stronger than in the GFR, for example – where they governed in coalition with the right-wing People's Party in a grand share-out government from 1945–66 before going on to win absolute majorities in 1971 and 1975. They virtually anticipated the Bad Godesberg programme in their own New Programme of 1958 and have transformed themselves into a catch-all party shorn of their traditional anti-clericalism. In Switzerland, the Social Democrats command roughly a quarter of the electorate and participate in the permanent all-party coalitions which are a feature of the country's political system. In Belgium and Holland their effectiveness has been reduced by linguistic divisions but favoured by the slow decline of religious loyalties in politics: they have often been part of governing coalitions, although currently out of office in both countries. Mention should also be made of Des O'Malley's Progressive Democrats ('Progos'), a new party in the democratic socialist tradition, which is seeking to break the long-established dominance of Irish politics by Fianna Fail and Fine Gael, two groupings with their roots in the Irish civil war. Last but not least, outside Europe the swing of the parliamentary pendulum has brought the Hawke and Lange Labour administrations to power in Australia and New Zealand respectively.

Conclusion

It is now time to draw the threads of this panoramic survey together in a necessarily brief concluding section. In domestic politics, democratic socialist parties continue to draw their dynamism from the motivations outlined at the start of this chapter. In economic recession, they are concerned to use state resources to promote employment-creating measures; they seek the maximum protection for welfare services and the amelioration of working conditions, not infrequently by the introduction of 'industrial democracy' reforms; and, starting from these premises, they present themselves as more competent to manage the economy than their rivals on the right. Often, though not universally, they look favourably upon incomes policies. They have become increasingly sensitized to environment issues – especially so, perhaps, in the German Federal Republic, where the Greens have been having an increasing impact on the political scene. They constantly have to manage internal tensions between what might be called the 'majoritarians' on the right who are acutely aware of vote-maximizing requirements and the ideologues on the left who are anxious to transform society in a socialist direction.

The countries of the Eastern bloc remain closed to democratic socialism by the ideological permafrost. The most recent demonstration of this has been the fate of the remarkable Solidarity uprising in Poland 1980–81. Soviet security requirements entail the continued enforcement of the Brezhnev Doctrine although its author is discredited by the current party leadership.

Nevertheless, one of the more notable developments in democratic socialism in the past seven years has been its anxiety to try to mitigate the asperities of East–West nuclear rivalry as the level of conflict over this issue has risen. Here again, democratic socialist opinion ranges along a spectrum. The French Socialist Party, for example, resolutely maintains the country's security policy unaltered in essentials; New Zealand unilaterally follows a 'keep-out' strategy on nuclear weapons; the British Labour Party has manifested acute withdrawal symptoms. The installation of Cruise and Pershing missiles in Western Europe, followed by the complex US 'Star Wars' initiative, have brought security issues to the forefront of the international scene. The commonest reaction among democratic socialist parties in countries which are members of the Western alliance has been to seek to act as a third force here also, by pursuing initiatives to try to break the deadlock between the superpowers without jeopardizing alliance unity on fundamentals.

Part V
Epilogue

Marxism, Communism and Social Democracy

Eugene Kamenka

Marx and Lassalle

Both Marxism and Social Democracy – as distinct from socialism – were born in Germany. Karl Marx, the greatest (though not the nicest or the most decent) of socialist thinkers, was reared in Trier, shaped by Kantian, Fichtean and Hegelian philosophy, excited by the radical critique of Eduard Gans, Ludwig Feuerbach and other Left or Young Hegelians and led to communism by Moses Hess and by the criticism of German conditions. His only direct, serious and prominent involvements in the wider political scene were in the Rhineland in 1842–43, and again, more seriously and more prominently, in 1848–49. The German labour movement, initially, may have owed as much if not more to Ferdinand Lassalle as to Karl Marx, stuck in exile in London for most of his life, never an orator and never at his best in dealing with people. There are those who believe that Lassalle's initially primary influence has never been eradicated. The 1875 programme that united the two wings of Marxists and Lassalleans was personally displeasing to Marx. But by 1890, the newly renamed German Social Democratic Party or SPD had largely accepted Marxism as the core of its ideology. By 1914, as Susan Tegel reminds us, it was the largest political party in Germany and the largest socialist party in the world. 'Orthodox' Marxism and 'revisionism' were formulated in its ranks and by its leaders. The language of Marxism, until the First World War, was German, even if the most exciting Marxist thinkers of the period – in economics, in law, on nationalism and in the formulation of socialist theories of the state and political government – were living in Austria–Hungary.

Despite an appalling interlude under National Socialism that has long, deeply and rightly tarnished modern Germany's moral, cultural and intellectual credentials, the role of Germany and of Germans in the working out and the initial discussion of Marxism, Communism and

Social Democracy remains immense. It was in Germany, through the electoral and recruiting successes of the SPD, even before the First World War, that Marxism was made to appear wedded to and capable of political democracy – rejecting conspiracy, dictatorship and terror, closely linked with an actual, conscious and decent working class. It was in Germany, too, that Marxism, even revolutionary Marxism, sought to absorb the great thought of the past and the exciting intellectual developments of the contemporary world. In the work of Karl Korsch and Georg Lukàcs, in the discussions at the Frankfurt Institute for Social Research, in Grünberg's *Archiv* and in the culture of the Weimar Republic generally, at least some Marxisms were saved from Lenin's concentration on power and ends and from Stalin's crude and opportunistic elevation of dogmatism and tactics. The gradual appreciation of the link between Marxism and European culture, and of the democratic and emancipatory moments in Marx's thought, came to the English-speaking world through a series of Marxist and Social Democratic German and Austrian thinkers driven from their homeland by the Nazi terror. No one interested in Marxist socialist theory and practice, and the relations between them and democracy, can fail to be interested in the history of the German SPD, to which this book is devoted. Here, Lenin and the Russian Revolution were criticized, as they were by the Russian (Menshevik) Social Democratic Party before it was ruthlessly destroyed, from a Marxist standpoint. Here, the working class and the trade unions and not only the revolutionary party were taken seriously; here, labour legislation and social legislation were drawn up and applied by people who saw themselves as socialists and often as democratic Marxists.

Marxism, for no other reason than the intellectual power and genius of Marx and his ability to weld together earlier competing socialist traditions, has put its lasting stamp on the language of socialism, in the Social Democratic as much as in the Communist camp. Nevertheless, the 100 years since Marx's death in 1883 have witnessed the disintegration of classical European Marxism as the ideology of and for the working class, as a science of society and as a principled, coherent plan for achieving a socialist future. In its Leninist form, Marxism has become, as George Lichtheim put it, an ideology for backward nations, its predictions to be proved false in the moment of success. In their democratic form, Marxism and Social Democracy have had to live with the failure of the working class to play the 'historic role' that Marx envisaged – the central theoretical problem for and in the history of the SPD. The proletariat, indeed, has become neither the most numerous nor the most revolutionary class. Proletarians are not so destitute that they have nothing to lose but their chains. They are no longer so free of property that they cannot help but usher in the society without property. At crucial periods, they and their leaders have proven more nationalist than internationalist, more self-seeking than 'universal'. The story of the SPD told in this exciting and important book is the story both of the disintegration of Marxism into its initial disparate components, welded together in a time-bound act of force and faith, and the story of the collective upward mobility of the working class, of the increasing socialization of capitalism from within, of the essential correctness, in short, of Bernstein's predictions and of Kautsky's rejection of the Leninist course as destructive of any relationship between revolutionary socialism and the working class.

Nevertheless, Social Democracy in Germany and elsewhere has much to be proud of. The Weimar Republic was, for a period, a social laboratory, seeking to harness knowledge, imagination and compassion to the work of producing a better society. The outstanding feature of the twentieth century, perhaps, has not been the actual securing of human rights throughout the world: our century has seen more horrors in this regard than many earlier ones, and some of them were caused by Germans of all walks of life. The outstanding achievement of the twentieth century, consummating work begun in the Enlightenment and during the nineteenth, has been the steady extension of the class of persons who count as human, entitled to compassion, opportunity, dignity and respect. Slaves, servants, workers, Asians, Africans, women, children and finally indigenous peoples have all been admitted, in theory at least, and to a large extent in practice, to the circle of those who are to be treated as fully human and whose sufferings and longings count equally with those of other people. Socialists have long been in the forefront of the battle for that, in Germany as elsewhere – though they have by no means been the only carriers of moral compassion, human sympathy and the recognition of the essential moral equality of mankind and though they have been as capable of lapsing from those ideals as many others.

Murderous Utopias

Yet the story of Social Democracy in the world today is not simply a 'we were right' story. Social Democrats can and should congratulate themselves on not having to accept responsibility for and defend either Nazism and fascism or the Bolshevik terror, the Stalinist purges, show trials and labour camps, the social catastrophes of Mao's Great Leap Forward and Great Proletarian Cultural Revolution, the murderous utopia of Pol Pot's Cambodia or the fact that the Soviet Union remains the strongest one-party dictatorship and the last major empire in the world. Social Democrats did not invade Hungary, Czechoslovakia and Afghanistan. They have not created, and they have mostly criticized and resisted, what the contemporary socialist humanist Steven Lukes rightly calls 'the grim, surveillance-minded demoralized world of contemporary "actually existing socialism" above all in the USSR and Eastern Europe [but also in the German 'Democratic' Republic] where civil society and public life have been destroyed and Marxist and moral vocabulary have been wholly devalued, the worthless currency of an empty rhetoric'. These horrors are more disturbing for our future than the doings of Chilean dictators and Haitian presidents, which smack of the past. But what democratic socialists gain in decency, in realism, in democracy, is also and can be presented as loss – in accommodation, withering away of revolutionary impulse and radical moral indignation, in willingness to go with the moderate majority and to abandon 'true socialism'. The Second World War, like most wars, produced both great social upheavals and a strong and widespread belief in a new world of freedom and social responsibility. Unlike the Communists, Social Democracy stood for both, and even conservative parties came more and more to accept the role of the state, of trade unions and of social legislation in promoting welfare and greater equality for all. What Professor Ralf Dahrendorf has called the postwar Social Democratic consensus and the doctrine of the *sozialer Rechtsstaat* – the democratic rule-of-law-based welfare state, – were the result. In Germany, this drama was played out in complex and often uncertain conditions. Yet it is startling how universal, how international, the political struggles and political issues in modern Western societies are, at least outside America. Some years ago, in Hamburg, I observed Helmut Schmidt's election campaign for a second term as chancellor at almost the same time as I watched the electoral campaigns in Australia and in Great Britain. It was incredible how similar the issues and the parties were: the Social Democrats or Labour Parties an uneasy coalition of right-wing and centralist working class, trade unions, left-wing intellectuals and students, with some professional groups, and loosely allied environmentalists and trendies, always ready to split off and not at home with workers; the Conservative Party also split between right-wing social and economic 'dries' and more liberal 'wets'. The terms were not yet fashionable then; the ideas were. In all three countries, electoral success depended on appearing to hold to the middle ground, repudiating the right and the left without disastrously alienating both of them. Those who wish to remain democrats have to pay a price. They have to turn from revolutionary rhetoric to welfare as the consumer sees it, from Marxist ideology to politics. That is what the SPD and all other great democratic labour parties have done, to the disgust always of some of their more radical members and to the disappointment of those who preach the urgency and overriding importance of a single issue, whether it be saving the forests, banning nuclear weapons immediately and one-sidedly if necessary, affirmative action for women or for indigenous peoples, freedom of information or a better deal for pensioners. Since the beginning of the 1970s, indeed, democratic socialists, to the distress of their left-wing colleagues, have had to accept a world of increasing economic interdependence in which the scope of government action is severely limited by the need to gain or retain international economic competitiveness and to keep an eye on inflation, employment and the decreasing tolerance of the electorate for ever-higher taxation and aspects of bureaucratic values and power.

End of Ideology?

The practical Western politician thus has much, surprisingly much, to learn from the practice and political history of the Social Democratic and Labour Parties in all parts of the democratic Western world. The extent to which this is so is brought out by the fact that they shamelessly borrow and repeat each other's ideas, tactics and slogans, but also each other's practical and sensible legislative arrangements and reforms – from pregnancy leave to worker-management committees, from holiday leave loadings to US-initiated equal opportunity tribunals, from various types of health insurance or free health service to the promotion of on-the-job training and late entries to tertiary education. All this, modern Western democratic societies have learnt to do and accept. In practice, it is only the range, scale and pace of such social legislation that is at issue between right and left, between Social Democratic and major non-socialist parties. The growing hostility to the state and its incessant demand for revenue is common to almost all parts of the political spectrum, but offset by even stronger demands that the state guarantee security and provide benefits – to the capitalist if you are a capitalist, to the worker if you are a worker.

Socialism was a nineteenth-century movement, a reaction against and a criticism of the coherent and self-confident elevation of the *Gesellschaft* principles and realities of nineteenth-century *laissez-faire* capitalism. To that *Gesellschaft,* socialists counterposed not one coherent social paradigm and goal, but a mixture of two conflicting paradigms. On the one hand, they elevated the egalitarianism and communality of the face-to-face *Gemeinschaft,* robbed of its traditional emphasis on status and hierarchy, but still held together by a common, pervasive ideology, that might leave the individual no room to breathe or think in. On the other hand, they elevated the technical rationality and state supervision extolled by Saint-Simonian socialism: the bureaucratic-administrative paradigm of the rationally planned and administered society. Marxists and Marx himself pretended that the *Gesellschaft* would be superseded by a society that was at once rationally planned and a free and communal association of producers capable of subordinating all social activities and institutions to universal human needs and desires that would engender no significant social or political conflict.

Today, almost no one believes this. For major political parties in Western societies the age of coherent and systematic ideology is over; so is their capacity to rely on a firm and unified, unshifting class base. In practical politics today, we seek increasingly an optimal mix between *Gemeinschaft, Gesellschaft* and bureaucratic-administrative approaches – not only to society, but to the family, the school, the legal proceeding, the workplace, the trade union and the political party. With an increasingly sophisticated electorate, democracy has, at least to some extent, weakened dogmatism and demagoguery. It does fragment interests and subvert principles: what it loses in firm direction and overriding commitment, it gains in plurality of thinking and testing of proposals. As long as Social Democracy continues, as the SPD has done, to take democracy seriously, this will be so. Socialism will remain a human socialism but will have less and less specifically socialist as distinct from 'progressive' doctrinal content. In Europe, historical traditions and past class antagonisms count for more than in the post-historical societies of the United States, Canada, Australia, Singapore. But everywhere sensible democratic socialists no longer believe that the nationalization of the means of production, distribution and exchange will in itself ensure either economic efficiency or the free classless society. Many, indeed, recognize that there is an important and fundamental social tension between political democracy and a nationalized economy. They elevate, here as in many other areas, a pragmatic mix of state action and private enterprise, of social responsibilities and individual freedoms. Above all, the conflicts and tensions of modern post-industrial societies and the structure of classes and interest groups within them, the popular base of Social Democracy and its various factions, are no longer well described by the classical (Marxist and pseudo-Marxist) languages of socialism. Increasingly, socialism becomes a set of often unrelated moral stances rather than a theory of society. In Germany, that evolution took place under very special conditions, but the outcome has proved much the same. It is apparent in the thought and work of Eduard Bernstein, as it was in the policies of West German Social Democracy under the chairmanship of Willy Brandt.

Bibliography

Primary Sources

Bebel, August (1971), *Woman under Socialism* (New York).
Bernstein, Eduard (1895), *Sozialismus und Demokratie in der grossen englischen Revolution* (Stuttgart); translated by H. J. Stenning as (1930) *Cromwell and Communism* (London), 2nd edn.
Bernstein, Eduard (1899), *Die Voraussetzungen des Sozialismus und die Aufgaben der Sozialdemokratie* (Stuttgart); translated by E. C. Harvey as (1909), *Evolutionary Socialism* (London).
Bernstein, Eduard (1901), *Zur Theorie und Geschichte des Sozialismus,* 3 vols (Berlin).
Bernstein, Eduard (1921a), *Die deutsche Revolution: Ihr Ursprung, ihr Verlauf und ihr Werk* (Berlin-Fichtenau).
Bernstein, Eduard (1921b), *My Years of Exile* (London and New York).
Bernstein, Eduard (1922a), *Das Görlitzer Programm der Sozialdemokratischen Partei Deutschlands,* 2nd edn (Berlin).
Bernstein, Eduard (1922b), 'Leipzig und wir', *Vorwärts,* No. 29 (18.1.1922).
Bernstein, Eduard (1930), *Entwicklungsgang eines Sozialisten* (Leipzig).
Braun, Adolf (ed.) (1906), *Ziele und Wege: Erläuterungen sozialdemokratischer Gegenwartsforderungen* (Berlin).
Forsdick, Raymond B. (1915), *The European Police System* (New York).
Hartig, Valtin (1925), 'Kulturbewegung im Sozialismus', *Die Tat,* vol. 16.
Hoegener, Wilhelm (1958), *Die verratene Republik: Geschichte der deutschen Gegenrevolution* (Munich).
Kampffmeyer, Paul (1930), *Eduard Bernstein und der sozialistische Aufbau: Zum 80. Geburtstag Eduard Bernsteins* (Berlin).
Karl Kautsky Papers, IISG Amsterdam.
Kautsky, Karl (1919), *Wie der Weltkrieg entstand. Dargestellt nach dem Aktenmaterial des Deutschen Auswärtigen Amtes* (Berlin).
Kautsky, Karl (1924), 'Die Frage der Kriegsschuld', *Vorwärts,* No. 427 (10.9.1924).
Landsberg, Otto (1931), *Die politische Krise der Gegenwart* (Berlin).
Löbe, Paul (1925), *Eduard Bernstein als Breslauer Abgeordneter* (Berlin).
Lukacs, Georg (1924), 'Der Triumph Bernsteins', in *Geschichte und Klassenbewusstsein* (Nieuwied and Berlin, 1968), pp. 591–7.
Mierendorff, Carl (1930), 'Gesicht und Charakter der Nationalsozialistischen Bewegung', *Die Gesellschaft,* vol. 7, pp 489–504.
Retzlaw, Karl (1971), *Spartakus. Aufstieg und Niedergang. Erinnerungen eines Parteiarbeiters* (Frankfurt).
Russell, Bertrand (1919), *Proposed Roads to Freedom* (NewYork).
Stampfer, Friedrich (1936), *Die 14 Jahre der ersten deutschen Republik* (Prague).
Sorel, Georges (1900), *Les Polémiques pour l'interprétation du marxisme: Bernstein et Kautsky* (Paris).
Tucholsky, Kurt (1975), *Gesammelte Werke,* 10 vols (Reinbek bei Hamburg).
Weyl, K. (1912), *Die Frau und die Gemeindepolitik* (Berlin).

Secondary Sources

Abelshauser, W. et al. (eds) (1985), *Deutsche Sozialgeschichte 1914–1945: Ein*

historisches Lesebuch (Munich).
Abendroth, Wolfgang (1972), *A Short History of the European Working Class* (New York and London).
Abraham, David (1981), *The Collapse of the Weimar Republic: Political Economy and Crisis* (Princeton).
Anderson, Evelyn (1945), *Hammer or Anvil? The Story of the German Working Class Movement* (London).
Angel, Pierre (1961), *Eduard Bernstein et l'évolution du socialisme allemand* (Paris).
Angress, Werner (1963), *The Stillborn Revolution: The Communist Bid for Power in Germany, 1921–23* (Princeton).
Ardagh, John (1987), *Germany and the Germans: An Anatomy of Society Today* (London).
Armeson, Robert B. (1964), *Total War and Compulsory Labor: A Study of the Military-Industrial Complex in Germany during World War I* (The Hague).
Auernheimer, Gustav (1985), *'Genosse Herr Doktor'. Zur Rolle von Akademikern in der deutschen Sozialdemokratie 1890 bis 1933* (Giessen).
Balfour, Michael (1982), *West Germany: A Contemporary History* (London).
Balser, Frolinde (1962), *Sozial-Demokratie 1848/9–1863: Die erste deutsche Arbeiterorganisation 'Allgemeine deutsche Arbeiterverbrüderung' nach der Revolution*, 2 vols (Stuttgart).
Berki, R. N. (1975), *Socialism* (London).
Berlau, A. J. (1949), *The German Social Democratic Party, 1914–1921* (New York).
Bertrand, Charles L. (ed) (1977), *Revolutionary Situations in Europe 1917–1922: Germany, Italy, Austria–Hungary* (Montreal).
Beyme, Klaus von and Manfred G. Schmidt (eds) (1985), *Policy and Politics in the Federal Republic of Germany* (Aldershot).
Bieber, H.-J. (1981), *Gewerkschaften in Krieg und Revolution: Arbeiterbewegung, Industrie, Staat und Militär in Deutschland 1914–1920*, 2 vols (Hamburg).
Boak, Helen L. (1981), 'Women in Weimar Germany: The "Frauenfrage" and the Female Vote', in R. Bessel and E. J. Feuchtwanger (eds), *Social Change and Political Development in Weimar Germany* (London), pp. 155–73.
Boll, Friedhelm (1980), *Frieden ohne Revolution? Friedensstrategien der Sozialdemokratie vom Erfurter Programm 1891 bis zur Revolution 1918* (Bonn).
Boll, Friedhelm (1981), *Massenbewegungen in Niedersachsen 1906–1920: Eine sozialgeschichtliche Untersuchung zu den unterschiedlichen Entwicklungstypen Braunschweig und Hannover* (Bonn).
Brandt, Brigitte (1984), *Erich Ollenhauer: Biedermann und Patriot* (Berlin).
Brandt, Willy (1971), *In Exile* (London).
Brandt, Willy (1986), *World Armament and World Hunger*, translated by A. Bell (London).
Braunthal, Gerard (1978), *Socialist Labor and Politics in Weimar Germany* (Hamden).
Breitman, Richard, 'Negative Integration and Parliamentary Politics: Literature on German Social Democracy, 1890–1933' *Central European History*, vol. 13 (1980), pp. 175–97.
Breitman, Richard (1981), *German Socialism and Weimar Democracy* (Chapel Hill).
Breuilly, J. and W. Sachse (1984), *Joachim Friedrich Martens (1806–1877) und die deutsche Arbeiterbewegung* (Göttingen).
Bridenthal, Renate (1977), 'Something Old, Something New: Women between the Two World Wars', in R. Bridenthal and C. Koonz (eds), *Becoming Visible: Women in European History* (Boston), pp. 424–44.
Bridenthal, R. and C. Koonz (1976), 'Kinder, Kirche, Küche: Weimar Women in Politics and Work', in B. A. Carroll (ed), *Liberating Women's History: Theoretical and Critical Essays* (Urbana, Chicago and London), pp. 302–29.
Bridenthal, R., A. Grossmann and M. Kaplan (eds) (1984), *When Biology Became*

Destiny: Women in Weimar and Nazi Germany (New York).
Bronner, Stephen Eric (ed) (1978), *The Letters of Rosa Luxemburg* (Boulder).
Brose, Eric Dorn (1985), *Christian Labor and the Politics of Frustration in Imperial Germany* (Washington, D.C.).
Broszat, Martin (1984), *Die Machtergreifung: Der Aufstieg der NSDAP und die Zerstörung der Weimarer Republik* (Munich).
Brüggemeier, Franz (1983), *Leben vor Ort: Ruhrbergleute und Ruhrbergbau 1889–1919* (Munich).
Bull, Hedley (ed) (1986), *The Challenge of the Third Reich* (London).
Carr, Jonathan (1985), *Helmut Schmidt: Helmsman of Germany* (London).
Carsten, F. L. (1972), *Revolution in Central Europe, 1918–1919* (London).
Carsten, F. L. (1982), *War Against War: British and German Radical Movements in the First World War* (London, Berkeley and Los Angeles).
Chalmers, Douglas A. (1964), *The Social Democratic Party of Germany* (New Haven).
Childs, David and Jeffrey Johnson (1981), *West Germany: Politics and Society* (London).
Comfort, Richard (1966), *Revolutionary Hamburg* (Stanford).
Conradt, David P. (1986), *The German Polity,* 3rd edn (New York).
Conradt, Sylvia and Kirsten Heckmann-Janz (1985), *'du heiratest ja doch!' 80 Jahre Schulgeschichte von Frauen* (Frankfurt).
Crosland, C. A. R. (1956), *The Future of Socialism* (London).
Cullingford, E. C. M. (1973), *Trade Unions in West Germany* (London).
Dahrendorf, Ralf (1969), *Society and Democracy in Germany* (New York).
Diehl, James M. (1977), *Parliamentary Politics in Weimar Germany* (Bloomington, In.).
Dominick, R. H. (1982), *Wilhelm Liebknecht and the Founding of the German Social Democratic Party* (Chapel Hill).
Dorpalen, Andreas (1983), 'SPD and KPD in der Endphase der Weimar Republik', *Vierteljahrshefte für Zeitgeschichte,* vol. 31.
Ebbinghausen, Rolf and Friedrich Tiemann (eds) (1984), *Das Ende der Arbeiterbewegung in Deutschland* (Opladen).
Edinger, Lewis J. (1956), *German Exile Politics* (Stanford).
Edinger, Lewis J. (1965), *Kurt Schumacher* (Stanford).
Edinger, Lewis J. (1986), *West German Politics* (New York).
Elder, N., A. H. Thomas and A. Arter (1982), *The Consensual Democracies* (Oxford).
Engelhardt, Ulrich (1977), *'Nur vereinigt sind wir stark': Die Anfänge der deutschen Gewerkschaftsbewegung,* 2 vols (Stuttgart).
Evans, R. J. (1976), *The Feminist Movement in Germany 1894–1933* (London).
Evans, R. J. (1980), 'German Social Democracy and Women's Suffrage 1891–1918', *Journal of Contemporary History,* vol. 15, pp. 533–57.
Evans, R. J. (1981), 'Politics and the Family: Social Democracy and the Working-class Family in Theory and Practice before 1914', in R. J. Evans and W. R. Lee (eds), *The German Family* (London and Totowa, NJ), pp. 256–88.
Evans, R. J. (ed) (1982), *The German Working Class 1888–1933: The Politics of Everyday Life* (London).
Evans, R. J. and Dick Geary (1986), *The German Unemployed 1918–1936* (London).
Feldman, Gerald D. (1966), *Army, Industry, and Labor in Germany 1914–1918* (Princeton).
Feldman, Gerald D. (1977), 'Socio-economic Structures in the Industrial Sector and Revolutionary Potentialities, 1917–22', in C. L. Bertrand (ed), *Revolutionary Situations in Europe, 1917–22: Germany, Italy, Austria–Hungary* (Montreal), pp. 159–70.
Feldman, Gerald D., Eberhard Kolb and Reinhard Rürup (1972), 'Die Massenbewegungen der Arbeiterschaft in Deutschland am Ende des Ersten

Weltkrieges (1917–1920)' *Politische Vierteljahrsschrift*, vol. 13, pp. 84–105.
Feldman, Gerald and Irmgard Steinisch (1985), *Industrie und Gewerkschaften 1918–1924: Die überforderte Zentralarbeitsgemeinschaft* (Stuttgart).
Fessender, P. L. (1976), *The Role of Women Deputies in the German National Constituent Assembly and the Reichstag, 1919–1933* (Ohio State University PhD Dissertation).
Fischer, Fritz (1967), *Germany's Aims in the First World War* (London).
Fischer, Fritz (1986), *From Kaiserreich to Third Reich: Elements of Continuity in German History 1871–1945* (London).
Fletcher, Roger (1984), *Revisionism and Empire: Socialist Imperialism in Germany 1897–1914* (London).
Foitzik, Jan (1986), *Zwischen den Fronten: Zur Politik, Organisation und Funktion linker politischer Kleinorganisationen im Widerstand 1933 bis 1939/40* (Bonn).
Fout, John C. (ed) (1984), *German Women in the Nineteenth Century* (New York).
Fowkes, B. (1984), *Communism in Germany under the Weimar Republic* (London).
Fromm, Erich (1984), *The Working Class in Weimar Germany: A Psychological and Sociological Study* (Leamingston Spa).
Gates, Robert (1974), 'German Socialism and the Crisis of 1929–33', *Central European History*, vol. 7, no. 4 pp. 332–59.
Gay, Peter (1952), *The Dilemma of Democratic Socialism: Eduard Bernstein's Challenge to Marx* (New York; Collier edn 1962).
Geary, Dick (1978), 'Radicalism and the Worker: Metalworkers and Revolution 1914–23', in R. J. Evans (ed), *Society and Politics in Wilhelmine Germany* (London), pp. 267–86.
Geary, Dick (1981), *European Labour Protest 1848–1939* (London).
Giddens, Anthony (1985), *The Nation-State and Violence* (Cambridge).
Gilcher-Holtey, Ingrid (1986), *Das Mandat des Intellektuellen: Karl Kautsky und die Sozialdemokratie* (Berlin).
Glees, Antony (1982), *Exile Politics during the Second World War* (London).
Glotz, Peter (1982), *Die Beweglichkeit des Tankers: Die Sozialdemokratie zwischen Staat und neuen sozialen Bewegungen* (Munich).
Goodrum, Richard G. (1969), *The German Socialists and National Unification* (University of Wisconsin PhD Dissertation).
Graf, W. D. (1976), *The German Left since 1945* (Cambridge).
Grebing, Helga (1976), 'Faschismus, Mittelschichten und Arbeiterklasse: Probleme der Faschismus-Interpretation in der sozialistischen Linken während der Weltwirtschaftskrise', *Internationale Wissenschaftliche Korrespondenz zur Geschichte der deutschen Arbeiterbewegung*, vol. 12, pp. 443–60.
Grebing, Helga (1977), *Der Revisionismus: Von Bernstein bis zum 'Prager Frühling'* (Munich).
Grebing, Helga (1985), *The History of the German Labour Movement: A Survey*, translated by E. Korner, rev. edn (Leamington Spa).
Gress, David (1985), *Peace and Survival: West Germany, the Peace Movement and European Security* (Stanford).
Groh, Dieter (1973), *Negative Integration und revoluntionärer Attentismus: Die deutsche Sozialdemokratie am Vorabend des Ersten Weltkrieges* (Frankfurt).
Grosser, Alfred (1974), *Germany in Our Time: A Political History of the Postwar Years* (London).
Gustafsson, Bo (1972), *Marxismus und Revisionismus: Eduard Bernsteins Kritik des Marxismus und ihre ideengeschichtlichen Voraussetzumgen*, 2 vols (Frankfurt).
Guttsman, W. L. (1981), *The German Social Democratic Party, 1875–1933: From Ghetto to Government* (London).
Hackett, Amy K. (1976), *The Politics of Feminism in Wilhelmine Germany, 1890–1918* (Columbia University PhD Dissertation).

Hagemann, Karen (1983), 'Frauen in der Hamburger SPD der Weimarer Republik', in Arno Herzig et al. (eds), *Arbeiter in Hamburg* (Hamburg), pp. 443–56.

Hamerow, T. S. (1958), *Restoration, Revolution, Reaction: Economics and Politics in Germany, 1815–1871* (Princeton).

Haupt, Georges (1986), *Aspects of International Socialism 1871–1914* (Cambridge).

Heckart, Beverly (1974), *From Bassermann to Bebel: The Grand Bloc's Quest for Reform in the Kaiserreich, 1900–1914* (New Haven and London).

Heimann, Horst and Thomas Meyer (eds) (1978), *Bernstein und der Demokratische Sozialismus* (Berlin and Bonn).

Hickey, S. H. F. (1985), *Workers in Imperial Germany: The Miners of the Ruhr* (Oxford).

Hirschfeld, G. (ed) (1984), *Exile in Great Britain* (Leamington Spa).

Honeycutt, K. (1975), *Clara Zetkin: A Left-wing Socialist and Feminist in Wilhelmine Germany* (Columbia University PhD Dissertation).

Hunt, R. N. (1970), *German Social Democracy 1918–1933* (Chicago); 2nd edn 1976.

Hyrkkänen, Markku (1986), *Sozialistische Kolonialpolitik: Eduard Bernsteins Stellung zur Kolonialpolitik und zum Imperialismus 1882–1914* (Helsinki).

James, Harold (1986), *The German Slump: Politics and Economics 1924–1936* (Oxford).

Kaelble, Hartmut (1986), *Industrialisation and Social Inequality* (Leamington Spa and New York).

Kendall, Walter (1975), *The Labour Movement in Europe* (London).

Kendall Rodgers, H. (1983), 'Eduard Bernstein Speaks to the Fabians: A Turning-point in Social Democratic Thought?', *International Review of Social History*, vol. 28, no. 3, pp. 320–38.

Kirby, David (1986), *War, Peace and Revolution: International Socialism at the Crossroads 1914–1918* (Aldershot and New York).

Kocka, Jürgen (1984), *Facing Total War: German Society 1914–1918* (Leamington Spa).

Kolb, Eberhard (1962), *Die Arbeiterräte in der deutschen Innenpolitik* (Düsseldorf).

Koonz, C. (1976), 'Conflicting Allegiances: Political Ideology and Women Legislators in Weimar Germany', *Signs: Journal of Women in Culture and Society*, vol. 1, no. 3, part I, pp. 663–83.

Korpi, Walter (1978), *The Working Class in Welfare Capitalism: Work, Unions and Politics in Sweden* (London).

Kubalkova, V, and A. Cruikshank (1985), *Marxism and International Relations* (Oxford).

Kuczynski, Jürgen (1957), *Der Ausbrach des Ersten Weltkrieges und die deutsche Sozialdemokratie: Chronik und Analyse* (East Berlin).

Labedz, Leopold (ed) (1962), *Revisionism: Essays on the History of Marxist Ideas* (London).

Langewiesche, Dieter (1982), 'Politik – Gesellschaft – Kultur: Zur Problematik von Arbeiterkultur und kulturellen Arbeiterorganisationen in Deutschland nach dem 1. Weltkrieg', *Archiv für Sozialgeschichte*, vol. 22, pp. 359–402.

Langewiesche, Dieter and Klaus Schönhoven (1976), 'Arbeiterbibliotheken und Arbeiterlektüre im Wilhelminischen Deutschland', *Archiv für Sozialgeschichte*, vol. 16, pp. 135–204.

Laqueur, Walter (1985), *Germany Today* (London).

Lehmann, Albrecht (ed) (1984), *Studien zur Arbeiterkultur* (Münster).

Lidtke, Vernon (1966), *The Outlawed Party: Social Democracy in Germany, 1878–1890* (Princeton).

Lidtke, Vernon (1985), *The Alternative Culture: Socialist Labor in Imperial Germany* (Oxford and New York).

Lindemann, Albert S. (1983), *A History of European Socialism* (New Haven and London).

Löwenthal, Richard (1974), *Sozialismus und Aktive Demokratie* (Frankfurt).

Löwenthal, Richard (1984), *Social Change and Cultural Crisis* (New York).

McKibbin, Ross (1984), 'Why was there no Marxism in Great Britain?', *English Historical Review*, vol. 99, pp. 297–331.

Maier, Charles S. (1975), *Recasting Bourgeois Europe. Stabilization in France, Germany and Italy in the Decade after World War I* (Princeton).

Markovits, Andrei S. (1986), *The Politics of West German Trade Unions: Strategies of Class and Interest Representation in Growth and Crisis* (Cambridge).

Marwick, Arthur (1979), *War and Social Change in the Twentieth Century* (London and Basingstoke).

Matthias, Erich (1971), 'German Social Democracy in the Weimar Republic', in Anthony Nicholls and Erich Matthias (eds), *German Democracy and the Triumph of Hitler* (London), pp. 47–57.

Mendelssohn-Bartholdy, Albrecht (1937), *The War and German Society: The Testament of a Liberal* (New Haven).

Meyer, A. G. (1985), *The Feminism and Socialism of Lily Braun* (Bloomington, In.).

Meyer, Thomas (1977), *Bernsteins konstruktiver Sozialismus* (Berlin and Bonn).

Miller, Susanne (1974), *Burgfrieden und Klassenkampf: Die deutsche Sozialdemokratie im Ersten Weltkrieg* (Düsseldorf).

Miller, Susanne (1978a), 'Bernsteins Haltung im Ersten Weltkrieg und in der Revolution 1918–19', in H. Heimann and T. Meyer (eds), *Bernstein und der Demokratische Sozialismus* (Berlin and Bonn), pp. 213–21.

Miller, Susanne (1978b), *Die Bürde der Macht: Die deutsche Sozialdemokratie 1918–1920* (Düsseldorf).

Miller, Susanne and Heinrich Potthoff (1986), *A History of German Social Democracy: From 1848 to the Present* (Leamington Spa).

Mishark, J. W. (1967), *The Road to Revolution* (Detroit).

Mommsen, Wolfgang (1981), 'The German Revolution 1918–1920: Political Revolution and Social Protest Movement', in R. J. Bessel and E. J. Feuchtwanger (eds), *Social Change and Political Development in Weimar Germany* (London), pp. 21–54.

Mommsen, Wolfgang and Hans-Gerhard Husung (eds) (1985), *The Development of Trade Unionism in Great Britain and Germany, 1880–1914* (London).

Morgan, David (1975), *The Socialist Left and the German Revolution: A History of the German Independent Social Democratic Party 1917–1922* (Ithaca).

Morgan, Roger (1965), *The German Social Democrats and the First International 1864–1872* (Cambridge).

Moses, John A. (1982), *Trade Unionism in Germany from Bismarck to Hitler 1869–1933*, 2 vols (London and New York).

Niggemann, Heinz (1981a), *Emanzipation zwischen Sozialismus und Feminismus: Die sozialdemokratische Frauenbewegung im Kaiserreich* (Wuppertal).

Niggemann, Heinz (ed) (1981b), *Frauenemanzipation und Sozialdemokratie* (Frankfurt).

Nolan, Mary (1981), *Social Democracy and Society: Working Class Radicalism in Düsseldorf, 1890–1920* (Cambridge).

Noyes, Paul (1966), *Organisation and Revolution: Working Class Associations in the German Revolutions of 1848–1849* (Princeton).

Offermann, Toni (1979), *Arbeiterbewegung und liberales Bürgertum in Deutschland 1850–1863* (Bonn).

Papadakis, Elim (1984), *The Green Movement in West Germany* (London, Canberra and New York).

Patch, Jr., William L. (1985), *Christian Trade Unions in the Weimar Republic,*

1918–1933 (New Haven and London).
Paterson, W. E. and I. Campbell (1974), *Social Democracy in Postwar Europe* (London).
Paterson, W. E. and Gordon Smith (1981), *The West German Model: Perspectives on a Stable State* (London).
Paterson, W. E. and A. H. Thomas (1977), *Social Democratic Parties in Western Europe* (London).
Peterson, B. (1977), 'The Politics of Working-class Women in the Weimar Republic', *Central European History*, vol. 10, no. 2, pp. 87–111.
Petzina, Dietmar (1986), *Fahnen, Fäuste, Körper: Symbolik und Kultur der Arbeiterbewegung* (Fulda).
Pore, R. (1981), *A Conflict of Interest: Women in German Social Democracy, 1919–1933* (Westport).
Potthoff, Heinrich (1974), *Die Sozialdemokratie von den Anfängen bis 1945* (Bonn-Bad Godesberg).
Potthoff, Heinrich (1979), *Gewerkschaften und Politik zwischen Revolution und Inflation* (Düsseldorf).
Prittie, Terence (1972), *Konrad Adenauer 1876–1967* (London).
Prittie, Terence (1974), *Willy Brandt: Portrait of a Statesman* (London).
Quataert, Jean (1979), *Reluctant Feminists in German Social Democracy, 1885–1917* (Princeton).
Ramos Oliveira, Antonio (1942), *A People's History of Germany*, translated by E. E. Brooke (London).
Reichard, Richard W. (1969), *Crippled from Birth: German Social Democracy 1844–1870* (Ames).
Richelbächer, S. (1982), *Uns fehlt nur eine Kleinigkeit: Deutsche proletarische Frauenbewegung 1890–1914* (Frankfurt).
Ritter, Gerhard A. (1976), *Arbeiterbewegung, Parteien und Parlamentarismus* (Göttingen).
Ritter, Gerhard A. (1985), *Die deutschen Parteien 1830–1914* (Göttingen).
Roehl, Fritzmichael (1961), *Marie Juchacz und die Arbeiterwohlfahrt*, rev. by H. Wachenheim (Hanover).
Rosenberg, Arthur (1936), *A History of the German Republic* (London).
Rosenhaft, Eve (1983), *Beating the Fascists? The German Communists and Political Violence 1929–1933* (Cambridge).
Roth, Guenther (1963), *The Social Democrats in Imperial Germany: A Study in Working-class Isolation and National Integration* (Totowa).
Rürup, Reinhard (1968), 'Problems of the German Revolution 1918–1919', *Journal of Contemporary History*, vol. 3, no. 4, pp. 109–35.
Rovan, Joseph (1980), *Geschichte der deutschen Sozialdemokratie* (Frankfurt).
Ruppert, Wolfgang (ed) (1986), *Die Arbeiter: Lebensformen, Alltag und Kultur von der Frühindustrialisierung bis zum 'Wirstschaftwunder'* (Munich).
Ryden, Bengt and Villy Bergström (eds) (1982), *Sweden: Choices for Economic and Social Policy in the 1980s* (London).
Ryder, A. J. (1967), *The German Revolution of 1918: A Study of German Socialism in War and Revolution* (London and Cambridge).
Saldern, Adelheid von (1984), *Auf dem Wege zum Arbeiterreformismus: Parteialltag in sozialdemokratischer Provinz Göttingen (1870–1920)* (Frankfurt).
Schellinger, Jr., H. K. (1968), *The SPD in the Bonn Republic: A Socialist Party Modernizes* (The Hague).
Schmädeke, J. and P. Steinbach (1985), *Der Widerstand gegen den Nationalsozialismus* (Munich).
Schmidt, Helmut (1985), *A Grand Strategy for the West* (New Haven and London).
Schönhoven, Klaus (1980), *Expansion und Konzentration: Studien zur Entwicklung der*

Freien Gewerkschaften im Wilhelminischen Deutschland 1890 bis 1914 (Stuttgart).
Schönhoven, Klaus (ed) (1985), *Die Gewerkschaften in Weltkrieg und Revolution 1914–1919* (Cologne).
Schorske, Carl E. (1955), *German Social Democracy, 1905–1917: The Development of the Great Schism* (Cambridge, Mass.).
Schuon, Karl Theodor (1986), *Politische Theorie des Demokratischen Sozialismus* (Marburg).
Smith, Gordon (1982), *Democracy in Western Germany: Parties and Politics in the Federal Republic,* 2nd edn (London).
Stachura, Peter D. (1983), 'Weimar, National Socialism and Historians', in Peter D. Stachura (ed), *The Nazi Machtergreifung* (London), pp. 1–14.
Stachura, Peter D. (1986), 'The Social and Welfare Implications of Youth Unemployment in Weimar Germany, 1929–1933', in Peter D. Stachura (ed), *Unemployment and the Great Depression* (London), pp. 121–47.
Steenson, Gary P. (1978), *Karl Kautsky 1854–1938: Marxism in the Classical Years* (Pittsburgh).
Steenson, Gary P. (1981), *'Not One Man! Not One Penny!' German Social Democracy, 1863–1914* (Pittsburgh).
Strain, J. (1964), *Feminism and Political Radicalism in the German Social Democratic Movement, 1890–1914* (University of California, Berkeley, PhD Dissertation).
Tampke, Jürgen (1978), *The Ruhr and Revolution* (Canberra and London).
Thönnessen, Werner (1969), *Frauenemanzipation: Politik und Literatur der deutschen Sozialdemokratie zur Frauenbewegung* (Frankfurt).
Thönnessen, Werner (1973), *The Emanicipation of Women: The Rise and Decline of the Women's Movement in German Social Democracy, 1863–1933* (London).
Trommler, Frank (1983), 'Working-class Culture and Modern Mass Culture Before World War I', *New German Critique,* vol. 29, pp. 57–70.
Ullrich, Volker (1982), *Kriegsalltag: Hamburg im Ersten Weltkrieg* (Cologne).
Wette, Wolfram (1976), 'Mit dem Stimmzettel gegen den Faschismus? Das Dilemma des demokratischen Antifaschismus in der Endphase der Weimarer Republik', in W. Huber and J. Schwerdtfeger (eds), *Frieden, Gewalt, Sozialismus: Studien zur Geschichte der sozialistischen Arbeiterbewegung* (Stuttgart).
Will, W. van der and Rob Burns (1982), *Arbeiterkulturbewegung in der Weimarer Republik* (Frankfurt).
Winkler, H. A. (1979), *Die Sozialdemokratie und die Revolution von 1918–1919: Ein Rückblick nach 60 Jahren* (Berlin).
Winkler, H. A. (1983–4), 'Eduard Bernstein als Kritiker der Weimarer Sozialdemokratie', *Annali della Fondazioni Giangiacomo Feltrinelli,* vol. 23, pp. 1003–27.
Winkler, H. A. (1985a), *Von der Revolution zur Stabilisierung: Arbeiter und Arbeiterbewegung in der Weimarer Republik 1918 bis 1924,* 2nd edn (Berlin).
Winkler, H. A. (1985b), *Der Schein der Normalität: Arbeiter und Arbeiterbewegung in der Weimarer Republik 1924–1930* (Berlin).
Winkler, H. A. (1988), *Der Weg in die Katastrophe: Arbeiter und Arbeiterbewegung in der Weimarer Republik 1930–1933* (Berlin and Bonn) (forthcoming).
'Workers' Culture' (1978), *Journal of Contemporary History* (special issue), vol. 13, no. 2.

Index

Index